KW-194-566

MUNICIPALITIES AND COMMUNITY PARTICIPATION

A Sourcebook for Capacity Building

Janelle Plummer

Research for
 Department for
International
Development

Earthscan Publications Ltd, London and Sterling, VA

UNIVERSITY OF PLYMOUTH

Item No. 9005409529

Date 17 DEC 2002 Z

Class No. 307·3416 PLU
Con. No. ✓

PLYMOUTH LIBRARY

First published in the UK and USA in 2000
by Earthscan Publications Ltd

Originally published in Great Britain in 1999
by GHK International

Copyright © Janelle Plummer, 1999

All rights reserved

A catalogue record for this book is available from the British Library

ISBN: 1 85383 744 X ✓

Design and layout by Brightmark, Pretoria
Printed and bound in the UK by Thanet Press Ltd, Margate, Kent
Cover design by Deirdré Bartie
Cover photographs (left to right) by GHK International, DFID, Andrew Cotton

For a full list of publications please contact:

Earthscan Publications Ltd
120 Pentonville Road, London, N1 9JN, UK
Tel: +44 (0)20 7278 0433
Fax: +44 (0)20 7278 1142
Email: earthinfo@earthscan.co.uk
http://www.earthscan.co.uk

22883 Quicksilver Drive, Sterling, VA 20166-2012, USA

Earthscan is an editorially independent subsidiary of Kogan Page Ltd and publishes in association with WWF-UK
and the International Institute for Environment and Development

This book originates from a research project funded by the UK Department for International Development (DFID).
The views expressed are not necessarily those of DFID

Printed on elemental chlorine-free paper

90 0540952 9

MUNICIPALITIES AND COMMUNITY PARTICIPATION

A Sourcebook for Capacity Building

This book is to be returned on
or before the date stamped below

- 5 DEC 2003

WITHDRAWN
FROM
UNIVERSITY OF PLYMOUTH
LIBRARY SERVICES

UNIVERSITY OF PLYMOUTH

PLYMOUTH LIBRARY
Tel: (01752) 232323
This book is subject to recall if required by another reader
Books may be renewed by phone
CHARGES WILL BE MADE FOR OVERDUE BOOKS

Acknowledgements

Various people were involved in the research phase that led to this publication and many others in the development and production of the final sourcebook. I am indebted to them all for their contributions, assistance, support and encouragement.

I would particularly like to acknowledge the local and UK collaborators for their research contributions: Mr Mihir Bhatt, Community Action Planning, Mr Ahmed Eiweida, Ms Sharadbala Joshi, Mr Rajendra Joshi, Mr K Gopalakrishnan, Sue Phillips, Richard Slater, Phillip Amis and Kevin Tayler. Thanks must also go to all those municipal officials, community representatives and other key informants who provided the wealth of experience documented in the case studies.

To those who helped to clarify and focus the framework and kindly commented on the final draft, I am very grateful, at the same time as taking full responsibility for this final version. I would particularly like to thank Sue Phillips, Social Development Consultant, for her generous support and ongoing comments and inputs; Richard Slater, IDD Birmingham, for his valuable and fitting illustrative material; and Mark Harvey for his tireless proof-reading. Thanks must also go to Jelle Van Gijn and John Kirke at GHK for facilitating the final stages of the work; Deirdré Bartie for the great care and attention to the design and layout of the final publication; and Jonathan Sinclair Wilson and Frances MacDermott at Earthscan for all their efforts.

I would also like to thank the Infrastructure and Urban Development Department at DFID for the Knowledge and Research Programme funding which made this research, the final sourcebook and further dissemination possible. Thanks to Michael Mutter and Peter Roberts for their assistance. I am also very grateful to all those professionals, officials, donors and project staff who have requested copies of the first edition and made this Earthscan edition possible.

My greatest thanks to Tommy and Mark Harvey for their patience and unending support, without which the publication of this work would not have been possible.

Janelle Plummer
July 2000

The case studies carried out for the Building Municipal Capacity for Community Participation research project provided the basis for the municipal experiences described in this sourcebook. The boxed illustrations throughout the text draw heavily on these case studies. The authors and researchers for each study referenced in the text were:

Ahmedabad:	Mihir Bhatt and Janelle Plummer with Rajendra Joshi
Bangalore:	Richard Slater
Cochin:	Janelle Plummer and Mr K Gopalakrishnan
Colombo:	Richard Slater
Faisalabad:	Community Action Planning and Kevin Tayler
Kerala:	Mr K Gopalakrishnan and Janelle Plummer
Nasriya:	Ahmed Eiweida and Kevin Tayler
Shrouk:	Kevin Tayler and Ahmed Eiweida
Surat:	Sharadbala Joshi and Janelle Plummer
Visakhapatnam:	Sue Phillips

Contents

List of Boxes

Box

Acronyms and Abbreviations

ADS	Area Development Society
AMC	Ahmedabad Municipal Corporation
BUPP	Bangalore Urban Poverty Project
CAP	Community Action Planning
CBO	Community Based Organisation
CD	Community Development
CDC	Community Development Committee
CDD	Community Development Department
CDO	Community Development Officer
CDS	Community Development Society
CHIS	Chinagadili Habitat Improvement Scheme
CMC	Colombo Municipal Corporation
CMOH	Chief Medical Officer of Health
CO	Community Organiser
CoC	Corporation of Cochin
CUPRP	Cochin Urban Poverty Reduction Project
DFID	Department for International Development
DPC	District Planning Committee
EIUS	Environment Improvement in Urban Slums
FDA	Faisalabad Development Corporation
FMC	Faisalabad Municipal Corporation
GO	Governmental Organisation
GoI	Government of India
GTZ	Deutsche Gesellschaft für Technische Zusammenarbeit
HI	Health Inspector
IAS	Indian Administrative Service
ILGUS	Institute for Local Government and Urban Studies
JPHN	Junior Public Health Nurse
KILA	Kerala Institute of Local Administration
KMA	Kerala Municipal Act
FDA	Faisalabad Development Authority
KPPC	Kerala People's Planning Campaign
MCV	Municipal Corporation of Visakhapatnam
MoUAE	Ministry of Urban Affairs and Employment
NGO	Non-Governmental Organisation
NHC	Neighbourhood Committee

NHDA	National Housing Development Authority
NHG	Neighbourhood Group
NUP	Nasriya Upgrading Project
ODA	Overseas Development Administration
PALM	Participatory Action and Learning Methods
PHD	Public Health Department
PMU	Project Management Unit
PRA	Participatory Rural Appraisal
PSC	Project Steering Committee
PSU	Project Support Unit
Rs	Rupees
SAP	Sector Action Plan
SIP	Slum Improvement Project
SJSRY	Swarna Jaynati Shahari Rojgar Yojana
SMC	Surat Municipal Corporation
SMT	Slum Management Team
SNP	Slum Networking Project
SO	Social Organiser
SPC	State Planning Committee
UBSP	Urban Basic Services Programme
UCD	Urban Community Development Department
UHSP	Urban Housing Sub-Programme
ULB	Urban Local Body
UPA	Urban Poverty Alleviation
UPO	Urban Poverty Office, DFID
VSIP	Visakhapatnam Slum Improvement Project
VTC	Voluntary Technical Corps
WASA	Water and Sanitation Agency
WPC	Western Provincial Council

Foreword

More than a third of the urban population of Africa, Asia and Latin America live in homes and neighbourhoods where conditions are so poor and infrastructure and service provision so inadequate that their lives and health are constantly at risk. The number lacking adequate provision for water, sanitation, drainage and health care is growing. So too is the number living in precarious homes at risk from floods and landslides, in part because more settlements are developing on hazardous sites, in part because of the lack of investment in reducing risks. In many urban centres, conditions have actually deteriorated for substantial sections of the population over the last one or two decades – for instance as water supplies have become more scarce, unreliable or expensive.

Municipal authorities remain the single most important influence on whether conditions will improve, remain the same or deteriorate for much of the urban population. But it is not only in what these authorities do (or do not do) but also in what they allow and support other groups to do. In particular, in how much they can work with the lower-income groups within their city, including the inhabitants of illegal or informal settlements and their community organisations. Many of the most remarkable and cost-effective responses to a lack of infrastructure and services have been achieved by partnerships between municipal agencies and lower-income groups. But the possibilities of developing such responses depends on the quality of the relationship between municipal agencies and low-income groups.

This sourcebook centres on the means to improve this relationship. Among all the literature on participation, this is the first book I know that focuses on municipal authorities. It is solidly grounded on practical municipal experiences and includes case studies of how municipal authorities established municipal–community partnerships. It provides a strategic framework to help municipal authorities to identify all the elements and processes that need attention if participatory approaches are to be realised. It is also based on a recognition of the formidable external constraints under which most municipal authorities operate.

The book does not underplay the difficulties facing municipal authorities, most of whom face great constraints – in personnel, in revenues, in equipment and in investment capacity. Decentralisation programmes have often increased their responsibilities but provided them with few additional powers and resources. But it does highlight how much can be achieved with limited resources through municipal–community organisation partnerships. This book also has particular importance both for higher levels of government (at national or provincial/state level) and for international agencies. Firstly, it is a reminder of the importance of well-functioning municipal governments for reducing poverty. Secondly, it is a rich source of case studies and analysis about how municipal authorities can incorporate one central component of 'good governance' – a permanent, participatory engagement with their citizens.

David Satterthwaite
International Institute for Environment and Development (IIED)
London

Introduction

Increasingly, governments of developing countries are adopting, in rhetoric and policy, the concept of community participation. In many cases, particularly where governments are pursuing decentralisation policies, the responsibility for addressing urban poverty lies with local government and accordingly it is the municipal levels of administration that are handed the responsibility for implementing policies advocating the participation of poor communities. However, most municipalities lack human and financial resources and many function through hierarchical structures and prescriptive approaches. Most are unlikely to have the capacity to change their approach with the same speed that policy makers can draft legislation, reformulate programmes and reconsider approaches.

A majority of local governments are dominated by engineering-led, capital intensive works and staffed by administrators and technical professionals who find the concept of community participation irrelevant. Other municipalities have little power, are under-staffed and under-skilled, and battle to fulfil standard municipal functions. At worst, constant transfers, the lack of resources and political pressures mean that municipalities are dysfunctional. The common experience appears to be that municipal officials have an incomplete knowledge of the potential and limitations of participatory processes. Even where there is a basic willingness to accept participation, municipal officials often lack skills and resources, and few policy makers and managers appear to appreciate the degree of difficulty, capacity building and commitment required to develop effective partnerships at the local level. Furthermore, the development community frequently lacks an appreciation or acknowledgement that the very nature of the conventional municipality is in conflict with the concept of participation and that the whole notion of community-municipal partnerships is somewhat incongruous.[1]

The prevalence of weak municipalities combined with the new paradigm for participation makes it necessary to consider, in pragmatic terms, just how community participation is to be seriously and sustainably adopted in the municipal delivery of services to the poor. If policy formulation toward increased participation is to become meaningful, it is essential that it is accompanied by efforts to improve the capacity of the government agencies responsible for implementation. Municipalities must be given the support needed to change their basic nature and to become responsive, flexible and accountable organisations that are able to work in harmony with communities.

Although it may be accepted in some spheres that municipal capacity building for community participation is urgently required, there is still considerable scope for improving the understanding of what exactly this capacity building entails. There is a need for understanding the problems that municipalities experience in implementing participatory processes, the options for their resolution and the range of areas in which capacity building needs to be undertaken.

Background

Many donor projects currently promoting participatory approaches have themselves been designed through non-participatory methods. Donors frequently impose generic ideas of participation on project objectives and methodologies and as a result municipal officials rarely initiate change voluntarily. Mostly they are cast into the domain of participation. While many officials are willing to attempt participatory approaches, many are deeply sceptical and nearly all ask for proof, tangible illustrations and evidence.

- **Where is community participation being undertaken elsewhere?**
- **How does it work in other cities?**
- **What problems have they had?**
- **How is the project organised in the municipality?**
- **Who is involved?**

- **How does a municipality communicate with a community?**
- **What are the roles of the municipalities and the communities?**
- **At what stage does the community get involved?**
- **Who leads the process within the municipality?**

Over the last decade, the adoption of participatory approaches in the delivery of urban infrastructure has dramatically increased. Yet, to date, there are still few examinations of the municipal perspective of participation and only limited documentation of the constraints facing those municipalities that undertake such a shift in methodology.

The research for this sourcebook was undertaken with Knowledge and Research (KAR) programme funding from the Infrastructure and Urban Development Department of the Department for International Development (UK) over the period June 1997 to March 1999. Following the development of a conceptual framework and a database of potential case studies, a fieldwork methodology was prepared and tested in the city of Ahmedabad in India. Detailed research was then undertaken in 10 locations in 4 countries. In India, where there are a number of municipalities with experience of community participation, case studies were undertaken in Ahmedabad, Bangalore, Cochin, Surat and Visakhapatnam, as well as one statewide initiative in Kerala. Studies were also carried out in Aswan and on the national level Shrouk Programme in Egypt, Colombo in Sri Lanka and Faisalabad in Pakistan. The aim of this research was to examine the processes of establishing municipal-community partnerships in service delivery,[2] to document the main issues identified by municipalities, the problems they encountered in promoting community participation and the solutions which were developed.

The range of case studies, including donor and local initiatives, exposed both vast differences and similarities in participatory approaches. On the one hand, a number of key themes emerged from the case studies. On the other, participatory approaches appear to be dependent on the social and cultural factors affecting the community and the administrative context of the municipality. A comprehensive analysis of the findings led to the development of a strategic framework for building municipal capacity for community participation. This framework places the vast range of issues into a coherent structure for discussion and action.

Purpose of this Sourcebook

The ultimate aim of this work is to bring about stronger and more sustainable forms of community participation which lead to a better quality of life for poor people. The underlying aim of this sourcebook is to consider the municipal perspective and support municipalities in the development of participatory approaches. With this goal in mind, this work is unapologetically concerned with municipal problems and lessons. While it assumes the need for municipal involvement in urban service delivery, it starts from the basic premise that introducing participatory processes is not easy for municipalities, and suggests that there needs to be greater recognition, from all actors, of the degree of difficulty of the task. Only once this is recognised will effective capacity building programmes be introduced.

The purpose of this sourcebook is twofold.

- First, it aims to provide a strategic framework for strengthening the capacity of municipal organisations and officials to implement participatory processes. It does so by documenting and structuring the basic elements underlying municipal-community partnerships.
- Second, it aims to provide a sourcebook of illustrative material. It documents tangible examples of the key elements of participation and municipal change, the opportunities and constraints of differing contexts and the procedures and activities that impact upon participatory processes. Through the dissemination of these experiences to municipal officials, it aims to develop greater confidence and familiarity with community participation.

This sourcebook is directed at those development professionals responsible for building municipal capacity for community participation: for trainers responsible for capacity building, and for those policy-makers and municipal managers committed to the process, and keen to broaden their understanding of the diversity and enormity of the task. The term 'municipal' refers to the local level of government commonly responsible for the delivery of urban services and infrastructure. This definition is not intended to limit the discussion or audience which, by its nature, is likely to be applicable to all forms of local government.[3]

Conceptual Framework

One of the primary problems encountered by government, agencies and organisations deliberating over participation in the last three decades has been the lack of consensus as to what is meant by 'community participation'. Unsurprisingly, actors consider participation with different agenda, opposing ideologies and distinctive goals. By extension, there is little consensus as to what participation should be. This debate is well documented[4] and forms an important background to the specific topic of this sourcebook for building capacity for community participation. This assumes the need for the participation of poor communities in service delivery and concentrates on unpacking the rhetoric of participation into elements which are tangible and achievable within the scope of the municipality. At the very least, however, it is essential that this introduction highlight some of the key issues and conflicts relating to participation, and that these are constantly re-emphasised in the capacity building process.

Key aspects of the participation debate

As early as 1969, Arnstein[5] introduced a number of important issues to the conceptual debate. In an effort to describe the way communities interacted with government in development projects, she established the idea of a ladder of participation which functioned as a continuum ranging from the most exploitative and disempowered to the most controlling and empowered. These ideas enabled theorists and analysts to describe various types of participation in terms of increasing degrees of decision-making. This process established a simple framework for describing:

- non-participation (manipulation and therapy);
- tokenism (informing, consultation, placation); and
- citizens' power (partnerships, delegated power and citizen control).

In 1983, Moser proposed that a simple distinction could be made, irrespective of context, between those development efforts which envisaged community participation as a means, and those which saw participation as an end in itself.[6] Participation-as-a-means implies that the people are mobilised with the purpose of **achieving a desired outcome** (for instance, improved water supply or drainage). It could involve bottom-up or top-down processes, but is commonly evaluated in terms of the measurable outputs of the process. Participation-as-an-end is not measurable in terms of development goals but in terms of the transfer of power. It is a process where the outcome is **itself increasingly meaningful participation in the development process**; and where the real objective is to increase the control of marginalised groups **over resources and regulative institutions**.[7] Moser suggested that the operational constraints on participation-as-a-means include inadequate delivery mechanisms, while the constraints on participation-as-an-end are structural and include institutional opposition to the redistribution of power and resources.

While Moser herself has since asserted that the important issue is not the creation of a simple distinction but the dynamic through which participation-as-a-means has the capacity to develop into participation-as-an-end,[8] this dichotomy has become well established and has strongly influenced the categorisation of participatory projects. For the purposes of municipal capacity building for community participation it is a helpful and contentious differentiation for discussion amongst municipal, community and NGO actors. In practice, it describes the fundamental distinction commonly, if incorrectly, drawn between socially-oriented and output-oriented goals which are often the seeds of conflict between various actors in the development process.

In 1987, after Moser devised the means-end distinction, Samuel Paul conducted an evaluation of a large number of participatory projects for the World Bank. His empirical analysis resulted in a more detailed explanation and the first conceptual framework for participation. It brought with it a greater distinction between the objectives, methods and degrees of participation. First, he identified 5 types of project objectives:[9] **cost sharing, efficiency, effectiveness, beneficiary capacity, and empowerment.** Second, he reinterpreted Arnstein's ladder of participation to describe the different levels of 'intensity' to which communities can participate in development projects. He defined community participation in terms of **information sharing, consultation, decision-making, and initiating action.** Third, his analysis identified three instruments of participation: **user groups, community workers/committees** and **field workers.** This contribution to the debate, while controversial, helped to disaggregate community participation further into a refined and tangible set of factors.

The nature and scope of community participation in urban management has been discussed further over the last 5 years. Schübeler's work for the Urban Management Programme, for instance, acknowledges that participation exists 'in a wide variety of forms, ranging from government involvement in community-based development activities to people's participation in government-directed management functions'.[10] He proposed a typology of four complementary, potentially co-existing, evolving approaches to participation:[11]

- the **community-based** approach focusing municipal efforts on supporting community development initiatives, enhancing organisational capacity and enabling participation and projects through the development of a supportive operating context;
- the government-led **area-based** strategy focusing on the physical area, service outputs, efficiency and cost-effectiveness, and typically including awareness building, group formation and strengthening and participatory planning;
- the **functionally-based** strategy aiming to develop a collaboration in which the community takes full responsibility for neighbourhood activities and the municipality takes responsibility for the necessary external service and infrastructure; and
- the **process-based** strategy considering participation as a broad concept for the entire process of urban infrastructure management through the decentralisation of delivery processes.

More recently, Abbott[12] has emphasised the potential of different types of participation and participatory processes in relation to the political context and proposes that the duality of open and closed governmental environments fundamentally influences the entire concept of participation. In particular, Abbott proposes that participation in the context of democratic governments ranges from manipulation to community control. From his experience in apartheid South Africa he clearly differentiates this from the empowerment approach, which he locates in the 'confrontational arena' where interaction between government and community is not possible.

Parameters underlying the strategic framework

For the purposes of this sourcebook it is necessary to set out a number of the principles (or assumptions) on which this research and the development of a strategic framework for capacity building in community participation are based. While these may be debatable and argued by proponents of different viewpoints, this sourcebook aims to provide an achievable starting point for municipalities, and to set parameters which acknowledge the current limitations of municipal attitudes and functions but which also establish a scope for participation which is meaningful. Four parameters of this work are described below:

☐ **Meaningful community participation involves decision-making.**

It is essential that exploitative or manipulative forms of community involvement are not recognised as participation. Meaningful community participation aims towards participation in decision-making processes. A typological description of the various forms/intensities of decision-making, and the situations in which they commonly occur, is shown in Box 4.15.[13]

☐ **The degrees of participation form a continuum.**

This principle (suggested by Arnstein) is essential to an understanding that community participation can evolve in the participatory process, and that increased capacity of all (including municipal) actors is one mechanism that can result in more meaningful forms of participation.

☐ **Enhancing community participation has empowering effects.**

Effective community participation in service delivery can result in a shift in the existing power relations between the poor community and external actors (municipality, service operators, donors, NGOs). It also inherently produces a shift in the power relations within the community by encouraging women and other marginalised groups to become involved in decision-making. This strategy acknowledges that participation can produce empowering effects within the context of output-oriented projects.

☐ **Objectives of participation are diverse, multi-layered, complex and individual.**

In practice, a number of individual, informal objectives and organisational, formal objectives define and affect the participatory process. A first step in capacity building for community participation is in the acknowledgement that objectives cannot and will not all be concurrent at the outset, but may change. An effective partnership is one which sees greater concurrence of the objectives of all actors.

If participation is to become an integral part of the way municipalities manage obligatory functions, there needs to be greater acceptance that the introduction of participatory processes will take time and capacity building, and that municipalities will not miraculously and spontaneously become overwhelmed with empowerment objectives. Participation-as-a-means is not in itself a defective notion for municipalities seeking to improve service delivery mechanisms. Rather than focusing on the conceptual distinction between means and end, this work therefore focuses on the importance of increasingly meaningful participation; first by stressing that exploitative participatory practices are removed from the agenda of municipalities and, second, by emphasising that evolution of participation is an essential aspect, and result of, capacity building and attitudinal change.

The role of the municipality

The lack of ethical and political convergence between municipalities and communities (and other agencies representing communities) has led to a great deal of questioning about the wisdom of involving governments in the participatory endeavour. Concerns are quite rightly raised that increasing government involvement will compromise the quality and output of participatory processes achieved by non-governmental actors through focused and skilled initiatives. While this is true to some extent at least, it is necessary to work with municipalities to bring about the scale of initiative likely to have broad impacts. In the arena of urban infrastructure, it is necessary to develop more integrated solutions to service delivery, and these are crucial elements of both effective participation and sustainable development. The other primary reason for pursing community participation and community partnerships with municipalities is that it is time to dismantle ineffective prescriptive approaches to service delivery. Not only will top-down, supply-led approaches continue to produce inappropriate and unsustainable infrastructure, but the inertia of this perspective will continue to undermine the participatory efforts of other actors.

Nevertheless, it is necessary for government to be aware that there are risks in 'institutionalising' participation. Experience of participation in rural areas provides ample evidence of many government-led projects that never really absorbed the essence of participation: projects that were rushed in order to spend budgets and projects that replicated methodologies produced by untrained and unskilled co-ordinators. Above all, many participatory processes have been pursued without attention being paid to the skills and organisational capacity of the actors responsible for the implementation process. This sourcebook aims to underpin such capacity building.

Structure of the Sourcebook

The organisation of this sourcebook corresponds with the structure of the proposed framework. Chapter 2 outlines the strategic framework for building municipal capacity for community participation and sets out the primary components covered in the subsequent chapters. Chapter 3 addresses the broader operating context of municipalities. It highlights the impacts of the political, legislative, policy and administrative operating context – a context largely outside municipal control. Chapter 4 considers the key elements of participation and the nature of municipal-community partnerships. This includes the need to develop an understanding of the factors influencing participation and the forms and options for participation in service delivery. Chapter 5 examines the instruments municipalities can adopt to develop participatory processes. It considers the vehicles of participatory processes and the interface between the municipality and the community. It also considers the potential role of external organisations such as NGOs in collaborations towards community participation and greater municipal capacity. Chapter 6 considers the implications of building partnerships in the context of a government institution. It examines the main elements of the municipality and the constraints of municipal attitudes, structures, systems and staffing. Chapter 7 presents the central component of municipal capacity building in a discussion on the management and leadership required to lever change in approaches. The final chapter provides a comprehensive and simplified framework for action. It sets out the full range of aspects affecting participatory efforts and acts as a checklist for action.

Each component of the strategic framework is developed through a combination of text and illustrative material. The text highlights the key issues and lessons of participation, while the case study illustrations provide specific examples of the problems experienced and solutions adopted by municipalities. These are intended to translate concepts into tangible form. To this end, the illustrations form the greater part of the sourcebook.

Notes
1. The incongruous nature of municipal-community partnerships was emphasised by Cernea:
    ...the two fundamental sectors in local development processes are the local governments and the local communities. But "community and bureaucracy are two evidently antithetical styles of social organisation" [...] which serve to distinguish the two major protagonists in planned development, the people and the state. Cernea (1988) p11.
2. The KAR research funding from the Infrastructure and Urban Development Department of DFID limited the scope of investigation to environmental improvements for the poor. Many initiatives were linked to or a part of multi-sectoral poverty reduction programmes. The capacity building approach developed seems applicable to broader contexts.
3. Other local government organisations include development authorities, line agencies, parastatals and specialist units of state/provincial government operating at the municipal level.
4. Early conceptual discussions about participation in the urban context include Moser (1983 and 1989), Paul (1987), Arnstein (1969), Rakodi (1983), Batley (1983). These are documented and discussed in Abbott (1996).
5. Arnstein (1969) p217
6. Moser (1983) pp3-11
7. Moser (1989) p47
8. ibid.
9. Paul (1987) p3. Paul's work has been criticised for this project orientation. See Abbott (1996) p37. Such criticism could also be levelled at this sourcebook. The key issue in support of the approach taken throughout this work is that the information needs to be relevant to municipal officials for capacity building to be effective.
10. Schübeler (1996) p3
11. ibid. p2-4
12. Abbott (1996) p113
13. Pretty (1994).

A Strategic Framework
for Municipal Capacity Building

The strategic framework presented in this chapter attempts to rationalise the key areas of concern to municipalities in building capacity for community participation. It is anticipated that this framework will form the basis for capacity building strategies and be moulded and adapted to respond to the specific constraints of a municipality undergoing a capacity building process. An important underlying message of this work is that social and institutional factors play a primary role in determining the most appropriate forms of participation in a given context and, accordingly, these factors will determine the key priorities of capacity building.

The External Operating Context

This strategic framework is located at the municipal level responsible for the delivery of services and infrastructure. While this framework is limited to actions that are within the scope of local government, it nevertheless emphasises the constraints and opportunities for participation created by the external factors that combine to form the municipal operating context. For municipal decision-makers seeking to implement participatory processes, it is necessary to understand where the municipality is placed in terms of participation, where they will find support and resistance, what laws or policies influence their capacity, and what the political milieu means to the development of participatory processes. The primary external factors likely to affect municipal capacity for participation include the political context, the legislative and policy framework and the administrative context in which the municipality operates. This information sets the context for municipal capacity building for community participation and provides a fundamental basis for the contextualisation of a strategy.

The Components of the Framework

The strategic framework is structured into four key components, each responding to a fundamental question asked by municipal officials about participatory processes. The analysis of *what is it? how do we do it? how do we support it?* and *who drives it?* aims to disaggregate this vast problem of 'participation' for municipalities and thus to expose the multitude of issues, factors and actors involved in, and affecting, participatory processes.

☐ Elements of participation
Develop appropriate and evolving forms of participation

The first component of the capacity building strategic framework is concerned with developing municipal capacity in the basic nature and elements of participation. It describes the key issues, outlines the wide range of factors that affect participation, and discusses the various options for community participation. Many municipalities need to develop greater knowledge and skills of these fundamental aspects of participation to understand the nature of municipal-community partnerships and to promote appropriate and meaningful participation. The strategic framework for capacity building includes:

- Understanding the objectives of participation
- Understanding the needs of the poor
- Alleviating the factors affecting participation
- Promoting options for participation
- Establishing evolving forms of participation

Box **2.1**   **Strategic Framework**

Building Municipal Capacity for Community Participation

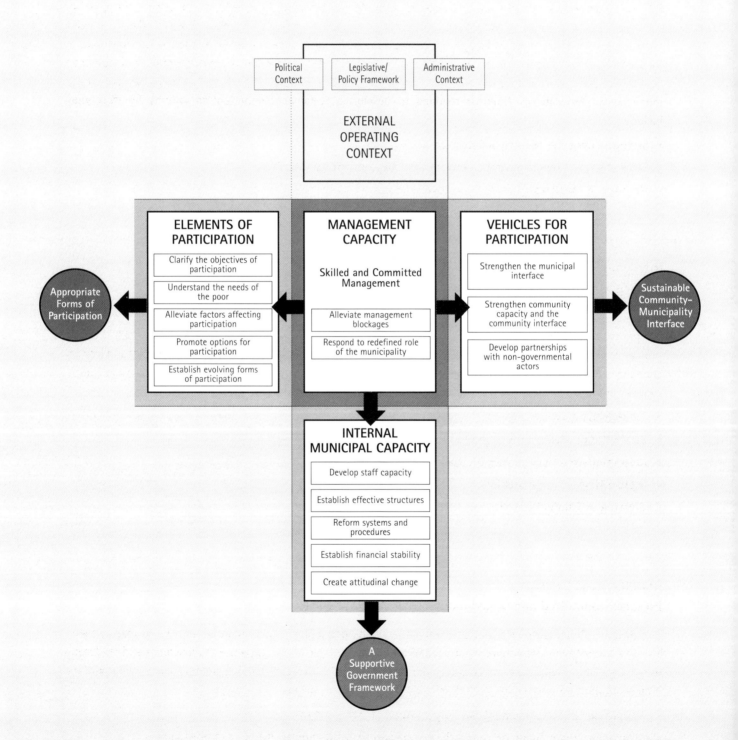

☐ Vehicles of participation
Develop a sustainable municipal-community interface

Effective community participation requires capacity to be built in those vehicles or means for carrying participation forward. The second component of the strategic framework therefore considers the actors and organisations involved in establishing the participation of the poor in the delivery of services and infrastructure, those actors working at the municipal-community interface. It describes municipal and community instruments, and the potential role of external actors in facilitating the development of participatory processes within the municipality. The capacity building required to develop a sustainable municipal-community interface may include:

- Strengthening the municipal interface
- Strengthening the community capacity and the community interface
- Developing partnerships with non-governmental actors

☐ Internal municipal capacity
Develop a supportive organisational framework

Many municipalities need to make significant internal changes in order to 'let participation in'. This third component considers the elements of the municipality (in terms of staff, structure, systems, attitudes and finances) and describes the areas of capacity building which are required within the municipality to create an enabling environment that underpins participatory processes. The capacity building needed to create a supportive municipal framework includes:

- Developing staff capacity
- Establishing effective municipal structures
- Reforming effective municipal structures
- Establishing financial stability
- Creating attitudinal change

☐ Management capacity
Establish committed and skilled management and leadership

The central component of the strategic framework is the development of committed and skilled management. This is the keystone of community participation within the municipality. Effective management and leadership will provide the driving force for change, the stimulus for the capacity building process and will support the implementation initiatives. Committed and skilled management means:

- Alleviating the management blockages affecting participation
- Developing a management approach that responds to the redefined role of municipalities.

The **External**
Operating Context

Overview

In the context of increased democratisation, the role of the people in decision-making has taken on greater relevance in development processes. Democratic trends, which promote a freedom of choice hitherto not experienced in many countries, have been followed by a shift toward the decentralisation of government to local levels, ostensibly a government closer and more reactive to the needs and requirements of the people. The whole point of decentralisation legislation is that it devolves power and responsibility to local levels of government and is not prescriptive beyond that. Yet, it is also at this level that resource constraints are most pronounced: the population of cities is increasing rapidly, existing services and infrastructure are deteriorating, and technical, managerial and financial resources are lacking. This has resulted in a collision of forces and in a conspicuous dichotomy of extended municipal responsibility with diminished municipal resources. This dichotomy seriously affects the poor inhabitants of cities, and has led to the seeds of change in the relationship between civil society and government.

This sourcebook is directed at the capacity building of municipalities in countries where this change is able take place. It focuses on operating contexts that are, to some extent at least, 'open to' increasing community involvement in development processes. This work therefore excludes oppressive states and military regimes[1] and narrows the context to those countries where engagement between community and government is possible.[2] Yet even within this narrower band of government behaviour there is significant diversity. At one, rare, extreme are those operating contexts which actively promote participation and are characterised by political commitment, legislative provision and policy and administrative support. At the other extreme (and more common) are those contexts which allow, albeit reluctantly, some form of donor-funded pilots of participatory approaches but where government ultimately falters at the suggestion of such radical change to the status quo. This chapter considers these characteristics of the external operating context and highlights the key role of policy-makers in creating a favourable environment for municipalities to pursue participatory processes.

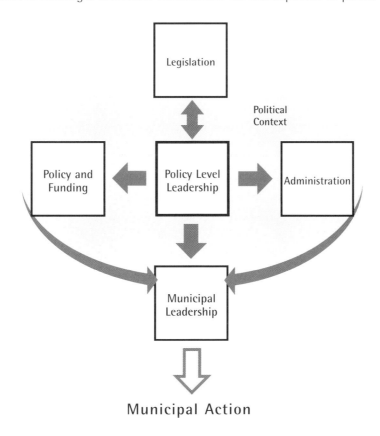

Box **3.1**

The Impacts of Political Change
Sri Lanka

Between 1979 and 1995, the prevailing political context in Sri Lanka and the subsequent policies and programmes for environmental improvements in poor areas provided an enabling framework for community participation. This framework was characterised by the Community Development Committee (CDC) structure and the Community Action Planning (CAP) methodologies which were promoted by national, provincial and local levels of government. The success of this framework, the supporting government action and the implementation through the Million Houses Programme established it as a forerunner to numerous participatory pilot projects in South and Southeast Asia. The processes and experiences are well documented.

Since that time, the experience of community participation in Colombo, and elsewhere in Sri Lanka, has changed and a new set of lessons about the impacts of the political environment has arisen. Before 1995, each tier of government was controlled by the same political party, and the unified position significantly enhanced the effectiveness of participatory efforts. The election in 1995, however, brought with it a change in the ruling party at national level and consequently different political ideas and interventions were prioritised. A fundamental uneasiness with the political motive of the CDC structure resulted in the withdrawal of political support for the committees, the community action-planning approach, and the institutional framework supporting this process. This withdrawal undermined 15 years' development of what had widely been considered to be sustainable and successful participatory processes. It is said to be a primary factor in the apparent collapse of the Community Development Committee movement. In this political environment, the Colombo Municipal Corporation (CMC), controlled by a different political party, has been constrained and municipal activity with communities has diminished.

The impacts of the eroded national level support after the 1995 election were exacerbated by the relations between the provincial and municipal level of government. Since 1996 the relations between the Western Provincial Council (WPC) and the CMC have been problematic, and it has not been unknown for the WPC to delay approval for CMC initiatives, particularly where delays would preclude the CMC reaping political benefit.

The promulgation of the 13th Amendment to the Constitution in 1987, which gave responsibility for supervising the management of Local Authorities to the Provincial Councils, created greater problems for the CMC and further undermined participatory processes. However, the Western Provincial Council (WPC) failed to fulfil the legal expectations of decentralisation, to share power and strengthen the capacity and resource base of municipalities, including the CMC, within its jurisdiction. It also failed to enact important statutes to provide the local level CMC with operational authority. As a result, the Municipal Corporation Ordinance is the applicable law and this places limitations on the functions of municipalities. There are several direct and indirect activities managed by the provincial level government. These include, *inter alia*, local government, health and education. The WPC, however, suffers from its own weaknesses, particular lacking technical capacity, policy co-ordination and resources, and some central government agencies, which enjoy far greater information and expertise, frequently by-pass the WPC in implementation processes.

CMC functions include improvements in the city environment, but they do not have the necessary control over the municipal administration. For important services (water, sewerage, electricity, housing for the poor, drainage) final decision-making authority is vested at national level. Key agencies are mostly controlled by the Ministry of Housing and Urban Development. Neither the CMC nor WPC has the authority to influence the activities of these agencies and as a result the activities and methods are frequently portrayed as encroaching upon the activities of the CMC.

The concertina effects of political manoeuvring have also been felt at the micro level, where previous successes were often the result of local and active politicians acting as champions to community participation and the CDC movement. More recently, shifting political objectives destabilised local level support. The change from ward committees to proportional representation also reduced the accountability of elected councillors to the electorate, thereby reducing the lobbying capacity of the urban poor. •

(Colombo Case Study)

This chapter emphasises that municipal action towards participation does not operate in a void, but in a broader context determined by external factors. Political, legislative, policy and administrative factors have a significant impact on the capacity of municipalities to meet their objectives. Each of these factors is reinforcing and inter-related and each determines the operating context of the municipality. Accordingly, objectives and processes need to be considered in relation to the constraints and opportunities of the external operating context, which is largely outside the sphere of influence of the municipality. It is critical to identify the key organisations and individual actors who lead that policy context and their potential impact on municipal level efforts. In some cases, political pressure, collective lobbying and donor influence can be brought to bear to alleviate constraining factors and develop greater support from higher levels of government.

The Political Context

In any context, the key factor determining the formation of municipal-community partnerships is the political background and framework for such action. Participatory processes which threaten a shift in existing power relations and change in the structure of resource allocation are generally not seen as harmless exercises in working with the poor, but as political manoeuvres which can affect the status quo. In the case of participation in service delivery, the effects are compounded by the capital-intensive nature of infrastructure and services which accentuate the impacts of politics on participatory processes.

The political context influences municipal functions at a number of levels. First, the general political milieu will influence the scope of participatory processes and the methodologies that can be used when pursuing participatory processes. A spectrum of political contexts exists: from one which is pro-active and supportive to one which allows participation to proceed unabated but makes no attempt to facilitate the process. The former scenario is not common but is illustrated by two case studies carried out in Colombo and Kerala, where politicians actively pursued participation in programmes, processes and institutions (see Boxes 3.1 and 3.2). The latter scenario is more common and frequently emerges in contexts where investment is conditional upon participation (such as donor-funded projects) and where municipalities are hoping to draw on community resources.

The second characteristic that affects participation is the dynamic nature of politics and government. Changes in political parties and ideologies can have a detrimental impact on projects driven by political motivation. While political support can lead participatory endeavours, the perception that a project is politically aligned creates a susceptibility that can threaten the sustainability of the project approach if that leadership is removed. In Colombo, the development of the Community Development Committees (CDC) and Community Action Planning (CAP) process over more than 15 years was rapidly undermined by a change in party at national level. At this point, the incoming government withdrew support for the participatory methodology and insisted on the disbandment of CDCs.

In the context of a tiered democratic system, potential conflicts between levels of government can also undermine participatory processes. Deteriorating relations between the state and the local levels of elected government heighten blockages and political manoeuvring. At the initial stages of the Colombo Urban Housing Sub-Programme, each governmental tier was controlled by the same political party. In the latter stages, conflict between the municipal level government and national level government constrained effective action in all aspects of poverty reduction (see Box 3.1).

Box **3.2**

A Supportive Political Context

Kerala People's Planning Campaign

Following the promulgation of the 74th Constitutional Amendment, the Government of Kerala enacted the Kerala Municipality Act (1994). This legislation outlines the explicit provisions and responsibilities for urban local bodies (and rural local bodies called Panchayats) in Kerala. The primary purpose of the Act is to bring the state legislation in line with the Constitutional Amendment, which aims to 'secure a greater measure of participation of the people' in planned development and local government affairs by granting Municipal Councils and Corporations constitutional status. This state level act not only provides a strong legislative framework for the decentralisation process in Kerala, granting power and authority to municipalities to function as an institution of self-government, but it entrusts the municipality with responsibility for planning and implementing schemes for economic development and social justice and explicitly provides for the participation of the Keralan people in the process.

The Kerala Municipalities Act (1994) was promulgated during the rule of the Congress-led coalition in state government (this initiative extended the work of the Congress-led central government in introducing the 74th Constitutional Amendment described in Box 3.4). However, in 1995, the election of the Marxist party in Kerala opened the doors to more radical efforts to decentralise decision-making and implementation. The leader of the party, Mr Namboodiripad, an innovative and respected figure, provided the motivation for the efforts and established the institutional mechanisms for implementing a new participatory approach to planning.

In July 1996, in the context of this legislative framework and committed political support, the newly established State Planning Board, chaired by the Chief Minister of Kerala, initiated the 'People's Campaign for Decentralised Planning', heralding an era in which the planning of local development would be carried out for the people, by the people. The decision in Kerala to move away from the existing top-down processes carried out in Delhi and Trivandrum was backed by two other crucial elements: a policy framework and effective policy leadership. The Finance Ministry subsequently allocated 35-40% of plan funds for municipal expenditure. The aim of the campaign was not only to empower municipalities to formulate development plans for the Ninth 5-year Plan but to facilitate a decentralised process involving the participation of the people at ward level.

Until this time major components of the five-year plans originated at central level, and the state level government was provided with a limited role in certain sectors such as agriculture and social welfare. Urban and rural local bodies had no role in the planning process, which ultimately failed to take into account local needs. In addition, planning was highly departmentalised and lacked acknowledgement of the integrated nature of development processes. The change in methodology for the preparation of the five-year plans in Kerala came about with the recognition that after eight successive five-year plans, the quality of life of the people had not significantly changed; targets had not been met; services, infrastructure and facilities were deteriorating rapidly and falling far short of demand; and economic constraints were limiting the capacity of government to successfully intervene. An acknowledgement of the limits of government resources was coupled with a concern that the people of Kerala remained passive and uninvolved in the development process.

The broad goals of the People's Planning Campaign are:

- to develop the commitment and responsibility of elected representatives;
- to activate the 'people' to become partners in a democratic development process;
- to develop the capacity of municipal officials to work with the people in a partnership;
- to mobilise the expertise of the private sector through voluntary assistance and;
- to mobilise non-governmental organisations to assist in the new approach to development.

The external operating context in Kerala for the Decentralised People's Planning Campaign was entirely favourable. Political will was combined with effective legislation, and the approach was developed through a policy framework, ably led by state level policy-makers who ensured that bureaucratic constraints were minimised. Funds were allocated to the initiative which ensured that the process of planning was meaningful. Political, legislative, policy and funding and administrative support was therefore established.

Despite this, implementation was hindered by the implementation processes at the local level and the lack of support and understanding of municipal level leaders. Political leaders at local government level sought visible results and immediate gain, and senior managers lacked the commitment and skills to bring about effective and co-ordinated planning. As a result, in the early years the planning process at local level did not meet the potential or the expectations of the state government. •

At a more local level, the stability of the political context can have a significant impact on the extent of municipal commitment to community participation and on the approaches carried forward. This is largely dependent on whether or not politicians engage in or ignore the whole issue of participation. The role and influence of politicians at the local level are an integral part of the management capacity of the municipality, discussed and illustrated through case study examples in Chapter 7.

The Legislative and Policy Context

The concept of a legislative and policy framework which grants municipalities decentralised powers and establishes obligations for community participation is incomprehensible in some political contexts. Yet during the 1990s, a number of countries pursuing more progressive approaches to democracy, notably India and South Africa, formulated and promulgated legislations which provide the resolution and a substantive foundation for people-focused approaches to development. While the South African legislation[3] followed the radical political change of the early nineties, in India the political reforms which preceded the 74th Constitutional Amendment (Box 3.3) were less marked.

While it is clear that a legislative framework does not replace political change, and legislation can be dormant in an unsupportive political context, there is also evidence that laws which enable, and policies which facilitate, community participation can provide a useful platform for municipal action. Experience suggests that this platform can support, simplify and accelerate the integration of participatory processes in municipal functions. An effective legislative framework, such as that found in some states of India,[4] provides greater certainty and constancy to the policy, programme and project environment and enables municipal officials to act with more certitude. These characteristics also promote sustainability and create the environment for widespread replication of participatory approaches.

However, this is not to say that with the enactment of legislation the tides are turned. It is necessary to keep a balanced view of what such laws can achieve.[5] In some cases, despite the formal enactment of decentralisation there is a powerful, informal dimension constantly influencing such processes. Devolving power to local levels removes political and administrative control at the state level, and, unsurprisingly, resistance and political manoeuvring are commonplace in the early years. The changing role of state/provincial government represents a significant shift from an authoritative to an enabling approach to development. In other cases, the meaning of the legislation is only narrowly interpreted as attitudes are unchanged, skills are undeveloped and organisational structures remain unreformed.

While both India and South Africa have enacted laws to enable municipal action towards increased participation, neither has effective local government structures in place, and neither provides support for those agencies obliged to implement this legislation. Despite the shift in their responsibilities, municipalities continue to approach their functions through the same conventional processes and structures. This is particularly noticeable with respect to planning processes in South Africa. Despite the apparent inclusion of communities in planning approaches through public meetings, in practice many municipalities are still pursuing blueprint approaches to planning and development. They are constrained by the burden of precedent and by insufficient capacity for developing alternatives.

The legislative framework for municipal-community partnerships is generally founded in those laws enacted to provide for decentralisation processes. The intention of decentralisation is to devolve decision-making and responsibility to local levels of government in order that the governing body is closer to the people it serves. While this accountability may be interpreted as promoting greater community involvement, this is not to say that decentralisation laws include provision for community involvement. The enabling environment for participation is often created through government policy.

Box **3.3**

74th Constitutional Amendment
India

While the ideology of decentralised governance is by no means new to India, it has gained near universal approval in recent times. Though overtly committed to decentralisation, India has witnessed several swings of fortune in translating this commitment into viable and sustained reality. The principal rationale behind decentralised governance is to create a milieu in which people can develop a recognisable stake in governance. This encompasses, *inter alia*, both participation and transparency. It will enable them to acquire access to information which in turn will render governance more transparent and also more responsive to public need. The key concept can be expressed in the terms **access** and **empowerment**.

The unpredictable changes surrounding decentralisation in India have affected institutions of local government in both the rural and urban areas. They have suffered from frequent dissolutions, delayed elections, paucity of funds and inadequate staffing. Continuous and strongly articulated demands from leaders committed to decentralisation, and an increasing awareness of the limitations of centralised governmental authority, finally combined with the global trend and international pressure for lower level, more effective and transparent government.

This resulted in the Government of India taking the step of conferring a constitutional status on Panchayat Raj Institutions (PRIs) in the rural areas and Urban Local Bodies (ULBs) in the urban areas. This was first attempted through the 64th and 65th amendments to the Constitution of India in 1989, but neither was passed by the Upper House of the Indian Parliament. A second attempt in 1990 also failed because of the dissolution of the Parliament. Finally, in 1992 Parliament gave its seal of approval to the Constitution (73rd Amendment) Act and Constitution (74th Amendment) Act, 1992 which were gazetted in April 1993. The 74th Amendment Act is thus the primary legislation prescribing the role and responsibilities of municipal governments. It is based on the principle that urban local government should be self-governing and encourages state governments to devolve to municipalities the power necessary for them to function as institutions of self-government.

One of the most important provisions of the 74th Amendment for community participation is Section 243s, requiring the constitution of Ward Committees in municipalities with a population over 300,000. The provision establishes a means for the participation of the people, sanctioning state governments and municipalities to develop participatory processes. It stipulates that the chairperson of the committee shall be the elected representative of the area (or one of the elected representatives in the case of a multi-ward committee) and establishes a responsibility for politicians to work with communities in decision-making processes.

Another feature which focuses on the participation of poor and vulnerable groups is the provision relating to the reservation of seats in ULBs. Seats are reserved in elections for Scheduled Castes and Scheduled Tribes in proportion to their population, with not less than one-third of the total number of seats for women. The Amendment thus provides for more even representation in democratic processes, protecting women and marginalised groups at the political level.

The Amendment lists the functions which are the preserve of urban local bodies (ULBs), while allowing state legislatures the freedom to make additions. Within the area of service delivery to the poor, these functions include, inter alia, urban planning, economic and social development, water supply, public health, sanitation and solid waste management, safeguarding the weaker sections of society, slum improvement and upgrading, and urban poverty alleviation.

The most vital aspect of the 74th Amendment is that it accords a constitutionally guaranteed status to Urban Local Bodies. It is no longer possible for a state government to dissolve any ULB and delay elections at will. Dissolution is permissible only after the ULB in question is afforded an opportunity for being heard and a new ULB must be constituted within six months of the dissolution. The significance of this constitutional mandate cannot be overemphasised. At one stroke it provides a permanence: for ULBs security of tenure and for protection against politically motivated suspension, supercession and dissolution. Since 1992 a number of states have promulgated legislation to enact these provisions, including Kerala. The Kerala Municipalities Act takes a further step in defining the role and composition of the Ward Committee. This state legislation has been used as the basis for a comprehensive participatory planning campaign (see Box 3.2). •

While the Kerala Municipality Act (1994) provides for municipal responsibilities and outlines the vehicle for people's participation, it was the immediate implementation of this act that set a unique policy precedent by defining and funding people's participation in the planning and budgeting process for the state-wide 9th Five-Year Plan (Box 3.2). In most cases, however, it is the policy framework for poverty reduction that introduces opportunities for more effective participatory processes. In India, for instance, national policy towards the rights of women is promoted through the pre-scribed role of women in community groups (Box 3.4).

To highlight the magnitude of policy change, it is helpful to consider this process from the perspective of resource-poor municipalities. In Kerala, for instance, municipalities are being instructed to fundamentally change the way they function, the way they make decisions and the way they execute their work. Through the eyes of senior municipal administrators, the act grants the municipality the powers for urban management and the policy hands it on to the people. Through the eyes of recently elected councillors, the policy has removed their purpose and power of decision. It is unsurprising that successful implementation is linked to innovative key individuals, and it is clear that capacity building is needed to promote understanding of policy as well as the skills for implementation.

In other cities in India, many reforms are still undertaken without a state enactment, and tell a very different story. The municipal reforms undertaken in Ahmedabad and Surat, for instance, were carried out under the umbrella of the 74th Constitutional Amendment, but Gujurat has not promulgated a state legislation to provide for municipal action and responsibility. Both municipalities are bound by the 1949 Bombay Provincial Municipal Corporation Act, which has little applicability in the current political and policy context. However, it is particularly notable that in the enabling environment created at the national level by the Constitutional Amendment, reform processes were achieved through innovative leadership in both cities, not through innovative state policy and legislation. Both municipalities were conferred with senior, strong, charismatic and steadfast leaders with ambitious objectives and relentless, uncompromising will. Both leaders interpreted the legislation in such a way as to enable the reforms necessary for a more efficient, accountable and able municipality (Boxes 7.2 and 7.3).

While supportive legislation can underpin municipal moves towards participation by prescribing the municipal duties and the methodology for participation, many participatory projects are developed in contexts where there is little or no statutory support or obligation but some other driving force. Frequently, administrative and political champions of participation find means to interpret legislation to meet their ends. In Egypt, for instance, the participatory processes prescribed in the Shrouk Programme appear to be compatible with those of the pre-existing Local Services and Development Funds, which enable funds to be accessed and controlled at the local level. Where there is no legislation underpinning municipal action, municipal leaders need to have the skills to review the legislation that exists and identify the constraints and opportunities for municipal action.

In Pakistan, by comparison, the development of participatory programmes is a struggle; a struggle which government during the mid to late 1990s allowed, but did not actively support.[6] The impacts of an unsupportive legislative and policy environment were seen in the power of the government over the people, the lack of support for municipal government and the lack of any sustainable action which threatened the status quo of top-down processes.

To be effective, legislation and policy must be immediately followed and reflected in implementation processes, in programmes and funding. Where there are well established programmes manifesting ambitious and increasingly participatory programmes, and even where there is holistic political support, implementation continues to be thwarted at municipal level by the chronic lack of capacity. Funding should therefore not only provide opportunity for the

Box **3.4**

The National Policy Framework for Poverty Reduction
India

The national policy framework for urban poverty reduction in India has evolved substantially over the last decade. The forerunner of these programmes was the Urban Community Development (UCD) Programme initiated in 1958. This programme was replaced by the Urban Basic Services (UBS) programme in 1981, increasing the focus on mother and child health care and improvements in water, sanitation, women's income, and health and education facilities. This in turn led to the UBSP, the first participatory poverty reduction programme initiated in 1990-91. It aimed to create a facilitating environment which would bring about improvement in the quality of lives of the urban poor. The UBSP aimed to achieve this through (a) community organisation mobilisation and empowerment of urban poor communities; (b) equipping communities for decision-making and community management; and (c) ensuring the convergence of the various government sectoral programmes for the urban poor. In theory, the UBSP was integrated with other GoI initiatives, including the Environmental Improvement in Urban Slums (EIUS) programme. Although they claimed to have involved communities, the focus of these programmes was largely technical, and participatory activities were limited.

Understanding at policy level of the role of the community undoubtedly evolved through this process. In late 1997, as a result of the experience gained and in the pursuit of a policy aimed at an integrated poverty reduction approach, the Swarna Jayanti Shahari Rojgar Yojana (SJSRY) was created, unifying under one programme both physical and social aspects of poverty reduction. One of the most noticeable features of the SJSRY is that all poverty alleviation programmes under the jurisdiction of the Ministry of Urban Affairs and Employment (MoUAE) will be channelled through community based organisations. Building on the experience of the pyramidal approach to community organisations from neighbourhood to municipal level (found in Kerala), the programme's guidelines set down the proposed structures and mechanisms for channelling funds.

The SJSRY adopts the model for community organisation that has been developed nationally under UBSP, consisting of Neighbourhood Groups (NHG) (an informal association of women living in a cluster of about 10–40 families who select one resident community volunteer (RCV) to represent them); and Neighbourhood Committees (NHC) (a more formal association of women from the neighbourhood groups located in close proximity and within the same electoral ward). It is suggested that NHCs should be registered under the Societies Registration Act to enable them to apply for grants-in-aid under various schemes. At the apex level is the Community Development Society (CDS), a formal association of all the NHCs at the municipal level. The CDS is to be the body for channelling resources to scheme beneficiaries as well as channelling information to government on problems and priorities through planning and feedback.

Although these structures are primarily women's organisations, and the intention is that women should represent household interests, the guidelines are flexible and allow for male participation as non-voting members. The national consensus is that women need space to participate equally in development.

Community Development Societies (CDSs) are expected to identify deficiencies in basic services within their areas and to prioritise possible interventions. These are then passed on to the Municipal Poverty Alleviation Cell, which is responsible for prioritising actions for the whole town and obtaining detailed estimates for carrying out those actions. The power to sanction schemes identified through this process rests with either the Municipality or the District Urban Development Agency. Work is then to be carried out 'departmentally' through the Community Development Society under the general control and supervision of the municipality.

The SJSRY guidelines set out some proposed mechanisms for participation. The scheme has potential for empowering poor men and women (women in particular) to express demands through community action plans which form the basis for allocation of poverty alleviation funds. The spirit of the guidelines, however, appears to be most concerned with using the NHG/NHC/CDS structure as a channel for government programmes and as a mechanism for identifying programme beneficiaries. The emphasis is more towards employment generation than empowerment. It is fair to assume that this programme will be implemented with participation as a means to an end rather than an end in itself, but the scheme does offer considerable potential for improving the effectiveness, efficiency and sustainability of urban poverty alleviation funds if necessary approaches and skills can be developed. •

implementation of participatory programmes, but should cover the costs of the capacity building and delivery mechanisms necessary for effective implementation.

The Administrative Context

Notwithstanding the close relationship of the administrative context to the other (legislative, political, policy) aspects of the external operating context, it is important to highlight the constraints placed on municipalities by the administrative framework outside their control. Commonly, municipal government, even in the context of decentralisation, has low status, and the roles, responsibilities and relationships between municipalities and higher levels of government have significant impact on the capacity of local level government to develop new processes for planning and managing services and infrastructure.

The structure and functioning, location and role of municipal government within the overall government bureaucracy differ considerably between countries. Notwithstanding the differences between the English and Continental systems of government, the conventional administration is characterised by departmentalisation, compounded by strict functional hierarchies and driven by bureaucratic control. Despite exceptions (see for instance Boxes 6.13 and 7.3) where efforts to introduce the organisational and managerial lessons of the private sector have led to reform, in the main, heavily bureaucratic administrations are prevalent in most developing countries and municipalities suffer from and perpetuate this norm.

The degree of control of the municipality (and other local level agencies) over decision-making in policy, programmes and implementation and ongoing maintenance of services and infrastructure also varies greatly between countries and between cities (although experience suggest this is less problematic for large municipal corporations). Much of the decision-making process is controlled by higher levels of government through the administrative apparatus, which may impose legal and regulatory obligations, may force informal requirements, and may exercise control through the financial dependence of the municipality. Typically, basic structures, staffing and financial procedures are determined to some extent by a higher order of government and affect capacity building processes (see Box 3.5).

In theory, the administrative structure and actions of higher levels should reflect and facilitate the requirements of the policy environment. Where this is the case, municipalities may find the support they need to implement participatory processes. The situation in Kerala in the implementation of the People's Planning Campaign illustrates such a unique situation where, mainly due to political pressure, procedural change was rapidly executed. In contrast, however, most state or provincial levels of administration lean to bureaucratic inertia. Participatory policies are frequently not accompanied by the necessary reforms to systems that would allow communities to become effectively involved.

Ideally, higher levels of administration act as 'enablers' and 'facilitators' of capacity building processes towards policy goals. In practice, however, the lack of supportive administrative machinery at higher levels of government can result in staffing, procedural and management barriers to promoting participation.

* Staff policy, procedures and placements are often determined at state or provincial level and seriously affect the actions of municipalities in poverty reduction and participation. For instance, the primary need for effective and skilled municipal managers is rarely prioritised, due to the low status of the municipality in the hierarchy of administrative posts.
* Junior staff, often those with the responsibility for working directly with communities, are transferred or appointed with indifference by provincial/state levels of government. Yet the lost skills and experience of participatory projects,

Box **3.5**

Constraints of a Policy and Administrative Environment
Faisalabad

Local government is not embodied in the Constitution of Pakistan. Functions are divided between the Federal and Provincial levels of government and local government exists only under the control of the provincial level, which delegates functions to the local level by promulgating ordinances. This lack of constitutional status allows provincial governments to suspend democratically elected local governments from time to time, replacing them with appointed administrators. In practice, local government has little power and looks to higher levels of government for all important decisions.

In Pakistan, the policy and administrative context for participatory processes is weak. While successive federal governments have introduced poverty reduction programmes for urban areas, these have invariably focused on physical improvements, primarily infrastructure, but also housing and land tenure. The implementation of these programmes has been top-down, with little practical provision for the participation of the intended beneficiaries. Some projects have involved waivers on infrastructure standards to facilitate the poor, but this has often meant that operating authorities have been reluctant to take over responsibility for services once they have been completed. There is little commitment to participation and no evolution of the participatory process. There is also no general provision for departments or cells dedicated to either poverty reduction or community mobilisation which might have been the champion of participatory processes.

However, the primary impact of the administrative operating context is the constant transfers at the highest management level. The Faisalabad Area Upgrading Project (FAUP) lies under the control of the Faisalabad Development Authority (FDA) and the key institutional partner is the Water and Sanitation Agency (WASA). Both the Director General of the FDA and the Managing Director of the WASA change with alarming frequency. Over the duration of the project there have been changes at least on a yearly basis. During the most difficult periods the change in leadership has occurred every few months.

Despite the recognition of the importance of supportive management for participatory processes in the project, capacity building of senior management in this context has been impossible. Just as one senior official has been made aware of the approach, he is transferred and the process of familiarising officials with the objectives, impacts and constraints of participation starts again. There has been little opportunity to build any depth of understanding and any commitment at this level throughout the project. As a result, the project still lacks a champion to take it forward.

Transfers are, to a large extent, due to the political instability in Pakistan over the last decade. Senior administrative posts are closely controlled by political leaders, and it is noticeable that appointees change with new political appointments. At the same time, senior administrative posts in Pakistan are laden with status and incentives. The lack of legislative provision for local government and the powerlessness of local government posts lead to constant change. Political motives dominate even if they cause massive disruption. The key administrative issue is that there is insufficient recognition of the instability this causes, and a lack of concern at the policy level for developing certainty amongst management staff at local levels. Permanence is required for capacity building, for effective planning and management and, ultimately, for sustainable institutions.

Given the lack of policy and legislative support, it is not surprising that participatory processes and initiatives are in conflict with a wide range of administrative norms, procedures and established policies. Externally-supported projects such as the FAUP can obtain waivers on standard administrative procedures in the short term, but their achievements are unlikely to be either sustainable or replicable unless a mechanism is found to institutionalise the changes, and policy is reoriented toward the creation of an enabling environment. •

(Faisalabad Case Study)

unfilled posts and appointments of staff without the necessary competency can undermine and cause serious delay to participatory projects.

- The incorporation of community involvement into municipal functions brings with it a need for change to the conventional procedures relating to contract procurement. These rules and procedures are frequently determined by state or provincial government and orders have to be issued to enable municipalities to act.

Policy Level Leadership

Box 3.6 provides an illustration of the influencing factors on municipal action in a number of urban locations. Several interesting points emerge from the analysis of these and other case studies.

- **Legislation and policy are not always necessary to bring about municipal change.**

  In the presence of a strong municipal leader, change can be effectively institutionalised, and municipalities can establish and explore participation by developing their own parameters, goals and processes.

- **Effective legislation is underpinned by strong policy leadership.**

  A supportive operating context is dependent on strong policy-makers operationalising legislation.

- **Effective policy and legislation are undermined by a lack of leadership at the local level.**

  It is absolutely vital to accompany supportive policy with capacity building at senior levels of operational management.

- **The external context is a unified apparatus.**

  External factors are linked, and negative influences can be counteracted e.g. effective policy leadership may offset ineffective legislation.

The primary mechanism in promoting a supportive or enabling context is to ensure committed and skilled policy level leadership. Effective policy leadership has a number of important impacts. In contexts where decentralisation is in place, the leadership plays a key role in promoting the spirit of the legislation, interpreting the legislation into policy and programme and funding commitments, ensuring that administrative systems support policy and blockages are removed, and, most importantly, in promoting attitudinal change. Skilled policy leaders will address training and organisational needs and devise mechanisms for developing the capacity needed at municipal level to make decentralisation reform meaningful.

In contexts where a legislative framework does not exist, policy level leadership is still the primary vehicle for promoting change. High level management plays a central role in the allocation of resources and facilitating donor funding. They have control over the introduction of pilots, and have the power to determine future priorities. Despite their struggles, participatory projects provide demonstration models for government and expose policy level officials to the rhetoric, the issues, and the opportunities of participatory processes in their own context. In this way prescriptive top-down methods of service delivery can be challenged by the development of other alternative models. It can be argued that projects such as Nasriya in Egypt had this effect and paved the way for the replication of participatory approaches in the nationwide Shrouk Programme. Project-based initiatives without legislation, policy and government finance are therefore important as demonstration tools on home soil. Senior central and provincial level officials and external agents play an important role in pursuing projects that influence attitudes and decisions of policy-makers.

Effective leadership at the provincial level inevitably means a greater awareness of the role and responsibilities of municipalities in decentralised frameworks. Inevitably the policy leader can help to ensure that municipal posts are

3

Box **3.6**   **The Impacts of the External Operating Context**
Comparative Diagrams

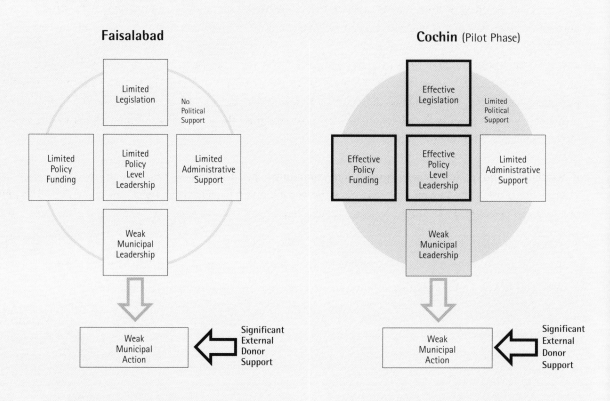

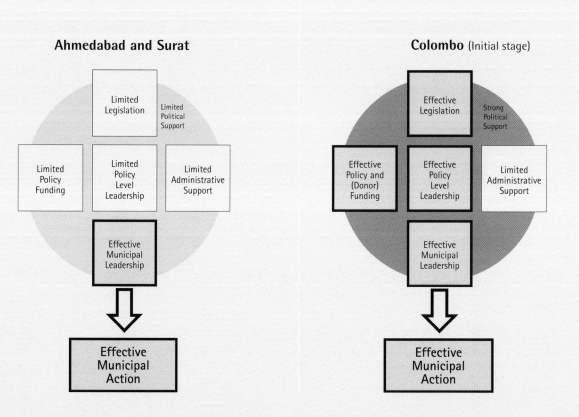

properly staffed as the key figure in the process of implementing policy is the Chief Executive Officer of the Municipality.[7] The appointment of skilled managers in a supportive context promotes the use of instruments available for participatory processes. In an unsupportive context, skilled and respected managers will orchestrate change in any case, pushing the boundaries of controlling frameworks, and frequently influencing higher levels of government.

The importance and characteristics of municipal leadership and management are discussed in detail in Chapter 7. However, in most contexts, control over municipal management lies with national, state or provincial levels of government and, as a result, a key to the integration of participatory processes lies outside the authority of the municipality. If decentralisation reforms are to be effective, decision-makers must recognise the value of positioning higher calibre management staff at the municipal level of government.

If legislation and policy reforms promoting community participation in service delivery (and other urban poverty interventions) are to be meaningful, they must be accompanied by capacity building at local level. The following chapters consider the content of the municipal capacity building required.

Notes

1. The 1999 military coup in Pakistan took place during the production stages of this book; the government in Pakistan prior to this regime was elected and could be said to be 'open' to an increasing involvement of communities in development. The impact of the military regime on participatory projects is not yet known.
2. This corresponds with the arenas of 'consensus' and 'inclusion' proposed by Abbott (1996) pp123-129
3. South Africa Development Facilitation Act (1994)
4. Not all states in India have followed the 74th Constitutional Amendment with definitive municipal legislation. Kerala and Andhra Pradesh were among the first states to do so.
5. See McAuslan (1993) p 241
6. McAuslan draws attention to the great contrast between the legislative context of India and Pakistan today. Whereas India is a country ruled by law and in which the courts are able to enforce protective laws for the poor, the legislative framework and institutions have lost this power in Pakistan. The long military rule established this situation and the political nature of appointments, the constant transfer of officials and the financial constraints underpin this inaction. Contrast is heightened by recent legislative changes, which enable participatory processes to develop in India. See McAuslan (1993) p 241
7. This includes municipal commissioners, secretaries, town clerks, city clerks etc.

DFID

The Elements
of Participation

4

Overview

In order to build capacity for community participation it is necessary for municipalities to enhance their understanding of what participation is and what it involves. The nature of participation and the municipal-community partnership varies considerably. Community participation is not only affected by the external operating context and the institutional context of the municipality itself, but by a multitude of community and project factors. In building capacity, all aspects of this contextual framework should be properly explored with the view to identifying constraints to and opportunities for community participation.

It is essential that municipalities develop a more detailed understanding of the livelihoods of the poor, the characteristics of poverty and the needs perceived by the poor themselves. This will be informed by a greater knowledge of the dynamics and social relations within poor communities and households and the identification of factors that affect the capacity of men and women to participate. It is also essential that municipalities develop a more informed understanding of the objectives of participation, the potential of community participation (when participation can take place, in what form, at what stage of the service delivery process) and what makes participation more sustainable.

This chapter describes the characteristics of effective participation and outlines the range of elements which municipalities need to address. Illustrations of key points are described, with examples of municipal initiatives and experience from Egypt, India, Sri Lanka and Pakistan.

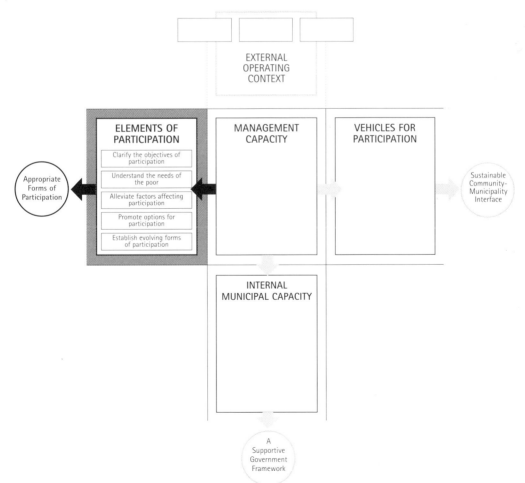

Box 4.1 **Project Objectives**
Comparative Table

	Objectives identified in project documents
Ahmedabad Slum Networking Project, India (SNP)	• to physically upgrade the slums in the city in a finite time frame by providing basic infrastructure; • to improve the quality of life of the urban poor in terms of health, education, skill upgrading, income generation and access to financial institutions; • to bring together in a partnership, the community, NGOs, the private sector and the municipality through which all efforts converge into a collaborative activity.
Bangalore Urban Poverty Project, India (BUPP)	• to design and test a model of sustainable comprehensive urban poverty alleviation that is based on the concept of enduring and effective popular participation (overall objective); • to constitute an institutional structure capable of stimulating and facilitating the processes of sustainable urban poverty alleviation; • to develop and test guidelines and procedures to make the institutional structure function properly; • to identify, formulate and implement a number of comprehensive poverty alleviation pilot projects at slum level; • to develop and test a monitoring and evaluation system.
Kerala People's Planning Campaign, India (KPPC)	• to empower municipal bodies to draw up schemes for the 9th 5-year plan within their respective areas of responsibility; • to develop the responsibility of elected officials and to equip them to work effectively in a new work environment; • to develop the capacity of officials in the various line departments to work under the direction of local bodies; • to mobilise the expertise of non-officials and the private sector to work in a voluntary capacity for the Campaign; • to mobilise the 'mass of people' to become partners in the development process; • to reorient the focus of Civil Society Organisations to mobilise their members to assist in the new development initiatives; • to institutionalise these changes by amending and updated current laws and developing new institutions and traditions.
Colombo Urban Housing Sub-Programme, Sri Lanka (UHSP)	• to mobilise urban communities to participate in development and to become organised for that purpose; • to facilitate the provision of basic amenities; • to safeguard amenities from theft and vandalism; • to play a primary role on the total development of the community; • to act as watchdogs of the process.
Nasriya Upgrading Project, Egypt (NUP)	• to improve living conditions in the area, partly by providing social and technical infrastructure; • to empower people by increasing their ability to participate fully in the decisions and activities that impact upon their lives; • to build an institutionalised capacity within government bodies in Aswan to elaborate sound housing and development policies.
Shrouk Programme, Egypt	• to transfer responsibility for the identification and ordering of priorities to the 'grass-roots' level; • to strengthen the processes of democracy and decentralisation; • to empower Egyptian communities.

The Objectives of Participation

In many contexts the widespread acceptance at policy level that people's participation makes a positive contribution to development processes has meant that the underlying reasons for involving communities are not communicated and discussed at the municipal level. However, a supportive policy context does not remove the need for municipal officials to be versed in the objectives of participation which underpin action. Like their counterparts from municipalities in countries with a less favourable operating context for community participation, it is vital that those involved in the process develop greater understanding of the various, layered and sometimes conflicting goals of involving communities in development initiatives.

The underlying rationale of government for promoting or responding to community participation is often 'instrumental' i.e. **to increase the effectiveness and efficiency of investment**. In the delivery of services and infrastructure, this is intended to result in interventions[1] that are more sustainable, targeted and appropriate than those delivered through traditional top-down municipal mechanisms. Some commonly cited instrumental or output-oriented objectives for involving communities in the delivery of infrastructure are:

- to provide infrastructure which is relevant to poor people's needs and priorities;
- to ensure infrastructure meets the needs of women and other marginalised groups;
- to utilise local knowledge and human resources;
- to improve the quality of construction;
- to improve the maintenance of infrastructure and services and decrease government responsibility for maintenance;
- to establish cost sharing arrangements; and
- to increase people's 'ownership' of services.

However, in the context of a rights-based approach to development, people's participation is seen as a means to a more fundamental end: **to strengthen civil society and democracy**. A strong and vibrant civil society is now generally regarded as being an essential component of poverty reduction. As well as directly improving efficiency, people's participation in infrastructure projects can provide opportunities for communities to lobby government and increase government accountability. Participation in infrastructure programmes provides opportunities for participants to learn about their basic rights, to develop negotiation and organisational skills, to mobilise community resources and to network with other deprived groups. The nurturing of existing skills and the development of new skills can have a widespread and long-term impact on poverty and on the relationships between the poor and government. Community participation may also lead to poverty alleviation through the development of income generation initiatives, as the participation of poor communities in construction can provide income-earning opportunities and the potential of developing new skills for longer term employment and income benefits. More specifically, the awareness of the impacts of gender relations means that government efforts are increasingly seeking to ensure women are centrally placed in participatory initiatives. This attempt to eliminate social exclusion results in a far more complex process than the functional aim of delivering services. The process of targeting women and other socially excluded groups changes traditional power relations.

A primary factor determining empowerment within project oriented initiatives is the content and objectives of the poverty focused project or programme (see Box 4.1). Traditional service projects focused on infrastructure alone often aim toward physical ends and do not place people at the centre of the process. Broader multi-sectoral poverty reduction initiatives which integrate education, health, income generation, and/or community development together with environmental improvements shift the focus to the people and such efforts have led the way to greater empowerment through delivery processes.[2]

Box **4.2**

Problem Identification and Needs Assessment by the Poor
Cochin Urban Poverty Reduction Project

In preparation for the design of the main phase of the Cochin Urban Poverty Reduction Project, the funding agency DFID (then ODA) commissioned a UK-based and a local Social Development Consultant to develop a comprehensive assessment of poverty in Cochin. Analysis of existing survey findings revealed that while some quantitative studies on poverty risk indicators were available, the information was not sufficient for the development of the DFID-funded project. It was therefore agreed that a qualitative assessment of the nature and extent of poverty in Cochin be undertaken to ensure in-depth assessments at community, household and individual levels. It was intended that this participatory needs assessment would supplement quantitative survey findings.

The Urban Poverty Profile Study was undertaken over a 3-month period by Corporation staff (mainly community organisers with some assistance from engineering and health staff). Intensive training was provided for all fieldworkers through a participatory tools and techniques workshop and a fieldwork pilot. The process adopted implicitly built the capacity of all those involved in the fieldwork, and provided a substantial opportunity for the community organisers to develop their knowledge of the problems of the poor and their skills in working with communities. The team were supported by the social development consultants and the committed involvement of the Community Development Project Officer of the Corporation of Cochin. Community Organisers were relatively well received by communities, were accurate in their documentation, and were active participants in the feedback workshop.

Information was collected using two methods. 100 focus group discussions were held with a cross-section of the poor including a broad range of vulnerable groups, user groups and other non-area based poor groups (such as street children and pavement dwellers). 100 individual case studies were also conducted. In addition, the assessment included detailed profiles of employment, training, credit, ownership, tenure security and infrastructure. A checklist, for each forum, was developed with the team before the fieldwork commenced.

Focus group discussions	Individual case studies
• Perceptions of poverty and wealth	• Activities and consumption patterns
• Key vulnerabilities/insecurities	• Income and assets
• Strategies during difficult times	• Family members' roles
• Access to services/resources	• Indebtedness/savings
• Environmental conditions	• Formal safety net/government services
• Community-based mechanisms of support	• Informal safety nets
• Community issues and priorities	• Seasonal issues
• Household priorities	

The primary purpose of the participatory needs assessment in Cochin was not only to provide a detailed assessment of the conditions and problems of the urban poor, but to disaggregate information about the poor and profile the conditions of women and other vulnerable groups. This information was then extended to provide indications of formal support mechanisms, as perceived by the poor, and to provide some insight into the coping strategies adopted by the poor in Cochin.

This UPPS provided the basis for the development of a poverty strategy and the demand-led approach to poverty responses in the subsequent Urban Poverty Reduction Project. •

(Jones, 1995)

The Needs of the Poor

A common shortcoming of municipal responses to poverty and interventions in poor urban areas is the lack of understanding of the nature and dynamics of poverty and the opportunities and constraints facing the poor. In many situations the understanding of poverty is limited to national statistics, poverty datum lines and other measurement systems which quantify poverty to a predetermined definition. Municipalities and municipal officials need to build an institutional and personal understanding of the scope of poverty in their area, the key characteristics of the poor, the problems they face on a daily basis and the main concerns the poor themselves have with the environment in which they live.

The constraints of limited knowledge

In the past, uninformed and partial knowledge about poverty and the needs of the poor has resulted in flawed judgements, which, when applied to the delivery of services and infrastructure, have in turn resulted in poorly planned improvements and unwanted, unmaintained and unsustainable services. A simple but relevant illustration is the amount the poor pay for services. It is widely assumed that poor households do not pay for services. As a result, municipalities do not offer them water connections, on-plot sanitation facilities or other levels of service routinely offered to higher income areas. In practice, however, many poor communities pay more for low standards of basic services (e.g. they pay more for water delivered by truck than others pay to have their water on tap). Such expenditure may not be evident in broad surveys, but detailed assessments of the needs and priorities of poor households and the use of their cash income would reveal this information on affordability and household priorities.

Inadequate understanding of the dynamics of poverty can also very easily result in environmental improvements by-passing their intended beneficiaries. Municipal officials promoting the construction of individual toilets in the environmental improvements of poor areas, for instance, may be causing living insecurity for the inhabitants. Some vulnerable householders have been known to opt for communal toilet construction (given the choice) as it helps to ensure that the less poor do not overtake their neighbourhood once services are improved. Conversely, and more commonly, many municipalities provide communal latrines without consultation with the community and without any consideration of privacy, security or community commitment to maintenance.

It is obviously critical that this general lack of understanding of poverty is reversed. Municipal knowledge of the poor's needs, their priorities and their strategies for coping with everyday and crisis situations is an essential basis for both delivering services and entering into partnerships. In the first instance, municipal decision-makers must recognise the need for improved knowledge of the nature of poverty, and then decide what information is needed (compared with what information is available). Where necessary and possible, quantitative forms of measurement should be supplemented with qualitative poverty assessments which provide a clearer picture of the assets of the poor (be they human, social, physical, natural and financial) and reveal a more comprehensive picture of the livelihoods of poor communities.

Participatory identification of needs and priorities

Developing municipal understanding of community needs and priorities will also provide an early opportunity to promote community participation. In participatory problem identification and needs assessments, partnerships can be formed with communities to collect information. This means municipalities embarking on assessments of how the poor themselves perceive their poverty. Methods such as focus group discussions, social mapping, individual and household discussions, preference ranking and transect walks will provide information to supplement conventional quantitative statistical surveys which may already be available. The process of collecting the information increases understanding and builds community confidence and capacity.

Box **4.3**

Defining Needs and Priorities
Shrouk

The Shrouk National Poverty Programme, implemented nationally in both rural villages and towns throughout Egypt, aimed to transfer responsibility for identifying priorities for poverty reduction initiatives to the grass roots level and to empower communities.

The nature and extent of poverty is detailed at a village/town level in an initial report. The report takes the form of a socio-economic profile or social map in survey sheets. It includes information on:

- available natural and material resources and the degree to which they are utilised;
- human resources and activities;
- the present quality and availability of local services;
- the activities of local NGOs and the resources available to them;
- social patterns and norms, social structures, communications and power relationships; and
- previous development experiences in the village unit.

While the Shrouk programme provides some guidance on the structure of the map, the hope is that the process will be open-ended, with more detail being provided by communities on issues of greater concern and interest.

Following the completion of the social map, the findings of the village profile are presented to the community. This is done through a series of focus group meetings. In each residential 'block', separate meetings are held for householders and for women. The investigating team and local leaders present the findings to the people and ask them to 'dream' about what they would like to see for the village over the next 25 years. A long list of dreams is drawn up based on the findings of the various meetings. The focus group discussions are also used to identify possible 'natural' leaders to be included in the Village Committee.

The Committee then examines the long list of 'dreams' and prioritises them in association with the technical team. The opportunities for addressing these needs are discussed and a list of potential projects is prepared. These are assessed in terms of their technical, financial, economic, social and environmental feasibility. Projects that are deemed to be feasible are nominated for inclusion in the Shrouk Village Plan. This specifies the roles and responsibilities of the different organisations and institutions for implementation and operation.

The term 'plan' is misleading, since the village plan is normally a simple table showing the list of projects required. It indicates:

- a short description of the project using simple words;
- an itemised budget including information on the labour and materials required;
- information on the expected project duration; and
- the size and form of the community contribution to the project.

The next stage of the process is the translation of the Shrouk Village Plan into a time-bound action plan and the development of proposals for specific projects. If technical drawings are required, the village committee sometimes looks for a technical volunteer to carry out the work. Otherwise, they leave the responsibility to the technical team to either prepare technical drawings or select a typical design. Proposals are sent to the Governorate for screening before being forwarded to the technical team. In theory, this compares the plan with the socio-economic data collected for the village and establishes the relationship of proposals to Ministry plans. In practice, the role of the team often primarily appears to ensure a timely response to proposals. Where it finds that proposals are affected by or duplicate existing ministry plans, it recommends modifications in plans to prevent any overlap.

The original intention was that this process would include a broad cross-section of the local community working under the support and guidance of the Shrouk technical team. It is unclear, however, if this process, in practice, included all groups in the community or if the process was dominated by the more influential people in the village. •

(Shrouk Case Study)

Poor communities can provide very detailed information about their poverty. Participatory needs assessments, such as that carried out in Cochin (see Box 4.2) provide essential information on:

- the characteristics of poverty;
- the specific needs and priorities in local neighbourhoods;
- the specific problems of vulnerable and marginalised groups;
- the poverty of women and the nature of gender relations;
- the types of external shocks and seasonal variability affecting livelihoods;
- household and individual coping strategies;
- perceptions of governmental and NGO support programmes; and
- aspects of poor people's lives which lack support and make them most vulnerable.

The outcomes of participatory problem identification and needs assessments provide municipalities with essential and disaggregated information on the poor's needs. In many prescriptive projects, it is evident that the poor are treated as a homogeneous group. In actual fact, poor communities are heterogeneous in all situations, and cultural and socio-economic differences can be accentuated in urban contexts. This type of disaggregation of the way people experience poverty has led to innovative projects which address intra-household inequalities and focus on gender needs and priorities (as seen in Visakhapatnam CHIS II). In infrastructure delivery, improved understanding of the primary role of women and girls, for instance in water collection and solid waste disposal, has led to services that are more gender-sensitive.

The process of carrying out needs assessments should be developed with the involvement of all staff (community organisers, health, planning and engineering professionals) as the qualitative and participatory study provides the opportunity for officials to learn about poverty and communities first hand (see Box 4.3). Experience of similar studies in Colombo, Visakhapatnam and Faisalabad reveals how this process builds the capacity of staff in participatory processes and builds trust between the community and the municipality. However, the absence of management from the fieldwork process means that field staff gain skills, understanding and sensitivity which managers do not gain. Results should be shared with those managers of service provision through forums that encourage discussion and raise general levels of awareness.

Building an understanding of poor communities in this manner does not preclude the necessity for technical surveys or quantitative data to inform technical feasibility of service solutions. Many engineering officials are threatened by the qualitative nature of such assessments, and as a result qualitative studies are not carried out at all or not with the same rigour as technical surveys. The community should be encouraged at a later date to assist in the preparation of demographic surveys and site surveys locating existing services and constraints. Promoters of participatory processes must impart the message that entering into participatory processes does not mean that technical standards and issues are compromised. Rather it means that the services delivered are wanted by the poor, that they meet their priorities and are delivered in such a way as to meet real, not perceived, needs.

Box 4.4

The Perceptions of the Poor
Ahmedabad Slum Networking Project

Interview with Champaben Arunbhai Patni

" After getting the land in Sanjay Nagar, I started to build a house on it. I brought mud from a nearby field and built the walls. I put a plastic sheet in the place of the roof and began to live there. In this way I made a kuccha (temporary) hut in Sanjay Nagar. After some time I became pregnant, but my husband was not keeping good health and returned to his mother's house. I didn't have any money and I didn't know how to work so I mortgaged my house to pay for the delivery of the baby and left Sanjay Nagar. When my son was one month old I began selling masala on the street and saving Rs.2–3 per day. In 1985 I joined the Self Employed Women's Association (SEWA) as a community leader to educate women and spread awareness about the organisation, about the bank, savings and loans. In 1993, I had saved the Rs. 2000 to get my house back and I went back to Sanjay Nagar. But there were no amenities there and I faced many difficulties, going to work, organising the children and throwing out the waste water.

I wondered how I could help to bring amenities to the place because the women would have to go to a nearby chawl to wash the clothes, and collect the cow dung and take it to the dumpyard. Only then could they fill up their vessels with water at the Rabaris House. Women couldn't enter the crematorium ground so 10–15 children would bring water for the crematorium. After a while, out of our own money, we got 4 public taps installed for 200 families. But these weren't enough for so many households and terrible fights broke up while waiting in the queue. We paid Rs. 600 for an illegal connection but that got disconnected. There was no gutter so everyone used to dig soak pits outside their house. This had to be emptied everyday but the municipal school opposite would not allow us to throw the water there. So where could we get rid of the waste water? – that was the big question.

There were public toilets in Sanjay Nagar, but outsiders used them and they were never cleaned. The water would overflow and our children would play in the mess, cow dung dumped there would make the place even dirtier. Then we heard about the Slum Networking Project. Uttarben and Nirajbhai came here and told us about it. The project could only be implemented if everyone agreed. But everyone did not agree. People didn't believe it. People thought that Sanjay Nagar was within the red line, and that the AMC had reserved it for another purpose. Many houses had been cleared away before, and people had received notices to remove their houses. Who's [sic] house would fall when was anybody's guess. That our houses would remain intact was beyond hope.

So we thought that these outsiders are vote seekers. Or since the land belonged to Arvind Mills, they are saying this and then they will take the land back. In other words, there was a lot of disbelief. But slowly by having several meetings with the leaders they began to convince them. They showed us Mr Varma's [the Municipal Commissioner's] letter. What facilities will we get? What will the total expenditure be? They explained how much we would have to pay and who would pay the rest. They showed us the Indore Slide Show. They showed us what the slum looked like before and how nice it became after the Slum Improvement was completed there. This way the people began to have a little more faith. After that, a meeting was held with Mr Asnani [the Deputy Municipal Commissioner] and he said 'we will do the project at Sanjay Nagar' " •

This interview was conducted by Preetiben Patel of SEWA Bank,
Translated from the original Gujarati and reproduced by kind permission of the SEWA Bank, Ahmedabad.

Factors affecting participation

A wide range of cultural and socio-economic factors can determine how, why and in what role marginalised sections of the society become involved in municipal partnerships. Municipalities seeking to develop sustainable participatory processes need to be aware of the factors which constrain and influence communities, and where possible to employ mechanisms to alleviate blockages to participation.   Key factors affecting the nature of community participation are described below.[3]

Skills and Knowledge

The existing knowledge base and the skills found in a poor neighbourhood are determining factors in the form of participation that a neighbourhood group is able or willing to take on. At the outset, communities are generally not familiar with the various aspects of service delivery and have little understanding of participatory processes or governmental procedures. Yet the poor can be very experienced in negotiating services and explaining physical and financial constraints. Micro-planning, which accommodates an iterative process, will build on existing knowledge and then incorporate the benefits of improved skills and knowledge gained through the project. As the confidence of communities increases, the nature of participation will evolve and priorities may change.

The scope of knowledge and skills already available within the community impacts upon community and individual participation. Political awareness, technical know-how and management skills may also affect the stage and form of participation. The availability of specialist trade skills – financial or accountancy skills, for instance – will promote more willingness and offer broader opportunities for participation in the construction stage of the project cycle. Successful municipal initiatives build on the existing knowledge and skill base as well as creating opportunities for developing that skill base.

Employment

Employment status may also significantly influence the amount of time the poor are willing or able to spend participating in projects. Men and women are less likely to be able and/or interested in giving time to participatory processes if they are in low wage employment with long working hours. Their work commitments may also mean that they can only attend meetings at certain times.   Yet community members with regular jobs are an important stabilising factor in the community; their access to cash may provide them with choices and they may be more willing to bring about change. Specific mechanisms need to be developed to suit the employment profile of the neighbourhood and to secure as much participation as possible.

Conversely, unemployed groups may be keen and able to participate in a range of initiatives. Unemployed youth are often an important motivating and organisational force. In Visakhapatnam, the active involvement of youth acted as a catalyst for confidence development and skills training.   Municipalities must make space for the employed and seize the opportunity which service delivery activities can provide for improving productive skills and creating new opportunities for the unemployed. In some contexts, income-earning activities introduced in association with community group formation and service improvement have proven to be an important cornerstone to participation and to people's ability to pay for services.

Education and Literacy

While education can not be easily separated from related factors such as economic and social status, aspirations, attitudes and skills, it is notable that education and literacy levels are key factors affecting a community's willingness and ability

4

Box **4.5**

Gender
Encouraging the participation of women

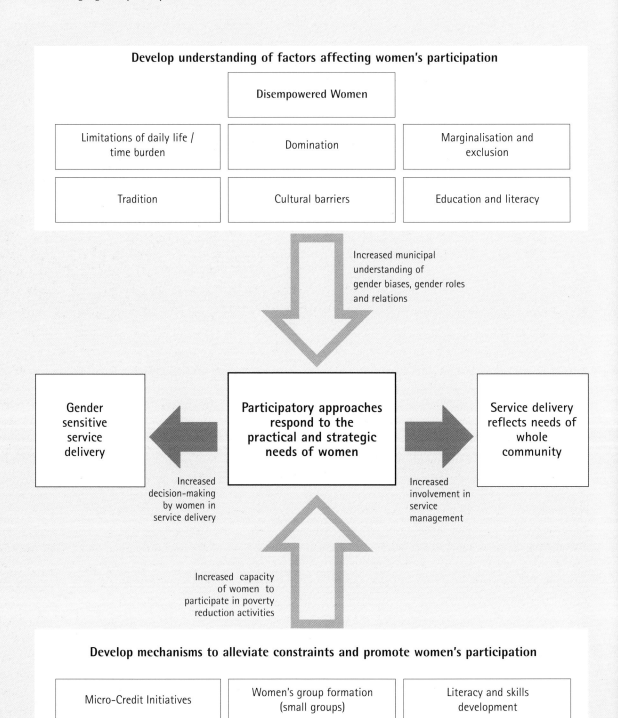

Develop understanding of factors affecting women's participation

Disempowered Women

| Limitations of daily life / time burden | Domination | Marginalisation and exclusion |
| Tradition | Cultural barriers | Education and literacy |

Increased municipal understanding of gender biases, gender roles and relations

| Gender sensitive service delivery | **Participatory approaches respond to the practical and strategic needs of women** | Service delivery reflects needs of whole community |

Increased decision-making by women in service delivery

Increased involvement in service management

Increased capacity of women to participate in poverty reduction activities

Develop mechanisms to alleviate constraints and promote women's participation

| Micro-Credit Initiatives | Women's group formation (small groups) | Literacy and skills development |
| Livelihood initiatives | Confidence building and leadership training | Appropriate time and location of meetings |

to participate, and on the degree and form of participation adopted. Literacy levels should affect the choice of strategies and mechanisms used to facilitate participation, and micro-planning tools and techniques may need to vary from literate to illiterate areas. Experience shows that PRA tools, in the hands of skilled facilitators, are an excellent means to secure the participation of illiterate women. Conversely, mobilisation of communities has been much easier in areas where education and literacy levels are higher, if facilitators are not adequately skilled to draw out the knowledge of illiterate people. As literacy improvements are rarely contentious, literacy can be used as an entry point to communities and as a binding element for the development of collective action.

Cultural Beliefs and Practices

Urban neighbourhoods are frequently characterised by heterogeneity of culture and religion and the culture of target groups is an important dimension determining participatory strategies and implementing methods. In many situations, however, development planning ignores traditional, formal and informal, systems of 'community' decision-making, and imposed approaches conflict with existing practices. As a result project activities prove unsustainable. Whilst participation in service delivery can bring with it some form of social transformation, this cannot be achieved unless there is a better understanding of how 'communities' work in the first instance and how the group relates to the rest of civil society. Inevitably, strategies and mechanisms for participation must reflect the cultural norms and practices of the project context.

Gender

It is well established that gender is a significant factor influencing participation (see Box 4.5). Men and women will often have different views and perspectives on infrastructure problems and requirements and it is important that these different views are known and are incorporated into project planning. Evidence shows that while there is a tendency for men to make the decisions about physical improvements in low-income areas, it is actually the women who are primarily involved in these activities. The collection of water is, in India for instance, generally the role of women and girls, yet decision-making over water supply preferences or the location of stand-pipes is frequently carried out by men. For municipalities entering into partnerships with communities, understanding the complexities of gender-bias in household allocation, gender roles and relations and the potential impacts of empowering women through the participatory process is essential. This understanding can then be applied by developing participatory approaches that take into account the practical and strategic needs of women, and by monitoring achievement of objectives.

Past experience has shown that it is important to create 'space' for women to articulate their views and participate equally in decision-making. The mechanisms required to create this space will vary according to the specific cultural context. In many cases, small, homogeneous, all-women groups provide a sensitive forum for women to express their views and to describe their problems and experiences. Initiating processes with a disaggregation of the community into small groups can promote the participation of the weaker and more vulnerable sections, and can enable them to develop confidence and consolidate their views before participating in the broader community forum. On the other hand, active women's groups can be contentious as lead forums for decision-making. Men are generally keen to be included in infrastructure related projects, and mechanisms which enable male participation, such as those included in the CDS system in India, should be considered (see Box 3.4).

It is also well established that women's participation in planning, design and implementation of infrastructure and facilities can contribute significantly to women's empowerment, can promote gender equality, and can also help to ensure that the facilities provided are appropriate to the needs of the whole community. This participation is, however, not without cost. In some places, this acknowledgement of the benefits of women's participation has led to dramatic increases in the workload of women. Poor women's multi-dimensional role in livelihood strategies, their relative vulnerability and their understanding of household poverty make it essential that they are key participants in poverty reduction efforts, yet their daily tasks leave them little time to do so. In order to improve (and not exploit) women's

4

Box **4.6**

A Strategy toward Gender Equality

In project agencies and amongst primary stakeholders

Working objectives	Entry points	Indicators	Assets and constraints
To mainstream gender in all aspects of project planning, implementation and monitoring	Organisations of workshops/ consultation for: • defining gender strategy • gender awareness • gender planning • responsibilities for gender devolved to all staff levels	• Reflection of gender concerns, implementation and monitoring of projects, project workplans	**Assets** Existence of NGOs/CBOs Gender aware core group Co-operation of municipal authorities Knowledge of participatory planning techniques
To sensitise men and women to gender inequalities and rights and responsibilities within home and community	• Legal literacy and gender awareness programmes at secondary and primary stakeholder levels • Dissemination of information • Gender training of a core group of trainers from primary /secondary stakeholders	• Nature and number of causes taken up regarding accountability of government and project authorities • Women organised around male violence/alcoholism • Challenging practices that perpetuate inequalities • No. of women / men trained in gender issues	
To mobilise men/women to define and prioritise their needs and subsequently around these self-defined needs for planning, implementation etc.	• Existing community organisations • Identification and mobilisation of community / government and external resources. • Develop procedures for information sharing and control authority for the community and define participatory indicators • Identification of vulnerable groups • Micro-planning PRA/PALM	• Ensure 50% participation of women in all spheres • No. of community groups formed, frequency of meetings and participation • Use of community based facilities	**Constraints** Lack of trained resources at local level Resistance at various levels - organisational and individual Time, regular follow-up Available space and time
To enhance women's capacity to take up leadership and managing roles at community level and in secondary stakeholders organisations	• Exposure visits between slums and cities to build confidence • Training for women councillors • Training for municipal staff • Network with other CBOs and create appropriate links with municipal authorities	• No. of contested seats • Active participation of women at various levels • Percentage of representation of vulnerable groups in ADS etc and frequency of attendance	

(UPO, 1997)

participation, incentive structures (such as training) can be incorporated which enable women to gain individually from the process.

A major shortcoming of many participatory processes is also the assumption that women are a homogeneous group. In reality, there are usually significant differences (with respect to culture, social and economic status) between women in one neighbourhood. These inequalities significantly affect their relative degree of participation. Accordingly, issues of dominance and representativeness need to be considered in women's groups as well as in the larger community organisation.

Social and political marginalisation

In addition to gender, there will always be other social inequalities within 'communities' (arising from age, occupation and economic and religious differences) which affect the willingness and ability of different groups to participate. The dynamics of groups within the community affect participation. Powerful individuals may dominate; women, children and vulnerable groups may be marginalised; and representatives elected at the outset may not ultimately be perceived as legitimate. Inevitably, economically and socially influential groups are more likely to have experience or confidence to see themselves in the participatory role and this 'control' or capture of participatory channels can act against the interests of more marginalised groups. This process of capture also means that opportunities for empowerment of marginalised groups through participation can be lost.

In this heterogeneous context, municipalities need to develop knowledge of different groups. Assessments need to be sufficiently disaggregated to expose the problems and needs of the range of sub-groups, and development processes must involve marginalised groups, even if the process is time consuming, difficult and not immediately productive.

Community views of participation

Participation will also depend on political views and motivating factors. There may be communities that view participation unfavourably owing to:

- political alignment;
- preconceptions of what participation means;
- the view that it is the Government's responsibility to provide them with services; and
- the inherent costs of participating (e.g. the loss of income earning time).

Perhaps the clearest message imparted by communities in the initial stages of participatory project development is their lack of trust in all forms of government (see Box 4.4). This lack of trust is inevitable. It has generally been acquired through an accumulation of municipal promises which, due to a lack of resources or commitment, were not fulfilled, and typically through the fear of eviction. The whole concept of the community participating in upgrading an informal settlement stands in contrast to previous prescriptive activities and threatening methods employed by municipalities. One of the main challenges for municipal managers is to reverse community perceptions and to build a new confidence in municipal actions. In most cases this will only come about through concrete action and visible change.

4

Box **4.7**   **Service Delivery**
Incorporating participation

e.g.	**Water**	**Sanitation**	**Solid Waste**

Household / Individual Need

Access to clean, reliable and adequate water supply	Access to hygienic means of waste removal	Access to solid waste removal

Actors   **Community Participation**

Neighbourhood Level Service

Individuals, households, neighbourhood committees / CBOs, NGOs, private operators (water kiosks etc), zonal offices, municipalities	Individual or neighbourhood water connection, neighbourhood lane level distribution pipes	Toilets, latrines, pits/tanks and household neighbourhood sewers	Bins, handcarts, organisation of labour (sweepers, waste collection)	Problem identification, implementation, community management, participatory monitoring
	Maintenance of distribution network (leaks, vandalism, damage)	Pit/tank emptying, removal of blockages	House-to-house collection, dumping, bin management	

Ward Level Service

Neighbourhood committees/CBOs, NGOs, private operators, zonal offices, municipalities, Line Agency (WASA) District Offices	Secondary distribution mains, pump stations	Secondary sewers, pump stations	Transfer stations, vehicular collection	Representation on ward committee, community monitoring of construction activities
	Maintenance of water mains	Removing blockages/ collapses; maintenance of pump stations and water mains	Collection service operations	

Municipal Level Service

Private operators, Municipalities, Line Agencies (WASA)	Trunk and distribution mains; bulk water supply, treatment and pumping	Treatment works/ trunk services/ pump stations	Transfer stations, disposal sites, incineration, recycling	Participatory planning, participatory monitoring, formal complaint systems
	Maintenance of mains, valves, infrastructure	Operation of treatment works	Operation of landfill/incinerator, recycling plant	

Factors affecting participation in service delivery

In order to understand the potential of community and municipal partners in the delivery of services and infrastructure, it is necessary to recognise that there are likely to be a number of possible roles for each partner, each role appropriate and relevant to a different situation. To examine the diversity of this involvement, it is helpful to disaggregate the problem of service and infrastructure delivery, and to consider the factors that affect participation. Examples of water, sanitation and solid waste services are illustrated in Box 4.7 and described below.

Types of service

Local government is generally responsible for the delivery of many different services: water supply, sanitation, drainage, solid waste, roads, paving and street lighting, and it is evident that poor communities can play a very different role in each type of service. Participation in water supply projects involving large scale construction may be problematic and complex to organise, and require more skills and attitudinal change on the part of line agency actors, while participation in solid waste collection, with the necessary resolve, can be organised more quickly and easily.

Levels of service delivery

Each service functions through a tiered structure at neighbourhood, ward, or municipal levels. In the supply of water, for instance, neighbourhood level improvements include handpumps, standpipes and private connections. The sense of ownership, the scale and the level of technology all make it possible for communities to become involved in the planning, management and/or delivery of water supply projects. However, at the primary and secondary levels of infrastructure (including water mains, pumping and bulk supply), partnerships are less frequently considered, ostensibly because the problem is removed from the community and the scale and complexity are accentuated. Apart from the limits this places on community involvement, the problem with making such a distinction is that the levels of service delivery are interlinked. Work carried out at one level is dependent on effective delivery at the other levels. A key aspect of a participatory strategy for service delivery should then be identifying mechanisms for linking participation at the neighbourhood (tertiary) level to the ward (secondary) and then to the municipal (primary) levels. In Faisalabad (see Box 4.8), where communities share in the cost of secondary infrastructure as well as financing the neighbourhood works, a linkage was achieved by introducing a community representative as supervisor for the construction of infrastructure at secondary level. This helped to ensure that tertiary level initiatives were not hampered by delays and by infrequent and insufficient water supply, and promoted a level of transparency and accountability on matters affecting the community.

Communities also have the opportunity to influence secondary and primary levels of service at the early stages if participatory problem identification processes are established. Many problems which communities identify at the micro-level cannot be solved without higher level inputs. The most obvious example is in water supply, where new standpipes are useless if there is a lack of water supply to the ward or municipality. In solid waste collection, initiatives at the neighbourhood level are frequently encouraged by municipalities as a first step towards community involvement. The success of these initiatives is, however, dependent on municipalities providing the necessary secondary level collection and transfer. Municipalities which have found ways to extend the community role to the secondary level (through labour, monitoring and management) are seeing greater success at both levels.

Stages of service delivery

Service delivery can be further disaggregated into project (construction) and post-project (operation and maintenance) stages. The resource constraints typical of municipal level of government have frequently led to community involvement

4

Box **4.8**

Participation in Service Delivery
Faisalabad Area Upgrading Project

Despite the lack of government policy promoting community participation over the four-year duration of the project, the Faisalabad Area Upgrading Project (FAUP) has promoted a range of participatory initiatives in co-operation with local level agencies. The modus operandi of the FAUP in relation to tertiary level infrastructure improvements is intended to respond to needs prioritised by the community (this is clearly specified in the project memorandum) and this community role in identifying projects at the outset has established an important base for ongoing participation in the various project and post project stages. It has also led to a broadened scope for participation at higher levels of infrastructure provision (with line agencies) not specified in the project design.

In response to community priorities, perhaps the two key areas of participation are in sanitation and water supply, but many communities also participate in solid waste initiatives, in street lighting and paving. Some of the key forms of this participation are discussed in relation to service types below.

Sewerage

At a tertiary (neighbourhood) level, communities are centrally involved in the planning and implementation process. With the technical assistance of the FAUP, community groups propose the works to be carried out, plan location of sewerage lines, contribute 50% of the costs of tertiary works (mostly in cash, although this can be combined with labour and materials), and the full cost (Rs.500, approx $10) of the household connections. Involvement in construction varies, but a key aspect of the control given to communities is the disbursement mechanism through joint community-FAUP bank accounts. At neighbourhood level, some communities become fully involved in the purchase of materials for instance, and subcontracting of building contractors. Minimum performance specifications have been agreed between the FAUP PMU and the Faisalabad WASA to meet both the standards required by WASA and the cost-effectiveness required by the community.

Community participation has also been extended into secondary infrastructure. This involvement arose due to the lack of performance by line agencies at the secondary level, and the constraints this was placing on tertiary upgrades. (In the context of Faisalabad, much of the secondary infrastructure to the poorer areas needs to be provided and is funded through the project.) Secondary level services were not progressing or were poorly constructed and the FAUP offices were able to introduce a non-contractual mechanism to involve communities in monitoring the works being undertaken. In 2 pilot areas, community representatives (both men and women) were given a basic level of training and a checklist of problems to monitor as infrastructure was constructed by contractors. Communities have proven to be diligent supervisors (flagging potential defects before they affect tertiary level systems e.g. pipes not laid straight/to fall, backfill not compacted) and the monitoring process has begun to alleviate programme and quality problems in secondary sewer construction.

Water Supply

At a tertiary level, communities are, similarly, involved in the planning, implementation and financing of infrastructure needed to deliver water at a household level, and this process led to their involvement in water distribution. Many communities highlighted the problems occurring at the secondary level (due to the non-performance of WASA supervisory engineers), which ultimately affected the performance of the newly constructed neighbourhood level infrastructure (e.g. mains not pressure tested, not flushed out). A system was therefore developed, like that for sanitation, whereby communities play a central monitoring role in construction. It is intended that this will be achieved through an Implementation Committee (comprising representatives from the community, WASA, FAUP and the contractor) which will promote community supervision to ensure extensive delays and performance blockages are overcome.

An extension of this has been the development of community monitoring in the much-ignored maintenance of secondary mains where blockages were causing tertiary level infrastructure (paid for by communities) to malfunction.

Solid Waste

Community-based solid waste initiatives in the FAUP have been limited to the tertiary level. In some areas there has been conflict between municipal sweepers and private contractors engaged by communities (because the municipal sweepers felt that this was their territory) and this has often placed communities in a difficult position. The partnership arrangement currently being proposed between FMC and communities (facilitated by FAUP) is for the municipality to provide cleaners and collection vehicles at specified times, and communities to provide and organise dustbins. Communities are expected to monitor sweepers, designate, prepare and partially finance the foundations for filter depot sites. Although there is scope for involvement at the secondary, collection level, this involvement has not been formalised and currently is limited to community labour for secondary level collection. •

in the maintenance of neighbourhood levels of service. A variety of lessons have been learnt from these initiatives.

- Communities are likely to be committed to maintenance regimes if they were involved in design and construction, and particularly if they shared construction costs. Sustainability is dependent on the ownership created through participation at all stages of the project cycle and not just post-project maintenance.
- Poor communities are able and willing to contribute to, and manage, maintenance funds.
- Community participation in operation and maintenance frequently results in municipalities and line agencies neglecting their own responsibilities. Community participation should mean the creation of an enabling environment in which the municipality is still accountable for their performance.

Quality of service delivery

This complex array of types, levels and stages of service delivery is further complicated by the need to consider the quality of service being delivered. Typically, municipal planners and engineers prescribe the service technology to be provided. They generally do not explain technological options to the poor, and do not build awareness of options available. As a result, poor communities are not involved in the decision-making process over the quality of service they can access. Yet experience shows that many poor communities have different needs and prefer options which are not offered to them. Experience reveals a variety of (sometimes unpredictable) preferences for urban infrastructure, some for higher levels of service and some lower (e.g. where users have opted for pit latrines rather than piped sewerage, or conversely private water supply connections rather than communal standpipes).

The impacts of supply-led decision-making are unfolding and include:

- Service supply which does not meet demand and leads the municipality into a low-level equilibrium trap (i.e. Municipalities do not provide the standard of service communities need, so communities do not pay for the service. As a result, the municipality does not collect sufficient revenue and cannot afford to improve the service).
- The marginalisation of poorest groups when municipalities increase service standards without concern for affordability.
- The lack of concern for social issues in the selection of service characteristics (e.g. in some areas, women's safety and security are threatened by certain types and locations of services).

The sheer number of variables in the delivery of services and infrastructure often underlies municipal justification for top-down approaches. While communities are likely to play a greater role in the planning and management of some services than others, there needs to be an understanding that community participation need not be limited to the neighbourhood level or to 'easy' services, and that the degree of participation and timing of community inputs will not necessarily be the same for each service type. Municipalities embarking on participatory service delivery need to consider service delivery in its disaggregated form and work with communities to develop more comprehensive strategies for participation which ensure service needs are met.

4

Box **4.9**

Community Action Planning
Colombo

In 1985, the Urban Housing Sub-Programme, a part of the Million Houses Programme of the NHDA in Sri Lanka, accepted the Community Development Committees (CDC) as the main instrument through which housing development programmes were to be implemented in settlements occupied by the urban poor. The primary mechanism adopted by the Housing Sub-Programme to integrate communities into the delivery of services and infrastructure was a participatory planning approach called Community Action Planning. Community Action Planning (CAP) processes were developed as a means to facilitate community participation in planning and development, enabling programmes for low-income settlement upgrading to be implemented locally, collaboratively and rapidly. For the first time, community groups were to be involved in decision-making about their settlement. CAP saw people as the main resource for development initiatives and not simply as objects or beneficiaries of development efforts. The Community Development Programme intended to use CAP in Colombo and later throughout the country.

In Phase 1 (1984-1987), the innovative Phase, CAP was limited to physical issues related to housing. Phase 2 (1988-1991), the consolidation phase, saw economic support for the community members of low-income settlements through self-employment. Phase 3 (1991-1995) focused on expanding the project to Urban Local Authorities outside the City of Colombo. Guidelines for the Community Action planning process were established in 1985 and the staff of the NHDA were trained in the micro-planning methodology.

In essence, Community Action Planning processes aim to establish a concrete plan for settlement upgrading through six primary steps:

- Identification - what are the problems?
- Strategies - what are the approaches?
- Options - what are the actions?
- Planning - who does what, when and how?
- Monitoring - how to follow up, what to learn.
- Presentation - how to make everyone aware of the proposals.

To support the process, a set of specific Action Planning Modules was designed to enhance the knowledge and information available to community leaders. Guidelines, procedures, and forms were developed for communities on a number of specific topics including micro-planning, CDC formation and strengthening, land regularisation and blocking out, community building guidelines, housing loan and information, community construction contracts, women's enterprise support, market links, community environmental health, and monitoring and evaluation.

All Colombo Municipal Council staff and Urban Local Authority staff who work at field level as technical inspectors, health instructors or community development officers are meant to have a working knowledge of the action planning methodology. National level (NHDA) staff conducted CAP workshops. However, despite intentions to replicate the process across Sri Lanka, the community action planning approach was mainly implemented in the Colombo Municipal Council area, and only in UBSP target areas has the importance of the CAP methodology been fully recognised.

At a community level, CAP was the predominant methodology used for community development processes. The settlers were familiar with this approach and believed that it was effective since it took into account their problems, allowed them to prioritise needs and to pursue a demand-led form of community development. A number of programmes arose from CAP as the participatory processes developed. These include an Enterprise Support Programme, a Women's Bank, a Community-based Monitoring and Evaluation of Settlement Improvement, a CAP Workshop Module Guidelines Series, and the Clean Settlement Programme.

In 1995, however, following a change in party at National Government level, the CAP process was abandoned along with the CDC movement (described in Box 3.1). The perceived political alignment of the Community Development Committee, and thus the Community Action Planning process, is said to be responsible for a change in approach. Despite these difficulties, the CAP process is still one of the most successful micro-planning processes undertaken with poor communities, and is used as a model for participatory planning in a number of parts of South and South East Asia. •

Options for community participation in the project cycle

A useful tool in broadening understanding of community participation in municipal service delivery is to consider the potential roles of communities in terms of the project cycle. This technique reflects the understanding that technical professionals have of their roles and responsibilities and presents community participation in terms which parallel their own understanding of projects. Communities should be encouraged to participate in the preparation of projects, the planning, construction, financing and monitoring as well as post-project operation and maintenance. The following section considers the key issues of community participation throughout the project cycle by considering project identification, planning, implementation, financing and monitoring. This distinction between stages is not intended to be fixed or inflexible.

Evidence from most case studies suggests that the form of participation will vary throughout the project cycle. This may be dependent on the capacity and willingness of the community and the municipality, or may be prescribed by the municipality as the role communities will play (see also Boxes 4.16 and 4.17).

Project Identification

Frequently the project identification stage is consumed by the speed at which projects are conceived, the demands of output-driven infrastructure projects and the dominance of donors. Often the project identification stage is not thought to be the domain of the poor themselves. Many projects are identified and initiated by government and donors, and poor communities (and sometimes municipalities as well) are only informed of the intention to carry out environmental improvements. Some are even informed that they will 'participate' in the activities designed. However, municipalities which have worked with communities to identify problems and needs before projects are identified appear to have benefited from greater community commitment. In the case of the Ahmedabad Slum Networking Project, for instance, community participation was very limited in the early stages of the project, but the AMC did insist that communities be encouraged to volunteer their neighbourhoods for upgrading. Neighbourhoods were not included in the citywide project unless they voluntarily elected to undertake the project. Through this rather stringent process, communities revealed a strong commitment to the financial contribution and service improvements in their area.

Project Planning and Design

The majority of service delivery projects undertaken by municipalities have been dominated by an engineering vision of what is required. The engineering-led approach prescribes for communities what they need, where they need it, how it will be provided, to whom and when. As end-users, communities, and particularly poor communities, have rarely made any of these decisions despite their knowledge of their neighbourhood and their needs. Increasingly, it is agreed that placing communities in this passive recipient position without a role in the planning process has led to a failure to meet the real needs of poor communities.

Participatory planning (action planning or micro-planning) aims to provide a mechanism through which community needs can be actively translated into needs-based neighbourhood level plans. The micro-plan implicitly aims to address the needs of all groups in the community; to enhance community ownership; and to make decision-making processes transparent. Through this process, services can be planned in isolation or as an integral part of wider responses to poverty reduction.

In order to achieve this, it is essential that participatory planning and design recognises the heterogeneous nature of poor communities and the constraints of being poor, and takes into account the very different needs of women, the vulnerable,

4

Box **4.10**

Outline of Micro-planning Process
Cochin Urban Poverty Reduction Project

As a result of a large number of transfers, the Cochin Urban Poverty Reduction Project main phase was led by a group of local officials different from the pilot phase, and the experience gained during the pilot phase was not institution-alised to any significant degree. Skills development in participatory tools and techniques (described in Box 4.2) was also lost. As a result, there was only limited local understanding of the requirements of micro-planning and the donor agency (DFID) tried to promote efforts by developing guidelines for the micro-planning process to be tested and undertaken in the main phase. The steps proposed are outlined below.

Step 1: **Preparation** (one day by Engineering, Health and Community Development Staff). This stage aims to collect information to help project staff identify the potential scope and complexity of neighbourhoods where micro-planning is to take place. It consists of the formation of inter-sectoral teams, the collection of secondary data, and a review of past work in the area.

Step 2: **Informal Contact with the Community** (Project staff with Neighbourhood Group (NHG) leaders and Resident Volunteers). This stage aims to establish contact with the community, to form an initial impression of the locality and to agree the steps of the micro-planning process. A letter is issued by the municipality to confirm the agreed times and dates of future meetings.

Step 3: **Multi-sectoral Visit (1) to Neighbourhood** (3-4 hours by inter-sectoral team with NHG leaders, Area Development Society (ADS) representative, at least 50% women, representatives from local NGOs). This stage aims to introduce the project in an open meeting forum, explain the planning process, the possible activities which the project could carry out, and the time frame for project implementation. The goal of this stage is to draw up a planning schedule with the community, to ensure communities do not raise their expectations and to record the nature of the information required by communities. Another possible activity is exchange visits to other colonies to illustrate specific types of relevant work (e.g. flood protection, sanitation systems).

Step 4: **Multi-sectoral Visit (2) to Neighbourhood** (1-3 days by inter-sectoral team with NHG leaders, ADS representative, at least 50% women, representatives from local NGOs). This stage aims to help different people and groups within the locality identify poverty problems and to indicate which problems may be addressed by different funding sources. It involves a process of problem identification, detailed discussions on key problems and solutions, the formation of sub-groups, a focus on women and vulnerable groups, and the identification of gender needs and relations. The outputs of the visit will include 'problem statements' (noting who highlighted the problem), and notes on technical feasibility and constraints.

Step 5: **Assessment of Cost and Feasibility/Draw up First Plan** (2-3 days, inter-sectoral team with management staff and other relevant officials). This stage aims to document a response to the problem identification and needs assessment in visit (2) by proposing possible activities, details of potential resourcing, possible programme for implementation, for review with the community. Engineering staff will be expected to estimate approximate costs of infrastructure works proposed, and to prepare options to ensure works fall within budgetary limits. A primary goal is the convergence of different sources of funding toward appropriate, cost effective solutions. To reduce expectations, proposals were categorised into short, medium and long term activities.

Step 6: **Multi-sectoral Visit (3) to Neighbourhood to Review Detailed Proposals** (1 day, participants as for previous visits). This stage aims to review the draft implementation plan, to address identified problems through available resources over a specified time period and to ensure that this plan is both transparent and owned by the community. This includes ensuring that the specific needs of vulnerable groups are addressed, and responses to health, education, credit, income generation, skills training and other non-service related activities, the details of environmental improvements proposed (e.g. cost, quality, options) and operation and maintenance. This step also provides the opportunity to discuss contractual options for implementing the works.

Step 7: **Finalisation** (2 days inter-sectoral team with departmental managers). This stage aims to finalise the micro-plan, activities, resources, programme and expected outputs at neighbourhood level for a final review meeting with the community.

Step 8: **Final Confirmation Meeting** (same participants as previous visits at a meeting held in the colony). This stage aims to gain final agreement from NHG leaders and the community on the micro-plan, and to formalise the process through a letter explaining the process of fund allocation and approval procedures. •

(Montgomery, 1997)

and specific users. This will mean that separate men's and women's discussions or even separate groups may be established at the outset, and that meetings are carried out with communities and groups in their own neighbourhoods at times which accommodate their different needs.

The process of micro-planning or action planning implies that municipalities are developing a respect for poor people's knowledge. The microplan developed should provide quite specific details on the content and methodology of an initiative, and should identify and prioritise poverty reduction and service activities as a response to needs. It will also document community and social assets and structures, economic, social and health problems and existing access to services (see Boxes 4.9 and 4.10).

Closely associated with the micro-planning stage is the project design stage, which details the precise layout, size, and specification of service improvements. Even where communities have been given the opportunity to become involved in broad brush planning, it is common for the next stage to be carried out in a prescriptive manner by engineering and town planning departments on the grounds that this is a technical input. This need not be the case. Empowered by information and choice, communities can and should play a central role in decision-making over such details. In Faisalabad, for instance, communities were centrally involved in the decisions over the specifications of sewerage and the locations of sewers. Community representatives generally exercised a high degree of user control over the details of the tertiary services provided.

Municipal experience of participatory planning methodologies has led to a number of important lessons:

- **Effective facilitation is the key to effective micro-planning.** These skills are frequently overlooked or missing. Inexperienced facilitators do not take an objective role in documenting community needs and priorities or confuse micro-plans with wish lists.
- **Participatory planning is difficult to achieve in the context of top-down, inflexible methods of working.** Not all municipal officials are able to immediately respond to the participatory process, and a **transitional stage** occurs, which is both prescriptive and participatory. More participatory decision-making can then be achieved with time, capacity building and facilitation.
- **There is a tendency for officials to be less rigorous in the documentation of a participatory process.** Capacity building should stress the rigour required, the need for accurate cross-checking and triangulation of information.
- **The time needed for participatory planning is frequently underestimated.** It takes trial and error and revision to find the most appropriate methods. Patience is necessary and it is not easy to maintain momentum.
- **Results will vary.** Officials should be trained in understanding the variance of results in terms of the nature of the participation (who was there, who dominated the meeting, where was it held, what time was it held, ratio of women to men etc) and the nature of the facilitation (dominated, social and technical expertise). At the same time, officials should be encouraged by diversity. Diversity of micro-plans can reflect the diversity of the socio-cultural and physical characteristics of a neighbourhood.
- **Participatory planning is a process of learning for both community and government.** Both actors will develop capacity and knowledge through the process. There will be a change in **perceived needs** with capacity building and greater knowledge of options. Mechanisms for iterative micro-planning are needed to absorb this change.
- **It is necessary to build community trust before effective exchange can take place.** It is important to recognise that this trust can also be undermined by raising the expectations of the community through such a detailed process.

Project Implementation

Community participation in the implementation of services and infrastructure projects can take the form of labour provision, partial or full community contracts for construction (e.g. septic tanks, drains), or in the provision of services

4

Box **4.11**

Public Participation in 5-Year Planning

Kerala People's Planning Campaign

The Kerala People's Planning Campaign (see Box 3.3) also known as the Kerala Decentralised Planning Campaign for the 9th Five-Year Plan was initiated at the sub-municipal (ward) level through the preparation of Ward Sectoral Plans. Ward Committees were established comprising, amongst others, the heads of education institutions, presidents of the Area Development Societies (women's community organisations) and Housing Colony Associations, industrial and commercial representatives, trade union representatives, local doctors, cultural NGOs and prominent citizens.

After establishing the Ward Committees, the first phase of the campaign aimed to identify the local needs and establish local development options through a process of consultation and participation achieved in Ward Conventions. These conventions aimed to give all members of the public a forum to discuss needs and priorities in their areas. Organised by the Ward Committees and held in schools and community spaces, each convention provided the opportunity for Councillors to promote the concept of community level planning to their constituents. Trained resource persons were available in each convention to facilitate the meeting and present the state intention of People's Planning for the 9th 5-year plan.

The conventions were sub-divided into 12 groups, each examining the needs of one sector (including education, water and health, housing and social welfare). Each group was facilitated by resource persons and the municipal officials of the relevant technical departments. A checklist was intended to guide the group through the process of identifying the problems and key issues of the sector, the needs and priorities, possible solutions, and appropriate local resources.

In the Water and Health group, for instance, the participants were asked to:

- identify those parts of the ward where supply or quality of water was inadequate;
- identify the number of households without access to adequate sanitation;
- identify problems relating to solid waste and drainage;
- identify solutions to problems of inadequate water supply;
- identify provision of public and private health care facilities in the ward;
- identify primary illnesses in the ward;
- identify key problems in public health centres (e.g. lack of doctors, medicines, infrastructure);
- locate and comment on public health centre availability;
- identify access to immunisation and health camps.

Through this analysis of problems and needs, each group formulated a report/plan for the group chairman (selected from the Ward Committee) to present at the municipal planning forum. Ward Committee reports/plans were collated by municipal staff and local resource persons into a Draft Development Report for presentation at a one-day municipal seminar chaired by the Mayor or Secretary, and through which a citywide plan for each sector was produced. This procedure was changed in the second year to allow Ward Conventions to examine all proposals in detail and recommend modifications at ward level before submission to the municipal level.

Each proposal aimed to include a beneficiary component of 25% of the project cost, either as cash/labour/materials. At the completion of Phase 3 in October 1997, 150,000 project proposals had been formulated within the state. The content of the Draft Development Reports required by the State Planning Department included the objective and beneficiaries of the proposal, the scope of work, a cost estimate, the mechanisms for funding, the mode of implementation, period of implementation, and the methods for monitoring and evaluation. The result, however, was that the projects were not developed to a standard which could be evaluated for funding. The lack of expertise of the participants involved in their preparation, and the lack of support from the relevant departments to the participatory process, meant that the process was yet to produce viable proposals. A Voluntary Technical Corps (described in Box 5.11) was therefore convened to address technical constraints. •

(e.g. solid waste collection). The more extensive involvement of communities is illustrated by a number of projects in India where communities have been encouraged to undertake 'community contracts' in which they price, tender, organise, manage and carry out infrastructure improvement works (see Box 4.12). Experience suggests that the success of such community contracting is largely dependent on supporting frameworks (local champions, key municipal officials, NGOs, private sector representatives), but successful initiatives provide evidence of the sense of pride and ownership, and commitment to maintenance, which is developed through community involvement in construction.

In the Nasriya project in Egypt, where project planning and design were carried out by technical consultants, community involvement was limited to labour provision in the sewer construction and the water supply system. Members were given on-the-job training on technical and participatory aspects of implementation, and masons and other skilled workmen were recruited as and when necessary. In co-operation with the project sociologists and community representatives, the infrastructure team was responsible for introducing project proposals, for mobilising communities, organising the work and demonstrating the project approach to government officials. In this case, it is suggested that the provision of labour met community needs and objectives and was not considered exploitative.

At its most unproductive, however, the use of community labour without choice is manipulative, exploitative and demotivating. Asking communities to provide manual labour for project construction is, in practice, exploiting the opportunity for cheap labour. Labour-based forms of participation in isolation from decision-making should be treated with caution. Municipal managers involved in labour-related participation must consider the broader impacts on the participatory process. It is then likely that they will ensure that communities agree to the rates that are paid, or that market rates are paid for work done.

At its most effective, the participation of the community in this implementation stage can bring about significant benefits. These include:

- **Employment:** Local people can provide labour in return for daily wages.
- **Skills development:** Skills can be developed in building-related activities such as bricklaying, shuttering, paving; management skills such as material procurement, organisation, supervision, co-ordination of subcontractors, financial management, book-keeping, negotiation, and procurement.
- **Management capacity:** The community can build capacity to work as a group, to undertake self-help improvements benefiting the whole neighbourhood; and to establish and consolidate a representative community organisation.
- **Cost reduction:** The cost effectiveness of community participation in implementing projects can enable more services to be provided or make service proposals more affordable. This is generally achieved by removing the contractor profit margin, using smaller subcontractors or specialist tradesmen with lower overheads, agreeing lower payments for community labour, and/or procuring materials at subsidised prices.

Despite the potential benefits for poor groups, a number of factors constrain communities from participating in construction initiatives. Primary amongst these is the lack of skills and equipment and the lack of financial capacity for the poor to undertake endeavours which put them at financial risk. Municipalities need to examine the issue of risk and ensure that efforts to involve communities are in fact not placing additional burdens upon them. It is helpful if municipalities alleviate these constraints by devising mechanisms (such as the support of the private sector) to provide the necessary back-up for community efforts. Illustrations from case studies include the mobilisation of private contractors to assist with cost estimates and quantity surveying, NGOs to assist with financial management and accounting, and consultants and contractors to develop necessary trade skills.

Innovative community contracting initiatives will also be hindered by institutional constraints and the resistance to

Box **4.12**

Community Contracting
Cochin Urban Poverty Reduction Project Pilot Phase

In the pilot phase of the Cochin Urban Poverty Reduction Project, the residents of Kissan Colony identified their priorities for environmental improvements through a locally developed micro-planning process. However, the cost estimate for the infrastructure works was considerably over the budget available, and as a result, the Corporation of Cochin began to discuss the possibility of the community becoming directly involved in the construction process.

In subsequent discussions, the community raised a number of important questions:

- Why do we have to build our own services when the rich people do not build theirs?
- Why should we sacrifice work opportunities to do this when it is the responsibility of the council to provide us with basic services?
- How would we manage a construction contract?
- How do we supplement our labour with technical skills?
- Where do we get the equipment? How would we pay for tools?
- How can we get assistance to prepare the quote?
- How would we manage the accounts when we do not have accounting skills?

Acknowledging the resource constraints of the community, the Corporation of Cochin (CoC) facilitated quantity surveying assistance from a local contractor and financial management assistance from the local NGO. The first community estimate was 25% higher than the budget. This was not well received by the Corporation, which was still quite unfamiliar with the concept and problems of community contracting. The council immediately insisted that the works be tendered to local contractors. In order that the community could be included in the bidding process, it was necessary for the CoC to waiver contract procedures, but the community, concerned with the financial risk, did not ultimately submit their tender. In the final event, the tender process failed to result in a better price, and the CoC asked the tenderers to agree that a community contract be pursued rather than the lowest bid. The community group was then finally approached to match the lowest bid (22% over the cost estimate). This facilitated an outcome, and an exchange of letters for the construction works took place between the Community Development Society chairperson and the CoC.

The two primary procedural hurdles arising at the outset were the requirements for a security deposit and an advance for the purchase of materials and equipment. The CoC sought state level approval to bypass these procedures, but Government Orders were not issued to allow the CoC to continue the process within the regulatory framework. Ultimately, the CoC exempted the community organisation from the need to pay the security deposit; however, the Secretary (the CEO) was reluctant to provide an advance which would enable them to purchase materials and tools. At this stage, the process stalled and ultimately the Executive Engineer and champion of the community contracting initiative signed for the advance in his own name. This facilitated the commencement of the works and, once the initial advance was closed, another advance was issued and so on throughout the contract. This informal action facilitated the financial arrangements for the project.

During the process of construction, a number of unforeseen circumstances arose which caused considerable problems for the community and for municipal officials. The convenor of the project committee took advantage of his position and illicitly extracted project funds from the ADS chairperson. This split the community and disturbed the goodwill and unity the community had established during the design and planning stages. Agreements previously made on the location of the septic tanks were rescinded and work came to a standstill. Residents complained to the Mayor and Councillors and the process was in danger of collapse.

It was also assumed that a community contract would remove short-cutting and the use of inferior materials. In practice, the Corporation found that once construction had commenced, the community ignored supervision and attempted to bypass building standards.

At completion, a range of lessons had been learnt. Specifically, the need for:

- high level management support to undertake new contracting arrangements;
- community expertise in construction and financial management;
- municipal efforts to alleviate the financial risk communities perceive; and
- procedural change in tender and resource mobilisation procedures. •

change. Establishing community contracts undermines informal or corrupt systems of remuneration. In order for community groups to perform the role of building contractors, it is also necessary for municipalities to reform formal contractual procedures and to facilitate the process financially. These procedural issues are discussed in Chapter 6.

Project Financing

A number of projects promote community participation by incorporating a community financial contribution to the cost of the works. Experience has repeatedly shown the link between the financial participation, the self-reliance of community groups, and improved accountability of municipal service delivery activities. The obvious benefit to municipalities is greater resource mobilisation, but cost sharing normally leads to increased sustainability through an increased sense of ownership of facilities and infrastructure, improved maintenance and increased life of the services. In many instances, the process also results in greater cohesion amongst the community. These benefits were achieved in Ahmedabad and Faisalabad (described in Boxes 4.13 and 4.14).

Evidence also suggests that projects which do not include cost sharing arrangements are not as likely to gain the same sense of ownership, the same levels of community maintenance or the same degree of sustainability. The opportunity for improving the self-sufficiency of communities is missed when communities are treated as beneficiaries. In Visakhapatnam in India, donor funding undermined community empowerment processes when communities were no longer required to contribute to the cost of basic services. Unfortunately, when this was realised, the reintroduction of cost sharing was blocked by political representatives.

It is essential, however, that municipal leaders recognise that community financing (be it through charges, taxes or direct cost sharing) means that poor communities become 'clients' in the process. This fundamentally changes relationships and places demands on municipal performance and accountability. For instance, while it should be incumbent upon the municipality to offer upgrading options to communities at all times, the need for openness is accentuated when the poor are paying, and the lack of access to information creates a primary concern for communities risking their own resources.

Municipalities also have an added responsibility to ensure they act professionally and in the interests of the partnership. This means that they must provide their share of finances, and provide it in a timely manner, and that they must facilitate the works to programme and to the agreed quality. Failure to do so can have an exaggerated impact on the poor. Informal accounts reveal that some community members in the Ahmedabad pilot project borrowed from moneylenders at high interest rates to meet their share of the costs. Municipal delays in financing their share placed an unacceptable financial burden on poor households who were paying interest but were not seeing the benefits of service improvements.

Ideally, proposals for community financing form part of a coherent and integrated participatory process. This would generally evolve from participatory needs assessments and micro-planning, which ensure community involvement in decisions made and propose cost sharing arrangements based on an understanding of community ability and willingness to pay.

Initiatives covering a number of service sectors (such as water, sanitation, drainage and electricity), and high levels of cost recovery, mean more attention must be paid to affordability. The urban poor generally spend most of their cash on survival but have proven repeatedly that they are able to save small amounts. Payments for services will be taken out of a limited monthly, weekly, or daily budget. Financial contributions and the facilitation of credit and savings schemes must be formulated on the basis of the ability of households to pay. This will vary considerably from the vulnerable households to the employed poor, and may vary seasonally. The Rs. 2000 per household contribution (approx $50) paid by the

4

Box **4.13**

Community Financing
Ahmedabad Slum Networking Project

In the pilot phase of the Ahmedabad Slum Networking Project (SNP) a partnership was established with poor communities which included a 33% financial contribution from each neighbourhood group. This amounted to a household contribution of Rs. 2000-2500 (approx. $60/household) for the cost of the physical works and a contribution of Rs. 100/household (approx. $2) to a maintenance fund. The municipal and private sector partners (Arvind Mills and the AMC) devised the rules of the SNP, outlining the roles and responsibilities of communities in the partnership.

The process for establishing infrastructure upgrading works in a particular neighbourhood began when the community approached the AMC and declared their interest in entering the Slum Networking Project and in meeting the terms and conditions set down. This stage required written commitment that they would contribute their 33% of the costs, and proof that 90% of the participant households have saved Rs. 500 (approx. $10) or more in a SEWA Bank (or other recognised bank).

If these conditions were met, the AMC then agreed to facilitate the partnership and the remaining funding for the project. The next steps included the:

- identification of an NGO to join the partnership;
- formalisation of the community organisation (NHG) as a society;
- establishment of a joint bank account (NHG, AMC and Arvind Mills);
- mobilisation of the private sector contribution; and
- facilitation of community funds for the remainder of the community contribution.

Once the community had deposited 60% of their contribution, the AMC agreed to carry out a survey in the slum area. When 70% of the households had contributed, the AMC developed the layout for the slum (in consultation with the NHG), and placed the tender. When 90% of the households had deposited their contribution, the AMC began construction of the agreed improvements.

Despite their lack of decision-making power, it is thought that the financial commitment of the community led to their involvement in monitoring the works, and a sense of ownership of the services installed.

(Ahmedabad Case Study)

Box **4.14**

Community Financing
Faisalabad Area Upgrading Project

In the Faisalabad Area Upgrading Project, communities have a commitment to sharing the costs of infrastructure works (see also Box 4.8). Under project guidelines, no tertiary infrastructure scheme can proceed until the community has raised a 50% share of the cost. The community share, together with that of the FAUP, is deposited in a joint bank account with one signatory from the community and a second from the project, normally one of the Social Organisers. The community share can also be in kind. It is usually left to the community to deal with any problems that may arise because some people are unable or unwilling to pay their share.

According to the Project Memorandum, a secondary infrastructure project should only proceed when it has received 50% of the costs from the benefiting community and when 30% of the related tertiary infrastructure costs have also been deposited into the community project account. In practice, this requirement has proved difficult to enforce and a number of lessons have been learnt:

- secondary infrastructure facilities normally link to a number of tertiary facilities and it is difficult to get the individual community groups that are concerned with tertiary projects to act in concert;
- most tertiary schemes cannot be implemented until secondary infrastructure is in place;
- the time required to plan and implement secondary schemes is usually much longer than that required for tertiary schemes. (The rule means that people must pay funds into joint bank accounts some time before they will be able to use them. The timetable for implementation is dependent on the successful completion of a secondary project over which they have very little control and many people are reluctant to commit their resources in this way.)

Project staff are currently working on the development of procedures to overcome this problem. One important aspect of their efforts has been the formation of organisations at the settlement level, drawing representatives from neighbourhood level organisations that in turn include representatives from lane level organisations. These organisations provide the settlement-wide forum through which proposals and their financing can be discussed.

(Faisalabad Case Study)

residents of Sanjay Nagar in Ahmedabad represents a repayment of about 15% of their average income, more for the poorest households. Other sources suggest that municipalities should restrict payments for infrastructure to a total of 10% of household income.[4] In the Ahmedabad pilot area, one (female-headed) household was unable to contribute its share of the costs. The rest of the neighbourhood paid this final share, showing their unity and willingness to pay despite their relative impoverishment.

Whether or not the poor are able to pay, they must also be willing to pay, and this, like their willingness to participate, will be influenced by their options, the way they perceive the project and their trust in the municipality. Municipalities can help to promote willingness by ensuring that services proposed meet the stated needs and requirements of poor communities and individuals, that the poor are involved throughout the project cycle in decision-making and that services are delivered on time to the agreed quality.

Project Monitoring and Evaluation

Despite the progress of participatory processes, efforts to involve the community in monitoring and post-project evaluation are very limited. If efforts towards community participation are to become meaningful, the monitoring and evaluation of projects must change in two fundamental ways. First, impacts must be monitored rather than inputs and outputs; and second, the poor themselves must be involved in the process. Once this is achieved, the monitoring and evaluation stage becomes an integral part of a participatory approach to service delivery and becomes an essential tool for management of change in that process.

Participatory monitoring and evaluation involves an active collaboration, a problem-solving orientation, and the generation of knowledge. It is characterised by a process where:

- indicators of success are identified by the community (including vulnerable groups) themselves (and combined with the time-quality-cost performance and output-driven indicators of conventional systems);
- the system is established at the outset and well ahead of evaluations;
- the focus is on simple, open self-evaluation, appropriate to local context;
- the mechanisms are ongoing and allow for necessary adjustment; and
- local people are empowered to initiate, review, and control the process.

The community evaluation carried out in Colombo was established to find out if goals had been reached from a community perspective, and to feed back information into future projects. The workshop process was held a year after the formulation of the Community Action Plan at a local community hall and included 35 representatives from the community, NGOs and CBOs and officials from the local authority and NHDA. The basic steps of the process included problem identification and classification, analysis of the benefits and limitations of the work carried out, and an analysis of the reasons for success or failure.

| Box **4.15** | Forms of Participation in the Delivery of Urban Services and Infrastructure |

Form	Characteristics	Objectives
Manipulation	The participation of the community is included for exploitative reasons. Communities are included in the service delivery process without positive intention or meaningful end. There is no participatory decision-making. Initiatives manipulate communities to obtain agreement to interventions or human and financial resources.	• free labour • cost recovery • meeting donor conditionality • political gain
Information participation	Many projects masquerade as being participatory but municipalities only impart or communities provide information. Communities are given information about municipal intentions. This information is controlled by the government body and decision-making is unlikely to be open to change. The process is not transparent, and the municipality is not accountable. and/or Communities share information with the municipality. There is no control over the way information is used and there is no feedback process.	• services in place and in use • minimising community resistance to proposed interventions (e.g. communities surrendering land to widen roads) • cost recovery
Consultation participation	Form of participatory service delivery found in municipalities with positive intentions towards participation, some limited capacity building, but little institutionalisation of processes. Forums are established through which communities can communicate their views on intended proposals. Information and decision-making controlled by government but may be adapted to suit local requirements. Group formation promoted. Greater accountability.	• services in place and in use • minimising community resistance to proposed interventions • ownership • sustainability • efficiency • cost recovery • targeting of vulnerable groups for more equitable development
Co-operation participation	Stronger form of community decision-making normally promoted by municipalities after some capacity building or policy change (or may be facilitated by NGOs). The municipality and the community co-operate in an alliance towards improved and demand-responsive service delivery. Communities are included in the process from an early stage. Generally more cognisant of the needs of women and other vulnerable groups.	• community capacity building • ownership • sustainability • efficiency • target vulnerable groups • cost sharing • possible objective is the empowerment of the community
Mobilisation participation	Communities are in control of decision-making processes and municipalities enter into initiatives as required by the community. Municipalities respond to the efforts of communities, or facilitate communities to control their own initiatives.	• community empowerment • community manages service delivery • cost recovery

(adapted from Pretty and Chambers, 1994)

Forms of Participation

The conceptual framework for participation outlined in Chapter 1 describes various categories which have been developed over the last three decades to attempt to describe forms or degrees of community participation. The ladder of increasing forms of participation introduced by Arnstein and later by Paul[5] is a useful tool for municipalities aiming to understand the potential degrees of participation.[6] This has been adapted in Box 4.15 to highlight the characteristics and objectives of participation in relation to municipal service delivery.

Exploitative participation

A primary aim of the table shown in Box 4.15 is to emphasise the difference between exploitative forms of participation and those that aim, strategically, to bring about sustainable forms of development. The increasing demands on the financial and human resources of municipalities that have accompanied decentralisation have often led to municipal action toward community labour or cost sharing under the name of 'community participation'. Concerns are, rightly, raised that government can use community participation as a mechanism to shed responsibilities. Experience provides illustrations of many solid waste initiatives or community maintenance schemes which failed because the sole municipal aim was to reduce their own expenditure and the needs and objectives of the poor communities were ignored. While the benefits of participation can and will be different for different actors, participatory processes that exploit the poor are to be actively discouraged.

From information participation to co-operation and mobilisation

Experience suggests that much of the participation in municipal service delivery projects starts out in the form of information-participation. In the early stages of the Visakhapatnam Slum Improvement Project for instance (see Box 4.18) communities were asked to either answer questions (to inform) or listen to solutions (be informed), but there was little exchange, dialogue or feedback. In other situations, communities have been told of environmental improvements to be delivered to them: new systems, locations and containers for solid waste collection or new locations and types of standpipes, and may also be told that they will share the cost.

- The technical nature of service delivery exacerbates the detachment of municipal officials, and there has been a tendency in the past to hide behind the 'enigma' of technical knowledge. While **information-participation** should not be seen as effective and enabling participation, the process of communicating, informing and being informed can form the basis of increased interaction with the community, and thence more substantial forms of participation

- **Consultation-participation** implies there is an element of feedback between the community and government and that decisions are not already made. In practice, effective consultation means that the process of design and implementation will be iterative and there will be an urgent need for municipalities to develop the capacity for flexible processes which make community consultative processes meaningful.

- **Co-operation-participation**, such as that seen in Colombo, implies that the decision-making role of communities is increased, that the participation results in a partnership between communities and municipalities, and municipalities may act more as facilitators than providers. In addition, communities should be encouraged to decide for themselves the nature of the role they will play in the partnership.

- In the strongest form of participation, communities seize, or are given control over, the delivery of an activity. Unlike the rural context, in urban service delivery initiatives complete control may be limited as work requires some linkage with municipal or line agencies responsible for higher levels of service. **Mobilisation-participation** may be achieved in the tertiary efforts of communities in solid waste management and maintenance of basic infrastructure, but even these initiatives must be co-ordinated with the municipality responsibility for collection or operation.

4

Box **4.16**

Ahmedabad Slum Networking Project (SNP) Pilot Phase
Forms of Participation in the Project Cycle

These simplified illustrations aim to show that community participation can be interpreted and developed in diverse ways, even within relatively similar operating contexts. In the SNP pilot phase, the AMC drew the community into the project as a financial partner. Technically, they had control over whether or not they entered into the process and played a role in management and post-project maintenance. However, the community had little involvement in the planning or construction process.

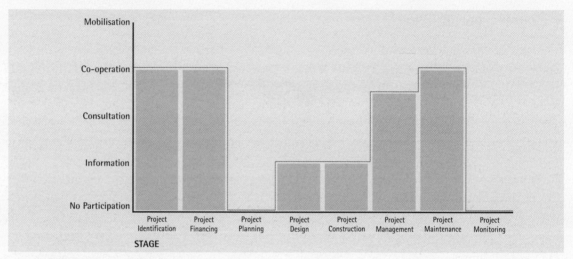

Project Identification: Co-operation
The commitment of the community is a critical step in the SNP partnership. The community must approach the Ahmedabad Municipal Corporation (AMC) and provide proof of funds for their financial contribution. In one sense this means the community has control over whether or not their neighbourhood is available as a potential partner for the AMC. In practice, if the community is under the threat of eviction they have little choice.

Project Financing: Co-operation
The community contributes 33% of the cost of the works.

Project Planning: No participation
The AMC designed the SNP as a package of basic services, and were inflexible unless a service already existed within a slum area. The community had no role in this process.

Project Design: Information
The AMC planners and engineers carried out the location, layout and design of the environmental improvements. These issues were considered to be technical decisions, not the domain of the community. Communities are informed of the planning and design of the services to be provided. While it may be that householders agreed to demolish parts of their houses to accommodate layouts, in practice they had little choice but to do so.

Project Construction: Information
The SNP did not adopt any form of community involvement in construction. The works were tendered as orthodox engineering projects, carried out by private contractors and supervised by municipal engineers; communities could not learn or earn from the construction activities.

Project Management: Co-operation - Consultation
The AMC is the Project Manager. Given their financial involvement, the community is asked to play a significant role in monitoring the construction of the project and ensuring that it is being carried out to their satisfaction. The technical supervision is carried out by an AMC engineer.

Project Maintenance: Co-operation
The services and infrastructure are maintained by the AMC. The community is responsible for smaller maintenance funded through a community maintenance fund established at the outset.

Project Monitoring: No participation
There was no participatory monitoring and evaluation of the project.

(Ahmedabad Case Study)

Cochin Urban Poverty Reduction Project Preliminary Phase

Forms of Participation in the Project Cycle

Box **4.17**

In the pilot phase of the Cochin Urban Poverty Reduction Project, an externally funded project aimed at a broad poverty reduction objective, the community participated in the planning and construction stages. This was achieved through needs assessments, micro-planning and community contracting. The community did not finance the works and were not involved in project management.

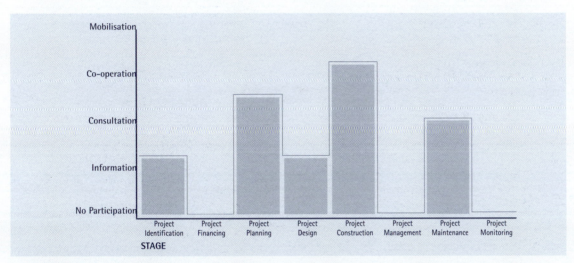

Project Identification: **Information**
The role of the community in the project identification was marginal. The Corporation and the State Government identified the project in conjunction with a foreign donor. The identification of the slums selected for the pilot phase was based on land pressures and ease of implementation.

Project Financing: **No participation**
The community is not involved in paying for infrastructure improvements or for the services provided.

Project Planning: **Co-operation - Consultation**
The principles of project planning were prescribed in the project documentation established at the outset between the donor (ODA) and the CoC. The process of planning in each individual colony included a participatory needs assessment and an attempted micro-planning process. While the intent was co-operation, the limited skills and experience and the attitudes of some of the staff resulted in a planning process which was actually sometimes more consultative than collaborative.

Project Design: **Information**
CoC planners and engineers generally carried out the layout and design of the environmental improvements. The CoC considered these to be technical decisions. Community discussions were held only to inform them of the design of the services to be provided.

Project Construction: **Co-operation**
The project pilot phases provided an opportunity for two colonies to fully participate in the construction stage. The community contracting initiative set up by a senior engineer resulted in a community activity supported with technical expertise from the Corporation, financial expertise from the private sector and management expertise from the NGO sector.

Project Management: **No participation**
The CoC is the Project Manager. Management decisions are not taken in consultation with the community.

Project Maintenance: **Co-operation**
The works completed are maintained primarily by the Municipality. The community is responsible for smaller maintenance, although there are no formal mechanisms for operation and maintenance.

Project Monitoring: **No participation**
There was no participatory monitoring or evaluation in the project.

(Cochin Case Study)

4

Box **4.18**   **Evolving Forms of Participation**
Municipal Corporation of Visakhapatnam

	Phase 1 Slum Improvement Project	Phase 2 Chinagadili Habitat Improvement Scheme (CHIS)
Project Identification	No participation	No participation
Project Planning and Design	Consultation • Neighbourhood Committees (NHCs) involved in infrastructure proposals. • No consultation on other components.	Consultation-Co-operation • Neighbourhood Committees (NHCs) involved in infrastructure proposals. Closer involvement in developing local plans.
Project Implementation	Consultation • NHCs provided some overseeing of construction, but no formal role.	Consultation
Project Management	Ranges from no participation to consultation • Programmes managed by Municipal Corporation of Visakhapatnam (MCV). • NHCs involved in management of community development (CD) and health programmes and workers.	Co-operation • Committees actively involved in decision-making and financial management.
Project Maintenance	Co-operation • Formal agreement between municipality and community groups on maintenance responsibilities. • NHCs responsible for maintenance and minor repair of neighbourhood level infrastructure and community halls.	Co-operation • Formal agreement and responsibilities developed.
Project Financing	No participation • 100% funding of infrastructure and social/health programmes by donor. • In theory, financial partnership between MCV and NHCs for maintenance.	Co-operation • More flexible financing arrangements introduced. • In theory, financial partnership between MCV and NHCs for maintenance.
Project Monitoring	No participation	Co-operation • NHCs co-operate with municipality and actively involved in monitoring programmes. At a strategic level each component has a monitoring committee including community representatives.

The participatory process in CHIS II (the second phase of the Visakhapatnam Slum Improvement Project) has been implemented since late 1996. Six-monthly Sector Action Plans (SAPs) are prepared for each sub-sector in Chinagadili by a multi-disciplinary team with the active participation of existing NHCs and indigenous community based organisations. Based on local needs and priorities, communities are able to select from off-the-shelf programme packages. Programmes offered by other organisations are converged through the planning process. SAPs are prepared in Telugu and are accessible to primary stakeholders.

Project staff identified the following benefits of the participatory process (as identified in Banashree et al, 1997):
• a shared understanding of the project process, purpose and appreciation of the views of other stakeholders;
• transparency of procedures and opportunity to raise and discuss issues and resolve disputes;
• NHC leaders valued the opportunity to participate as partners.

Some of the key constraints affecting the development of participatory processes include:
• time-consuming official procedures;
• limited interest of elected representative;
• local project office not vested with powers or support to function with any degree of autonomy;
• process still tends to be dominated by limited number of individuals who see their role as middlemen or patrons.

(Visakhapatnam Case Study)

Establishing appropriate and evolving forms of participation

There is no perfect form and no simple formula for community participation. The influence of the social and institutional context described above means that achievable and appropriate participation could and should be of a different form in each and every context. The range of services and aspects of service delivery will create a multitude of entry points and opportunities, and the degree of municipal openness and capacity will further influence the participatory approaches adopted.

In practice, effective participatory approaches are not ideal; static models of participation, introduced by external agents, and the forms of participation, are not so much objectives as indicators of the types of participation achieved.[7] From the vast range of participatory initiatives undertaken by municipalities it is possible, however, to draw out some basic parameters of effective and sustainable participation. These are described in terms of **appropriate, beneficial** and **evolving** participation.

☐ Appropriate participation

The concept of **appropriate participation** implies that the municipal-community alliance is relevant to the context. This means that participation should be:

- developed in relation to socio-economic and cultural factors;
- developed in relation to the community and municipal institutional context;
- developed and agreed with the community; and
- developed, where possible, around **existing community initiatives** and opportunities.

☐ Beneficial participation

Beneficial participation aims to describe participation which empowers a range of both community and municipal actors involved in the partnerships. For communities, this means that the process should create stronger communities more able to access services and to control aspects of their lives through increased decision-making. This means that participation should be:

- aimed towards **increased community decision-making**;
- aimed towards **increased community capacity** (knowledge, skills, access to information); and
- developed to **involve all groups** within the community, particularly women and marginalised groups.
- developed to ensure that service delivery meets municipal objectives; and
- developed to ensure that municipal officials perceive benefits as individuals (e.g. to carry out their job more effectively).

☐ Evolving participation

The notion of **evolving participation** emphasises the importance of acknowledging constraints at the outset and allowing participation to be developed and moulded to suit the changing capacities of both the community and the municipality. This evolution of participation may be expressed in the municipality and community undertaking different roles, in greater trust and confidence, and in a change in community actors (such as the emergence of empowered community members replacing traditional leaders).

Within this approach the role of the external agent should be in providing capacity building and support for municipalities and communities to find the most appropriate means of working together and then to extend this support to enable participation to evolve as time, confidence and experience accumulate.

Notes
1. The idea of participation leading to more effective outputs is that categorised by Moser as participation-as-a-means. See Moser (1989) p84.
2. This section has been developed with the assistance of Sue Phillips.
3. This section has been adapted from the Conceptual Framework produced for the research with key inputs by Sue Phillips.
4. Tayler and Cotton (1993) p154. In the urban context of Pakistan, Tayler and Cotton state that:
   'based on the assumption that 20-30% of household income is available to pay for shelter and related services, and allowing for other aspects of shelter, the aim should be to restrict payments for infrastructure to about 10% of household income".
5. Arnstein (1969) p 217; Paul (1987) pp4-5
6. Paul's categories were originally established to describe the participation in 50 World Bank projects, from the urban housing, population, health and nutrition, and irrigation sectors but are equally meaningful here.
7. Abbott (1996) pp142-143

The Vehicles
of Participation

Overview

The vehicles of participation include those instruments[1] or mechanisms that facilitate the development of participatory processes. In relation to municipal service delivery, the primary vehicles of community participation can be disaggregated into the **municipal team, community organisations** and **non-governmental organisations.** In order to make each of these vehicles effective in the participatory process it is essential that both the individual and organisational capacities of these vehicles are enhanced.

This chapter considers the problem of *how* municipalities develop community participation in relation to the municipal-community interface. The first section considers the nature and capacity of the municipal side of the interface: the way the municipality addresses the community through key municipal actors. It describes the lessons learnt through a diverse range of municipal approaches to working with communities. The second section considers the community side of the interface and the elements of building community capacity to enter into partnerships. This specifically considers the lessons of community organisations and the skills needed to participate in service delivery projects. The third section considers the role of the NGO sector in supporting municipalities and communities to achieve effective partnerships for the delivery of services, and is supported by illustrations of partnerships in which NGOs have played a primary role in facilitating the participation of the community.

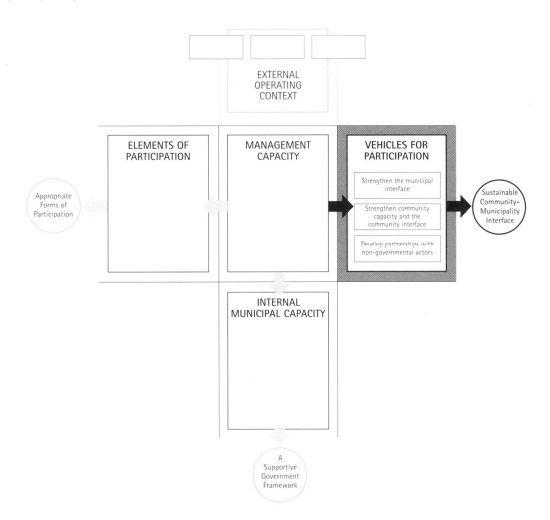

5

Box 5.1   The Municipal Interface with the Community

Comparative Table

	Characteristics of municipal interface	Key constraints and opportunities
Cochin Urban Poverty Reduction Project *(Pilot Phase)*	• Community Organisers (formerly Junior Public Health Nurses) with CD Project Officer. • Multi-sectoral team with senior engineer playing key role. • Training provided through project • Honorarium workers nominated in local neighbourhoods.	• COs well accepted by communities. • Trained in participatory techniques through project, but COs unskilled and without authority or status in municipal organisation. • Evidence of men COs being paid and promoted more than women. • Project officer managing COs did not have sufficient seniority. • High staff turnover and transfer of trained staff. • Limited NGO involvement at the outset, but developed through pilot project.
Ahmedabad Slum Networking Project *(Pilot Phase)*	• Main link with communities developed through NGO as intermediary and Community Development workers. • AMC project managers and engineers unskilled at working with communities. • COs limited involvement.	• Link through NGO was relied upon despite different objectives and disagreements. • Inadequate skills from AMC problematic as NGO role did not include service delivery. • Senior managers promoted participation, and underpinned NGO link, important in building community confidence. • Lack of convergence of SNP and government poverty reduction programmes resulted in lost opportunity for capacity building.
Visakhapatnam Slum Improvement Project	• Community Organisers (men) • Community Development Officers (women and men), located in UCD Department. • Women honorarium staff in neighbourhoods.	• Community Development staff unrecognised within the Corporation at project end. Blockage on promotion of UCD staff. • Community Development staff frequently allocated to other project work. • Women CDOs suffered marginalisation at work and at home.
Bangalore Urban Poverty Reduction Project	• NGO partnerships providing links and support to communities. • Programme Support Unit played co-ordinating / management role (between government departments and NGOs/ community groups).	• Lack of adequate training and skills for community liaison staff in PSU. PSU perceived as being part NGO, part GO. Assumed role of NGO when NGO capacity and skills proved limited. • NGO agenda varies significantly and orientation is not always flexible. • NGO-community relations improved through project mainly due to resource availability.
Colombo Urban Housing Sub-Programme	• Health Instructors (HI) from Community Development Department. • 75 men and 75 women. • Effective training in community development, health, and community mobilisation. • High level management support underpinned initiative.	• Well-trained interface staff resulted in effective formation of community organisations and project activities. Tendency for HIs to dominate communities resulted in some dependency. • Low salaries, poor benefits, with limited promotion opportunities, especially for women. • Committed and effective in the short term but dependent on political support. • Location of municipal interface in Public Health Department of CMC provided strong departmental backing.
Faisalabad Area Upgrading Project	• PMU Social organisers (SOs) main link with communities. • SOs (men and women) mostly college graduates (social work or with technical skills). Extensive training at outset. • SOs interface mainly with local activists.	• SOs involved in project decision-making and key members of PMU team, although women SOs marginalised within PMU and community. Frequent turnover of staff. • Success of project outputs related to SO skills, community skills and dependent on relationship with community leaders. • Time needed for community to build confidence in outsiders.

The Capacity of the Municipality to Interface with Poor Communities

The development of participatory processes in poverty reduction initiatives is fundamentally affected by the way in which the municipality interfaces with the community. Experience suggests that the nature and capacity of the municipal side of the interface are frequently taken for granted, and rarely given the same concern as the community side. Yet lessons also show that the nature of the organisation or team, and the capacity of the officials delegated to work with communities, will have a profound influence on the community participation which is achieved and the degree to which the process is institutionalised. Different approaches taken by municipalities to this interface are shown in Box 5.1.

An effective interface is underpinned, first, by a sensitivity to the poor and the capacity to develop a rapport with communities; second, by the skills to mobilise participation or respond to existing participatory efforts of communities; and third by organising officials effectively and creating a link into municipal functions. These characteristics do not, however, on their own, lead to institutionalisation. In order to achieve effective integration of participatory processes, the vehicle employed needs to have sufficient status and authority within the municipality. This is demonstrated by the Colombo illustration in Box 5.2.

Key factors requiring consideration include:
- the municipal actors who will be given the municipal interface role (Community Organisers, Health Officers, Engineers, Administrative Managers) and whether they act individually or as a multi-disciplinary team;
- the roles and responsibilities of these actors;
- the skills and experience needed to carry out this role (e.g. understanding of poverty, gender awareness, participation, technical knowledge); and their capacity to work effectively with all parts of the poor community (e.g. women and vulnerable groups);
- the skills development required;
- the municipal official to whom they are responsible;
- a municipal champion;
- the level of authority they have to ensure they are effective (e.g. they may be marginalised themselves) and the status they have to promote the ideology of participation within the municipality;
- the means they have of communicating with politicians and managers; and
- the support required from external organisations.

Most of these factors are readily illustrated through a consideration of the roles and experiences of different municipal actors. Issues of skills, organisation and attitudes merge with issues of gender and social status to create very specific constraints in different contexts.

The Fieldwork Interface

The municipal interface with the community in South Asian countries is commonly carried out by community or social organisers working as junior officials within municipalities. They are organised on a geographical basis and generally report to middle level managers in a community development cell or department. Frequently, and characteristic of the community organisers (COs) found in Indian municipalities, the interface role is played by partially skilled or unskilled junior government officials. Commonly these organisers have been outreach workers in Health Departments (e.g. Junior Public Health Nurses), with some experience of working in Women and Child Health Clinics in low-income areas,[2] although others may be career Community Organisers. Many of these COs are women with limited education, poorly paid compared with their male counterparts and less likely to receive promotion. If donor-funded, these community organis-ers may be given training on the scope of their new roles and on the nature and extent of government programmes

Box **5.2**

Health Inspectors as Community Organisers
Colombo Municipal Corporation

The Community Development Department (CDD) of the Colombo Municipal Corporation (CMC) is under the authority of the Health Education Division of the Public Health Department. The Head is the Chief Medical Officer of Health (CMOH), one of the most important and respected figures in the Corporation. The Public Health Department is highly regarded. Both the CMOH and the Mayor's interest in the Community Development Department were imperative for its successful functioning. It gave the department status in the CMC and in the minds of community leaders and residents of urban slum and shanty settlements.

In January 1979, the CMC began training Health Instructors (also known as Health Wardens or Public Health Officers) to work in urban low-income communities. Their task was to win the trust of community members and to convince them of the importance of organising themselves into committees in order to receive basic amenities. At present there are 150 Health Instructors (75 male and 75 female). This gender equality is in accordance with a council resolution.

The training programme was designed to enable Health Instructors to act as intermediaries between the CMC and the urban poor. The programme took place over a period of three months and was conducted under the guidance of the District Medical Officer of Health and the Assistant Chief Officer of Health of the CMC. The programme consisted of residential training for three weeks and non-residential training thereafter. The Health Instructors were trained in:

- community development (development of basic infrastructure facilities);
- primary health care (nutritional education, environmental education);
- communication (mobilising the community); and
- groups and group dynamics (conducting group discussions, types of groups, group behaviour and formation).

Initially, 100 Health Instructors were trained and sent to slum and squatter settlements. The visits aimed to establish a dialogue with community members on their health and education needs and to mobilise the communities. Their mission was also to convey the importance of forming committees within the poor communities to develop basic infrastructure facilities and interface with government. The Health Instructors ultimately became a central part of the community mobilisation. They were able to support communities to microplan their neighbourhoods and did not overly influence or change plans. Community feedback reinforces the respect many of the Health Instructors enjoyed, and stresses the fact that the Health Instructors did not even receive bribes or rewards for granting housing loans.

'They would bring their sarong and stay after meetings. They were committed to the project' and the support of the communities through the process. It is said that these officers were pro-poor, 'they were the few that knew about development.'

There are a number of valuable lessons from the approach adopted in Colombo. In the initial stages, an effective municipal interface was achieved because:

- high level officials were located in important institutional roles and actively facilitated and supported the participatory process;
- the CD Department was located in a powerful department of the CMC under a respected manager;
- the training programme for officers before they went to the field provided them with essential skills for mobilising the communities.

At present, however, the CMC does not have sufficient Health Instructors with adequate training to address the requirements of all the poor communities in the city. Communities feel that Health Instructors do not come to their settlements enough and are not available for regular meetings. Low salaries and meagre benefits are some of the key problems of the current system. Health Instructors also have very limited promotion opportunities due to a lack of qualifications. Women enjoy fewer promotion opportunities than men. The average salary for a Health Instructor in 1998 was Rs. 5,500 (approx. $125) per month, with a travelling allowance insufficient to cover costs. These conditions have prompted some change in the salary structure and levels and promotional prospects, but these have not yet been implemented. ●

targeting poor communities. Evidence suggests that many poorly educated Community Organisers develop a very close rapport with local communities and, despite their lack of formal training, are able to promote or respond to community participation. However, while most appear to have positive attitudes towards the poor and are committed to participatory processes, this is not always the case, and recruitment practices need to recognise this role is not appropriate for everyone.

The role of these municipal officials can be politically and socially vulnerable, particularly for women (see Visakhapatnam, Box 5.3). Their limited education means they are not treated as part of the professional team, and are frequently given additional tasks to perform. Many women COs complain of being marginalised by their co-workers and families because of their work, and also harassed by the men in poor neighbourhoods. For these reasons staff turnover is high. The appointment of women managers can be a helpful means of reducing gender inequalities for more junior staff if they themselves do not suffer from marginalising practices within the municipality. Municipal management should be aware of the problems likely to arise in their specific socio-cultural and administrative setting, so they can introduce procedural measures and gender awareness strategies to alleviate difficulties in the workplace.

The appointment of honorarium workers to act as a liaison with the community is another relatively well established method of developing a municipal-community interface. Honorarium workers (usually active local women or local kinder- garten teachers) generally have a wealth of knowledge about their neighbourhoods and are a rich source of information on householders, vulnerability and poverty. They form key members of community mobilisation and project implementa- tion teams, but are frequently poorly paid and undervalued.

Increased standing and recognition of the role of community organisers and voluntary support staff are critical for the development of more effective municipal-community interfaces. Many COs have established a successful interaction with communities, but their lack of authority and means of communicating with decision-makers restricts their efficacy. They require supportive management and a link person (such as the head of the community development department) to carry their message to politicians and senior administrators. The efficacy of this link will play a key role in whether or not they can achieve their project and personal objectives. Without higher level support, participatory approaches are not disseminated or absorbed by the municipality as a whole, and junior officials are left to propagate national level policy with little or no support from those municipal managers responsible for policy implementation.

In some cities, external agents have introduced other approaches to suit the context. In Faisalabad, for instance (see Box 5.4), 'Social' Organisers are employed from a cadre of university-educated social workers from middle class sections of society. They have gained their knowledge of the poor through training and work experience. They are able to communicate project-related problems and issues with other project professionals, and some have technical backgrounds and are able to impart information about service problems and options. The professional standing of these social organisers is also beneficial in some aspects of project level decision-making processes.

While skilled catalysts or facilitators, such as the FAUP Social Organisers, play a critical role in mobilising communities and developing productive participatory processes, there is also a concern that they are more likely to lead communities than facilitate them. At its worst, this tends to undermine the opportunity for empowerment evident when communities, sometimes by necessity, develop their own self-sufficiency. Inevitably a balance has to be found between supportive and dominating practices in order to ensure progress continues after project support ceases.

Box 5.3

Community Organisers
Visakhapatnam

In the urban poverty alleviation work being undertaken by the Municipal Corporation of Visakhapatnam, interaction with the community is performed by a team of Social Workers and Community Organisers working within an Urban Community Development Department (UCD). Despite the existence of the UCD department since 1979, it continues to sit outside normal government structures and CD staff continue to be somewhat of an anomaly. This has resulted in an absence of promotion and career development for staff, particularly apparent when CD staff compare themselves with colleagues in other departments who have regular salary reviews and promotion prospects.

In the context of Indian bureaucracy, this lack of opportunity for improved status is a primary constraint on staff efficiency and capacity. The blockage in promotion prospects for social workers in UCD also led to the creation of a new layer of staff under the Community Organisers, which seems to have resulted in significant overlaps in responsibilities and the creation of too many 'bosses' and not enough field staff. It has also limited the responsibility given to Community Development Officers to work in the field, and honorarium staff are now used more frequently for routine CD tasks. The inevitable resentment amongst more senior Community Organisers has been emphasised by the selection of a job title which attributes apparent seniority to CDOs ('officers' rather than 'organisers'). The lack of clarity over the Community Development staff's roles and responsibilities also impacts upon the allocation of tasks. CD staff spent only half their time on project activities during the project period. The rest of their time was spent on processing housing and loan (NRY) applications. This problem was aggravated by intensive use of CD staff for campaigns (surveys, mass literacy and election works), causing major disruption to their work.

The cumulative impact of these administrative issues has led to a gradual decrease in staff motivation and morale. Staff stressed the importance of training and exchange visits as important morale boosters, but ultimately the lack of recognition of their role has had a detrimental effect on their capacity to interface effectively with the community. •

(Visakhapatnam Case Study)

Box 5.4

Social Organisers
Faisalabad

The primary institutions involved in the Faisalabad Area Upgrading Project (FAUP) (Faisalabad Development Authority, Faisalabad Municipal Corporation and the Water and Sanitation Agency) have virtually no involvement in community and social development. Community interaction in the FAUP was designed to be carried out by a team of Social Organisers (SOs) based in the FAUP PMU who supplement the sectoral specialists in Infrastructure, Health, Education and Enterprise Development. The Social Organisers recruited are a group of professional and semi-professional staff. All SOs are graduates and many have postgraduate qualifications in social science. On the whole, their status is probably higher than that of social development staff on some other projects as they have the capacity and status to enter into open debate with their technical colleagues. However the willingness to enter into debate is frequently hindered by significant levels of conflict with management staff. During project implementation, there were two SOs, an assistant organiser and a diploma engineer for each of the four FAUP pilot project areas (population 10,000 - 25,000). The original group of SOs received intensive training in participatory approaches and methodologies. Training in participatory methodologies continues (with less intensity), although much of the information and processes is transferred through peer learning.

It is noticeable that the greatest success in facilitating community participation in infrastructure projects has been achieved by Social Organisers with a technical background. This suggests the importance of recognising the need for technical knowledge on services and infrastructure in complex urban situations. The problem with expecting all Social Organisers to develop such technical knowledge is that there is a wide range of activities covered by the FAUP, and it is not realistic to expect Social Organisers to have a basic level of knowledge about all these activities. One possible response is to promote more of a multi-disciplinary team approach to interfacing with the community. The other option being pursued is to allow PMU Social Organisers to concentrate on developing systems and structures within the community and to facilitate initial links with line agency technical officials. Their skills would then be supplemented by officials from the Community Infrastructure Unit (a unit developed within the WASA to work in poor areas) who would develop community knowledge and skills relating to community-based approaches to water and sanitation provision. The key concern with this approach is that the Social Organiser frequently 'protects' the participatory process, and this may be undermined if CIU officials do not have the same commitment to community participation. •

(Faisalabad Case Study)

The Multi-disciplinary Interface

In order to facilitate physical improvements in low income areas, it is frequently necessary (and desirable) for officials to work in teams and for engineers to accompany community organisers and NGO representatives. Being the beneficiaries of purely technical educations, the community skills of engineers carrying out this role are commonly limited to begin with and their attitudes are not always conducive to the promotion of participation. This was exemplified in many municipalities in Kerala, where engineers were reticent to promote the participatory planning process directed by the state policy in the People's Planning Campaign.

The involvement of engineers is vital, and needs to be facilitated through skills development and attitudinal change. In those cases where municipalities have achieved successful community participation in service delivery, it is interesting to note that the efforts of the CD Department have been supported by the work of a sympathetic engineer. However, most senior engineers responsible for staffing environmental improvement projects have not recognised the need for engineers to have community skills, and do not pass this message on to their staff. In the early stages of the Ahmedabad pilot phase, despite the effective role of the NGO as facilitator of the partnership, the engineers involved were quite detached from the process. A junior engineer supervising sewerage works, partially financed by the community, had no training in working with communities, did not see the need for such training for engineers, nor for the participation of the community in the overall process. Such differences in view affect relationships established with community groups. Later experience in Ahmedabad also suggests that, with experience, 'soft' engineers emerge from participatory efforts if they are given the time and space to become involved. Municipal capacity building must encompass skills development and place an emphasis on defining appropriate roles for actors involved at the interface with communities. Ensuring that officials work in teams helps to protect the participatory spirit and to ensure that technical viability and knowledge are valued. (The skills required by these different actors are described in Chapter 6, see Box 6.6.)

The Management Interface

The effectiveness of the municipal interface with the community not only depends on routine interaction with community development and project-related officials. Junior officials rarely have the authority to dictate expenditure or to determine levels and types of service improvements. Community fieldworkers need to be supplemented and strengthened by senior management presence at important decision-making forums. This will provide the opportunity for communities to see signs of high level support for the partnership; will underpin the efforts of the fieldwork staff; and will enable senior officials to develop first-hand knowledge and strengthen further the municipal side of the interface.

Municipal CEOs inevitably adopt different styles of working, and not all leaders will take to community-oriented work. Many successful projects have been led by charismatic leaders who, through public meetings, informal visits and the media, played a central and visible role in the process of building community commitment. The reforms in Gujarat in India were both led by Municipal Commissioners with a high public profile, willing and keen to address constraints directly, as the situation required.

Local champions and politicians also play a key role in establishing an effective municipal interface with the community. Often this role is promotional: to encourage communities to participate, to explain the motives of the participation and to build confidence that the municipality is serious in its efforts to form a productive partnership. (The changing role of administrative and political managers is developed further in Chapter 7.)

Box **5.5**   The Diversity of Community-based Organisations
Comparative Table

Group	Key characteristics	Key constraints and opportunities
Community Development Society (CDS) (Cochin, India)	• Women's groups working in parallel to political structures. • Funded by municipal government under direction from the state. 2% of municipal revenue must be allocated to CDS. • A hierarchical structure starting at neighbourhood group (NHG) level, combining into area development societies (ADS) at ward level and community development societies at municipal level.	• Men may be marginalised from community decision-making. There are reports of physical abuse of women due to the disempowerment of men. • Provided for in state legislative framework. • CDS chairperson is powerful in community, invited to participate in a large no. of decision-making forums. • CDS is active due to the financial base, but threatening to political representatives, increasing vulnerability.
Ward Committees (Kerala, India)	• Committee constituted to represent the people of the wards and work with elected councillors on planning and budgeting for local area development. • Chaired by the elected Ward Councillor. Up to 50 members are prescribed by legislation (including ADS representative). • Men and women form committee. • No further reservation for women or disadvantaged groups.	• Utilised as a primary vehicle for Kerala People's Planning Campaign. • Committee is an integral part of the political structure. • Provided for in state legislative framework. • Not proven as an effective vehicle for targeting the poor.
Neighbourhood Committees (NHC) (Visakhapatnam, India)	• NHCs grew out of women's groups, but now have both men and women. Some women's groups still run in parallel. • One volunteer represents 10 households. • NHC plays a financial role in MCV projects, but has little role in ongoing service delivery once project completed.	• Tend to be dominated by key individuals, often traditional leaders. • Women marginalised in infrastructure projects, with clearer role in CD activities. • Many inactive and unrepresentative. • Perceived as externally imposed rather than indigenous groups. NHCs have evolved during the project towards a more sustainable form which built on existing CBOs.
Slum Development Teams (SDT) (Bangalore, India)	• Slum-wide organisations, representing all interests and geographical sub areas; formally registered; bank account holders; equal male and female representation. • Responsible for drafting the slum development plan which is the primary mechanism for demand-led improvements and for monitoring and evaluation	• Ran in parallel with statutory CBOs. • Formed by project to carry out project based activities, but intended to be long term. Unsustainable when the central purpose or key activities of the groups have been removed. • Non-representative, traditional leadership, male dominated, marginal women's involvement, externally driven, ignored existing community groups, separate savings and credit groups have become an important alternative group for women.
Community Development Committees (CDC) (Colombo, Sri Lanka)	• Democratically elected organisation from poor households; numbers depend on the size of the slum garden; weekly meetings attended by municipal representatives. • Rules and regulations established.	• Achieved significant success in early stages. More recently the lack of direct funding, and the political situation, appear to have threatened sustainability. • Externally driven. • Leadership considered critical for sustainability.
Lane, Neighbourhood and Area level organisations (Faisalabad, Pakistan)	• CBOs were intended at lane (30-40 households), neighbourhood (100-200 households) and area levels. • All three levels operate simultaneously, lane level focuses on service provision while area level focuses on income generation. • Registered with Social Welfare Department.	• Lane level organisations not sustainable post-project, too small and inactive. • Neighbourhood level most successful and active, and the more likely to influence government. • Possible to develop commitment to short-term projects but difficulty in maintaining interest in long-term projects. • Externally driven model imposed and requiring significant external inputs.

The Community Interface and Community Capacity

While poor communities have detailed knowledge of their problems and their needs, they are frequently hindered by their lack of familiarity with participatory processes. Just as municipalities have traditionally functioned in a non-participatory way, communities have been treated and acted as beneficiaries. As such, many communities have little experience in the planning, management and delivery of services and infrastructure. Most community organisations are weak and most members lack the necessary knowledge, skills and access to information which are needed for them to interact and negotiate with government. Municipal support is frequently necessary to facilitate community capacity building not only for empowerment ends, but to enhance the capacity of the community to act as a potential partner in service delivery projects.

Although the capacity building of communities is not the topic of this guide,[3] it is necessary for municipalities to understand community capacity building and to develop a better understanding of their responsibility and role in strengthening communities to join partnerships. This section deals with the key elements which make up the community capacity: organisation, leadership and skills. Basic knowledge of these issues is essential for municipalities to support and respond to the community side of the interface.

Community Organisations

The development of effective community-based organisations (CBOs) is a fundamental aspect of community mobilisation and an important aspect of the municipal-community interface. Just as it is necessary to identify and refine the way in which the municipality will organise itself to facilitate community participation, local communities must organise themselves and most will need some form of support to do so. At their most effective, community organisations will not be confined to the life of the project, but will play a dynamic role in the mobilisation and self-sufficiency of the community thereafter.

The last two decades have provided a wealth of experience of the nature and sustainability of groups and organisations (see comparative table Box 5.5). A number of factors characterise the sustainability of urban community organisations and the participation of members of the community. Key factors affecting existing and proposed CBOs include:

- **The members and leaders of the community organisation**

  Is the community organisation representative of the community? Who attends the meetings and makes decisions? Do traditional leaders dominate the group? Are leaders trusted? Do they have the skills and knowledge to mobilise the community in the short term, to work with municipal officials, to create an ongoing driving force?

- **The marginalisation of vulnerable groups/individuals**

  Which groups are they? Are women members of the community organisation? Are they able to speak freely? Are they simply instruments for communicating male views? Are there opportunities for vulnerable members to participate and be heard?

- **The political status of the community organisation**

  Does the community organisation work within the norms of political acceptability? Does it function effectively? Do political factions threaten sustainability?

- **The objectives of the CBO**

  What are the existing objectives? Are the ends empowering or physical? Are these convergent with service delivery objectives? Will project goals undermine existing objectives and goals? Does the organisation have a post-project raison d'être?

- **The ownership of the group**

  Is the group a municipal or donor construct, or has it emerged from existing or indigenous organisations? Has the structure of the group been imposed?

Box **5.6**

The Formation of Neighbourhood Committees
Visakhapatnam Slum Improvement Project

The NHCs (Neighbourhood Committees) in Visakhapatnam were introduced through the Visakhapatnam Slum Improvement Project (VSIP), to represent 'community' interests in their areas. Consisting of both men and women, the NHCs are seen as the interface between residents and the Municipal Corporation (MCV) for planning and implementing urban poverty programmes. At the same time, NHCs are promoted as organisations which should mobilise people in their area to 'help themselves' to develop their own areas. The NHC was a development of the earlier concept of *mahila mandals* (women's organisations) which had been promoted under the Urban Basic Services initiative. VSIP was considered to have a broader community-wide focus than the UBS and therefore it was felt that both men and women should participate. In some areas, *mahila mandals* were continued as a separate group for 'women's activities' but many were merged with the NHCs.

In principle the NHC requires one volunteer for every 10 households, although criteria were modified to reflect social and geographical realities. In practice, the NHCs tend to be dominated by a limited number of individuals, often traditional leaders. Women tend to play a marginal role in relation to infrastructure (which is seen by men as a male domain) but have tended to play a more prominent role in health and community development programmes.

One initiative undertaken by the Corporation has involved NHCs in financial management of UPA programmes, and so one of the main responsibilities of NHCs has been the payment of honorarium staff such as teachers and health work-ers. The Corporation pays salaries to NHC bank accounts. These accounts also contain monies collected from the community, income derived from the NHC activities. To maintain accountability, a Community Development Officer of UCD is co-signatory to the account. The financial role of the NHC in Visakhapatnam is likely to increase in the future with the implementation of the national community-based urban poverty alleviation programme (SJSRY) which envis-ages all UPA programmes being channelled through community-based organisations. The experience of the VSIP has pro-vided a sound experience for the implementation of the new policy.

An impact assessment study carried out in 1997 (DAG, 1997b) found that large sections of the population had no connection with their NHC and were unaware of its activities. It also found NHCs to be quite inactive in many upgraded areas two years after the completion of the project. It appears that NHCs were considerably more active at an earlier stage when infrastructure was being planned and implemented. When infrastructure works were complete and CD and health programmes were up and running, NHCs had little actual role in the ongoing delivery process. It appears that there has become little motivation for maintaining an NHC, except to maintain an identity to secure benefits from future urban poverty alleviation programmes that require the NHC to exist as a vehicle for delivery. As such, most NHCs have established themselves as a means of implementing MCV programmes, but not as a body with a separate identity or one that actively represents or works on behalf of the community for other purposes.

One of the limitations of the participatory approach adopted in VSIP which contributed to the problems described above is the lack of a clearly defined strategy for involving NHCs in planning and delivery of services. It was never very clear from the outset, therefore, what, specifically, NHCs were to do. The focus was on NHC formation. The target-driven culture also resulted in the NHC model being applied comprehensively across all slums as another CD target-driven activity. This was exacerbated by traditional government and donor monitoring preoccupations with quantitative targets rather than quality or participation.

Phase 2, the Chinagadili Habitat Improvement Scheme II (CHIS II), provided an opportunity for UCD to review the experiences and lessons of VSIP and to develop mechanisms for greater and more representative community participation in the planning and delivery of Corporation services in poor areas. In the Chinagadili phase of the work, UCD staff developed the NHC concept with the view to making NHCs more active as partners in service planning and delivery, more representative of women's views, and more permanent. With the introduction of the 74th Constitutional Amendment and reintroduction of elected representatives and ward level committees for decentralised decision-making (see Boxes 3.4 and 3.6), it was also necessary to define the relationship of NHCs to these democratic processes. It is expected that this process of neighbourhood committee development will lead to more responsive targeting and longer term sustainability of project inputs. •

Experience suggests that the development of sustainable and representative groups is difficult. Without capacity building, community organisations are characterised by a number of constraining features. Many of these constraints are illustrated through the description of the Visakhapatnam and Colombo Community Based Organisations in Boxes 5.6-5.9 and outlined below.

☐ Domination and representativeness

Commonly, CBOs are dominated by the most powerful male members of the neighbourhood, are aligned or divided by political factions, and are exclusive in their approach to decision-making. Case study evidence suggests that the degree of representativeness achieved will depend on socio-political and cultural complexities. In India and Sri Lanka, where democratic processes are established, there is greater potential for community organisations in urban areas to be inclusive, and for the leadership of community organisations to be elected by relatively fair means. In many situations, however, traditional elders dominate community-based organisations and poverty reduction activities channelled through the CBO may not reach the poorest. Although it appears that visible and communal benefit of infrastructure improvements makes them less open to appropriation than more focused activities, decision-making processes must promote participation of all groups irrespective of status. Only in this way will service delivery be appropriate to the heterogeneous nature of poor groups.

☐ Gender

Case studies highlight the vast range of membership of community organisations, from the all-women CDC and CDS of Sri Lanka and Kerala, to the mixed Slum Committees of Bangalore, and the all-male organisations found in a vast majority of contexts. In India, all-women community organisations have, on the whole, provided a successful model for replication in appropriate socio-cultural contexts. The establishment of women's CBOs has led to massive improvements in the capacity of women to participate, to make decisions and to manage neighbourhood activities. However, in some situations, the empowerment of women and the opportunities for women created through the process have led, inevitably, to the exclusion of men from the decision-making process and discontent. Officials should be aware of the risk of women being abused and women acting as puppets for male family members. Efforts to establish this involvement (through parallel groups or participation without a vote) may undermine the women's groups.

☐ Building on existing organisations and livelihood activities

Ultimately, community organisations need the format, power and support to operate effectively. Evidence suggests that this is often likely to be achieved by building on effective existing organisations or indigenous groups, which may already be explicitly or implicitly supported by elected representatives, informal leaders and the broader community. Evidence also suggests that organisations developed around specific ongoing and tangible activities such as micro-credit groups or water committees are bound by a raison d'être and display more sustainability than project groups.

☐ Vulnerability and the building block approach

In organisational contexts where men and traditional leaders dominate decision-making processes, it is essential that weaker groups are given the space to participate in the early stages of capacity building. This can be achieved, for instance, through the development of smaller focused groups with particular goals (literacy, vocational training) which can then feed into the broader community groups when some capacity is built. This building block approach to group formation particularly encourages women and other vulnerable groups to participate. Community Organisations can function successfully at the neighbourhood level (comprising 15–25 households) or at a broader settlement level. In Cochin, the small (women-only) neighbourhood level groups (NHGs), come together first into Area Development Societies at Ward level and then into one Community Development Society for the Municipality. This case study provides a useful illustration of a formalised, pyramidal model already achieved in Kerala and to be replicated throughout India under the SJSRY poverty reduction programme (see Box 3.4).

Box **5.7**	**The Evolution of Neighbourhood Committees**
	Visakhapatnam

Since the introduction of the 74th Constitutional Amendment, the Urban Community Development Department in the Municipal Corporation of Visakhapatnam has tried to work out mechanisms for working more closely with Ward Councillors in project areas. This has been most systematically addressed in Chinagadili Habitat Improvement Scheme (CHIS II) (see also Box 5.6). Here the Ward Councillor is a formal member of the Project Steering Committee (PSC). The immediate objective of this initiative is to gain political support for the project. The longer-term purpose of this collaboration is primarily to create more transparent and representative channels for allocating municipal resources (traditionally, resources are allocated on the basis of political patronage). However, the involvement of the Councillor has not always been successful. The Councillor does not attend or take an active role in meetings and has failed to fulfil commitments, but the principle and mechanism for collaboration have been established and are perceived as important achievements.

The other critical issue that has arisen is the degree to which NHC members and leaders accurately represent communities. Although there is a model formula for NHC representation, in practice NHC members tend to be a combination of interested and active individuals and traditionally powerful individuals/groups. Women have tended to play a marginal role except in health and education activities. This is not necessarily a problem where the 'community' as a whole is satisfied that those individuals are acting in their best interests, but this is not always the case.

The VSIP impact assessment (DAG, 1997b) found that NHCs were most representative and successful in small slum areas and areas made up of single caste groups. In the majority of areas, however, large numbers of residents had no involvement in the NHC, knew little or nothing of its activities and felt that it was dominated by certain political affiliations or caste groups. This problem is not unique to Visakhapatnam. Most interestingly, however, this domination was less marked in the city of Vijayawada, with high levels of political awareness amongst the poor, a city with a long communist tradition). In Vijayawada, NHCs tended to be more mixed, leadership was more contested, people were more aware of NHC activities and project benefits were more widespread in the community.

In recognition of these limitations, community workers in Chinagadili introduced new mechanisms to try and ensure that NHCs were more representative. One notable feature of recent NHCs is that they recognise existing community-based organisations (sangams) (the earlier Visakhapatnam Slum Improvement Projects ignored indigenous groups) and seek to include these organisations. Project staff started by identifying existing organisations and then promoted NHCs, not as an alternative or competing organisation, but rather as a complementary vehicle for area improvements.

This approach seems to have been appreciated by local groups. Although the NHC concept is externally introduced or imposed as a mechanism for accessing municipal resources, it is possible it will continue to have a life after the end of the project. The concept of working together for mutual benefit has been introduced for the first time and the process strengthened individual sangams. Where social groups (particularly women) did not have an existing organisation or were not represented by existing sangams, MCV has promoted the participation of these groups in NHCs.

NHCs are required to have 50% women members. In addition, women are encouraged to form their own groups. This has primarily occurred through the formation of savings and credit groups (a response to a need identified by the women themselves). These savings and credit groups provide the space for women to develop their confidence and skills to participate in larger forums.

The case study of Visakhapatnam provides an illustration of a range of issues concerning community organisations including: the role and importance of promoting gender equality, the representative nature of the group, the potential of political alignment, and the experience of building on existing groups. It also provides an example of what role a municipality can take in supporting the development of community capacity and organisation. Most importantly it shows the potential role of a community organisation within a project and the evolution which can take place with time and capacity building. •

Community Leadership

In all case studies without exception, the effectiveness of community organisations has been dependent on the capacity of community leadership. Effective leadership is not only a matter of skill but of commitment shown and support received for that role. Effective leaders display, for instance, leadership skills, confidence, the capacity and willingness to shoulder the burdens of representing the community, the capacity to engage all groups, and the strength to avoid the domination of powerful members of the community. The collapse of the CDC movement in Colombo described in Box 5.9 has been ascribed in part to the lack of capacity of leaders.

Community Skills

In order for communities to become partners with municipalities and other actors, it is absolutely crucial that they be given the opportunity to develop the skills and knowledge they need to act. These will include:

- **institutional knowledge** which provides them with an understanding of how the municipal machine operates and the constraints and opportunities;
- **participatory skills** which include the tools and techniques of participatory planning such as needs identification, social mapping, micro-planning;
- **technical knowledge and information** on options, advantages and disadvantages, costs;
- **negotiating skills** which enable dialogue with other partners;
- **conflict and dispute resolution** skills to manage the dynamics of the community organisations;
- **confidence-building,** particularly for women;
- **literacy and numeracy skills** which empower and facilitate more significant roles in decision-making and management;
- **financial management skills** which create accountability and transparency and are essential to building community confidence and trust.

A common cause of the lack of community skills, is actually a **lack of access to information.** In the past, government officials have controlled community access to information and the government has relied on technical knowledge to justify a lack of communication with communities. The importance of information and choice was illustrated in the Cochin Pilot Phase, where communities opted for twin-pit latrines over septic tanks once they had been given complete information on the ramifications of each.

This lack of skill is also a **lack of access to the bureaucratic process.** Communities do not necessarily have the knowledge of the constraints and opportunities of municipal systems and structures, or of how to make their way through complex institutional processes. These skills are developed with ongoing experience, and municipalities must facilitate improved access through training and exposure and through reform to the procedures and structures which limit community access (see Chapter 6).

The development of capacity amongst communities is an incremental, evolving and long-term process. In many municipal-community partnerships focused on service delivery, communities are **not given sufficient time** to develop capacity. The emphasis on outputs is often reinforced by the need for politicians to see results within their term in office, and for administrators to work to annual budgets. Given these conflicting demands, municipalities need to consider how they can allocate the necessary time for community capacity building see Box 5.15).

Box 5.8

Formalising Community Organisations
Community Development Committees, Colombo

In 1979, the Colombo Municipal Council initiated the **Community Development Committees** (CDCs), sometimes called Community Development Councils, as the primary vehicle for the implementation of the newly reorganised Urban Basic Services Programme (UBSP) in Sri Lanka (see Box 4.9). The aim was to mobilise the participation of, and organisation within, urban low-income communities to facilitate the provision of basic amenities. At the outset, it was intended that the Community Development Committees were to act as a permanent tool for the comprehensive development of the community and the environment. From the municipal perspective this would specifically facilitate the urban poor to negotiate with government to receive basic amenities. With the assistance of the Health Instructors (see Box 5.2) tasked in mobilising and facilitating the organisation of communities, the first CDC was registered at the CMC in 1979, and by 1998 a total of 623 committees had been registered.

All members of the CDC are members of poor local communities. The CDCs have adopted the traditional organisational structure of Chairman, Vice-Chairman, Secretary, Assistant Secretary Treasurer, and a committee of five ordinary members. Generally the number of members depends on the size of the gardens (the larger slum gardens having many more members). The office members are chosen through a simple election process whereby each adult member of the community has a vote. There are simple rules and procedures, and in 1992 the CMC formed a constitution with CDC leaders to formalise the rules and encourage their use.

When CDCs were first introduced, the poor people participating in these committees had little or no educational background and had no experience in teamwork. CDCs gave them their first experience of working as a team to achieve a specific goal. In order to establish an effective organisation at the outset, Municipal Health Instructors acted as Secretaries to the CDCs for approximately a year, then as Assistant Secretaries, withdrawing completely after two years. This approach aimed to motivate community members and reinforce the importance of CDCs for the development of the community. CDCs then adopted the traditional organisational structure of office holders and a committee of five ordinary members. The office bearers are elected from among the poor families participating.

The CDCs and members of the garden meet weekly to address problems. These meetings are held in the local community hall and are attended by the Community Development Officer and municipal team. They are an attempt to address problems and resolve disputes at the grassroots level. The CDC played a number of roles on behalf of the communities in land regularisation, the identification of landless families, the demarcation of plot boundaries and in settling conflicts among families. In the housing construction phase of the Housing Sub-Programme, the CDCs helped in obtaining loans, and providing access to service organisations to improve infrastructure networks (including drains, footpaths, corridors etc). When a community member requires a certain service, s/he approaches the CDC in the garden and, pending the validity of the request, the CDC submits it to the CMC.

If problems, issues and conflicts cannot be resolved at the slum garden level, they are brought to the District Council and Habitat Unit at the District office. There is one district office in each of the six districts of the city. Meetings are held monthly and are chaired by the Deputy Medical Officer. The Assistant Chief Education Officer serves as Secretary. The meetings are attended by the District Engineer, Officers of the National Housing and Community Development Committees, and community leaders. They constitute an attempt to solve problems at the district level. If all else fails, issues are raised at the HCDC meeting, held every two months at the Mayor's office. This meeting is chaired by the Mayor and attended by the Heads of the 13 Departments of the CMC, NGO representatives and other government officers. The HCDC was utilised as a successful 'problem solving' forum for the community to voice their problems and opinions. This forum also acts as a venue for inter-departmental co-ordination, implementation monitoring and the discussion of issues raised in the CAP workshop.

Funding for CDCs was provided by UNICEF via the UBSP for the period 1979 to 1996. Every year the CMC, CDC leaders and the members of the community prepared an Annual Work Plan at District Level. This was a plan of building works for all communities in the district in the following year. The CMC submitted the plan to UNICEF and funds were allocated accordingly. According to a CMC ordinance, the CMC cannot allocate funds for CDCs, the CMC does not have a budget for this purpose and the allocation of resources through the National, Provincial Council and Local Authority budgets has been inadequate. •

The Sustainability of Community Organisations

Box 5.9

Community Development Committees, Colombo

Despite the success of the Community Development Committees in Colombo and the model the CDC has provided for many community-based organisations, the aim of the CDC as a permanent tool for comprehensive development has not been realised. Many are said to no longer exist, although there is little agreement (and no criteria to judge) whether they are defunct or whether they are inactive or dormant due to a lack of funding. Despite their earlier success, it is only in recent years that the important lessons of the Colombo Community Development Committees have been exposed. These lessons address the sustainability of the CDC as a mechanism for communities to work together and interact with government in planning and development initiatives in the long term.

The CDCs were established to carry out **short term development objectives**, and once their objective was realised there appeared to be no reason to sustain them. CDCs were **externally driven**, conceived and established by the CMC, and it is thought that this may have affected communities' sense of **ownership**. The role of the municipal officials in establishing the organisations facilitated progress in the short term. They acted as both facilitator and supporter, but also as leader. When officials withdrew, the activities of the community faltered and some partnerships declined. A key lesson is that the primary role of the municipal officials at the outset, to some extent, detracted from the long-term mobilisation and empowerment of the community, particularly where officials failed to transfer obligations and responsibilities. It is argued that communities need to own and run their own organisations and that this is preferable even if the organisations lack the capacity at the outset. Conversely, many reports suggest that without municipal support the CDCs are likely to have collapsed well before they had a chance to demonstrate their potential to the community; and that an 'independent' organisation, developed outside the purview of the CMC, may not have been accepted by the political wing.

Good leaders have proven vital for the success of the committees and action planning processes. The collapse of some organisations has also been attributed to leaders being unable to perform basic functions (setting objectives, planning activities and managing projects) and unable to understand the necessity for post-project meetings. CDC leaders' education, status, experience and values are important factors explaining the sustainability of some CDCs and not others. In some cases, abuse of power by CDC leaders removed the trust and confidence of the community. For instance, some acted as 'gatekeepers' for the community, enjoying contacts with bureaucrats or political actors and extracting bribes from householders wishing to benefit from initiatives.

While **political affiliation** of CDC leaders has also caused problems within committees in Colombo, in other less politically overt situations CDCs provided a focus for co-operation between people of different backgrounds and political affiliations, and provided 'horizontal' linkages which increased collective community capacity to access service improvements.

CDC successes and failures have often been attributed to the role played by **political actors**. Some politicians (irrespective of political party) actively sought to weaken CDCs. They wished to be seen as the main benefactor (of land, housing, water, clinics) in return for public acclaim and votes. CDCs threatened political patronage because the poor took credit for community improvements themselves, particularly where action planning processes were used.

Funding shortages proved a major problem. Lack of funds to CDCs restricted opportunities for direct service delivery and severely limited indirect activities. The hidden costs of the CDC (travel and administration) in lobbying government and holding meetings is carried by the leaders themselves, and the lack of any payment or reimbursement is said to affect the motivation of the leaders. In some communities, their lack of regular income and the time needed to survive are said to have had significant impact on their capacity to participate. The lack of financial resources is said to have, ultimately, hindered the capacity of the organisations and the CMC to promote community participation.

The recently formed **Federation of Community Organisations** is the next stage in the development of sustainable community-based organisations. It attempts to integrate community organisations, to bring people with different interests together, and to promote co-operation between different groups, neighbourhoods and social classes. The Federation attempts to remove the vulnerability of smaller organisations, and to increase the organisational capacity of CDCs by obtaining resources and ensuring more equitable resource distribution. •

Box 5.10   Role of NGOs in Developing Community Participation

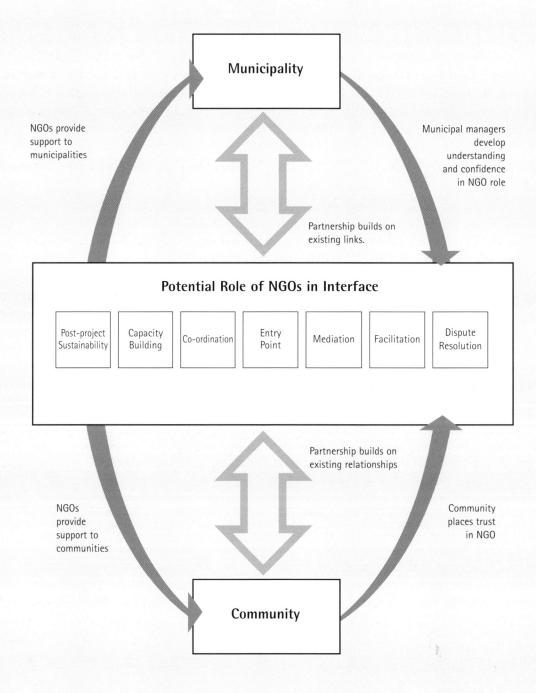

Partnerships with Non-governmental Organisations

In the light of rapid urbanisation and the deterioration of existing infrastructure, local government decision-makers are acknowledging that they simply do not have the resources, skills or organisational foundations to meet the statutory responsibilities of decentralisation. In conjunction with efforts to strengthen internal capacity, municipalities are, increasingly, looking outside the government for support in a number of sectors. This is particularly significant in the field of community development and participation where municipalities are weak, but where many NGOs have a track record and have developed experience of working with communities. Mechanisms for mobilising communities for promoting participation in the delivery of services and infrastructure, described earlier in this chapter, can be significantly strengthened by including non-governmental actors and other parts of civil society in the development of partnerships with the poor.

The inclusion of the NGO sector in this strategic framework assumes that the municipality plays a primary role in the delivery of services and infrastructure within the city; it does not envisage that the NGO sector will absolve the municipality from its responsibilities through independent NGO efforts. In the urban context and in most, but not all, service sectors in cities, NGO initiatives have been very necessary but are not always efficient or replicable. In many contexts, there is an opportunity to develop open and sensible partnerships with NGOs and to utilise this third sector as an important vehicle for implementing participatory processes.

Undoubtedly this approach requires significant capacity building and attitudinal change. Once municipalities have built an understanding of the key requirements for developing community partnerships and have acknowledged the need for assistance, they are in a position to identify gaps in their capacity and options for bridging these gaps by utilising resources from outside government.

The potential role of non-governmental organisations

The role of NGOs in building municipal capacity for community participation will depend on the capacity, skills and agenda of both the municipality and the NGO sector in a given context. Commonly, however, the attitudes and skills needed for promoting community participation are more prevalent amongst NGOs than government and this creates opportunity for municipal-NGO alliances. Ironically though, it is the stronger, more innovative municipalities, with a better skill base and less need for support, that seize the opportunity of working with external organisations and have gained vital experience of NGO partnerships. The potential role of the NGO sector in the development of a community-municipal interface is illustrated in Box 5.10 and includes:

☐ the NGO as mediator and entry point

Perhaps the key role that NGOs can play in the development of partnerships is that of mediator between the municipality and the community. In the early stages of establishing community participation, NGOs can help facilitate initial discussions, develop community confidence and trust and provide a supporting framework for community action. Frequently where municipal-community relationships do not exist, and particularly in areas where NGOs have established an active supportive role, the NGO can create an entry point for municipalities to approach communities.

☐ the NGO as facilitator

The NGO frequently supplements the skills of the municipality by acting as a facilitator. This may include assistance in project identification, participatory needs assessments, and micro-planning in the project development stage and training in management or technical skills in the implementation stages. It may also include the development of employment opportunities.

Box 5.11

Drawing on the Resources of Civil Society
Kerala People's Planning Campaign

One of the primary difficulties in the early stages of the Kerala People's Planning Campaign (see Boxes 3.3, 3.5 and 4.7) was ensuring the viability of projects proposed by Ward Committees. A review of development projects (from all sectors) in March 1997 revealed that the majority of the 10,000 projects developed throughout the state were not viable proposals which could be included in the Development Plan. As a result, a significant change in the methodology of the campaign was proposed and an additional stage was introduced to provide technical and financial appraisal and assistance such that projects could be modified and made practicable prior to the approval process.

The Kerala State Planning Board thus proposed the concept of a Voluntary Technical Corps (VTC) to strengthen the capacity of the local bodies, to counter the lack of technical expertise and the lack of commitment of all government officials. The VTC was intended to utilise the resources of civil society by drawing on the services of retired technical experts and professionals. The request entailed volunteers (with post-graduate degrees and officer-level experience) to spend one day per week providing local government bodies with technical assistance on project plans and budgets. 50-60 experts were required for each *panchayat*, or municipality. To initiate the process, volunteers were brought together in district level conventions for briefing on the requirements of the position. More than 4,000 retired professionals and government officers joined the Voluntary Technical Corps within 2 months. Subsequently, they each attended an orientation course intended to build capacity in the campaign's objectives and methodology and to develop skills for the technical, social and financial appraisal of local level plans. Municipal officials were also trained in what to expect of the VTC. This has been most successful in Trivandrum, where a large number of retired state government officials and well-respected professionals provided the support needed to strengthen the Kerala People's Planning Campaign.

The Voluntary Technical Corps performed two primary roles:

- the appraisal of plans and projects for technical and financial viability;
- the provision of technical assistance to local levels of government.

Both roles were vital for municipalities which were constrained by a lack of skills to develop proposals and by a lack of commitment to the process being undertaken.

Expert Committees, comprising VTC experts and relevant government officials, were formed at block, district and municipal levels. These committees acted as an advisory arm of the District Planning Committee. Tasks were clearly confined to appraising and suggesting modifications which would make projects viable. Their role was not to change priorities or proposals. Completed plans were then recommended to the District Planning Committee for approval. As the process developed and the VTC's role became more established, the expert committees were also given the power to approve technical revisions and, within certain financial limits, to approve budgetary adjustments, grant time extensions, resolve disputes and carry out final inspections.

The formation of the Voluntary Technical Corps from civil society assisted the government in translating unskilled people's planning into viable, budgeted proposals. In the first year of the KPPC, the VTC had a direct and positive impact on the technical and financial feasibility of projects produced, and this underpinned the participatory planning process. The introduction of the Voluntary Technical Corps at a relatively late stage in the planning process showed that the senior officials responsible for the campaign were able and willing to monitor progress, review results and adjust procedures to produce more effective results. They achieved this despite organisational difficulties and limited capacity. In the second year of implementation, the VTC provided the necessary sectoral expertise and experience throughout the whole annual planning process, and continued their transitional role of supporting the process while government structures slowly adapted.

However, despite the fact that VTC skills underpinned the KPPC and enabled the completion of the annual planning process, it is widely thought that the Voluntary Technical Corps is unsustainable in the long term. Two key lessons were learnt from drawing these resources in from civil society. First, by-passing unwilling or unable existing administrations does not ultimately build their capacity and create a sustainable process; and second, technical expertise, such as that provided by the VTC, should be formalised to maximise effectiveness. ●

the NGO as co-ordinator

The NGO can also play an important role in co-ordination in the planning and management of services and infrastructure. The non-governmental sector can frequently bring together the formal and informal sectors into functioning and cost-effective delivery systems. They are ideally positioned to develop sensible and effective systems at the neighbourhood level, and to work with municipalities to ensure successful integration into broader service networks.

the NGO as capacity builder

The attitudes of municipal officials towards communities are frequently insensitive and uninformed. Many NGOs have a wealth of knowledge about communities and can assist in municipal capacity building for community participation, either by demonstration or by more formalised training programmes led by skilled NGO workers. Municipalities have reported that working with NGOs can have the hidden benefit of skill development as staff learn from their non-governmental counterparts. Such skill development can then open options for direct partnerships in the future.

the NGO as a provider of community development expertise

As partnerships develop, an NGO can continue to assist in communication and interaction processes. Some municipalities have relied on the NGO to fill the role of community organiser in the development of the community roles and responsibilities and in the establishment of community organisations.

the NGO in dispute resolution

Throughout the project cycle the NGO can assist both the community and the municipality to understand and communicate requirements, and if necessary, assist in negotiation and dispute resolution processes amongst the community and between the community and the municipality.

the NGO in post-project sustainability

The NGO sector is also well-positioned to assist municipalities and communities in ensuring the sustainability of service delivery. The skills, resources and experience of NGOs often lend themselves to a role in ensuring post-project sustainability. Many NGOs see their success in terms of facilitating robust mechanisms for communities themselves to plan and manage, operate and maintain their services at the tertiary level.

Factors affecting NGO capacity

It is not the purpose of this work to dismiss established fears and conflicts between the government and non-government sectors. While many NGOs are able to facilitate community participation in the delivery of infrastructure and services, not all have this capacity and not all make good partners. Factors affecting NGO capacity to become effective partners include:

- the **advocacy agenda** of many of the strongest NGOs (an NGO entering into partnership with government will need to consider the potential conflict with its own established agenda);
- the **legitimacy** of the NGOs involved (not all NGOs have proven to be legitimate when involved in projects involving large budgets and lengthy programmes);
- the capacity of the NGOs involved to undertake the **scale of work** required without rapid scaling up;
- the **technical capacity** of the NGOs to facilitate service delivery projects (NGO attempts to broaden their scope to include service delivery have not always proven straightforward. Alternatively, NGOs may be experienced at the neighbourhood level and may lack an appreciation of secondary/primary level infrastructure requirements);
- the capacity of the NGOs to work in **partnerships** (NGOs do not automatically know how to work in partnerships; most need to develop skills and understanding of government practices).

Box 5.12

NGO Involvement

Bangalore Urban Poverty Project

In the Bangalore Urban Poverty Project (BUPP), non-governmental organisations cover a broad range of activities and roles in slum improvement works. Most NGOs are facilitating organisations, which have proven to be capable of organising development programmes with both local and/or donor funding. These NGOs include Rotary, Lions Clubs and similar associations, religious organisations, and a range of independent organisations. They demonstrate vastly different skills and capacities in a range of sectors, including community development, women's development, child-care facilities, vocational training, physical slum improvement, and housing.

In the past, many of the Bangalore-based NGOs involved with the urban poor have been able to raise the consciousness of the people. Initially NGOs in Bangalore saw their role in the project as a temporary one, as instrumental in empowering local communities or vulnerable groups within communities, and ensuring activities were not dominated by the elite.

At the outset, relations between governmental and non-governmental organisations in Bangalore were considered to be fragile and co-operation had to be established on unfamiliar territory. Government officials misunderstood the capacity and objectives of the NGOs and their representatives, and NGOs mistrusted government officers and dismissed them as uninterested in development issues. Despite this, there was a joint recognition that a collaborative approach was necessary to assist the poor and weaker sections of society improve their access to social and physical services.

The project envisaged that NGOs would become involved in two primary roles. Firstly, they were to provide services to the Slum Development Teams (community-based groups established by the project). Secondly, they were to participate in the management and decision-making with respect to the programme as a whole through the membership of the Project Steering Committee (PSC). (The PSC was introduced as a useful way of bringing partners together to discuss strategic issues. In practice, however, the committee was diverted away from a partnership focus to day-to-day operational problems.)

NGO support aimed to:

- assist in the selection of slums to be taken up in the programme and assess the strength of the local community in slums selected;
- establish or strengthen working contacts with the communities of selected slums and assist the poor communities to set up Slum Development Teams;
- assist the Slum Development Teams to prepare, draft and implement Slum Development Plans;
- assist the Slum Development Teams in accounting and operating bank accounts;
- indicate training needs of the slum populations (and possibly other parties) involved in the programme and to organise and/or to participate in training sessions concerned;
- liaise between the Slum Development Team and the Programme Support Unit; and
- assist in monitoring and ongoing evaluation of the Slum Development Plans under implementation.

Despite the clear definition of the NGO role in the project, NGOs have not provided the intended support for SDTs. One of the most important differences between BUPP as designed and implemented has been that the Project Support Unit (PSU) has played a more direct role in SDT formation and strengthening than originally envisaged. This has arisen for two main reasons. Firstly, not all NGOs have the capacity or skills to take on this role. Secondly, NGO interests vary enormously and it was an incorrect assumption that service-oriented organisations would want to take on community development work. A more in-depth analysis of NGO interests would have highlighted this issue at an early stage. Although most NGOs support the SDT philosophy, few are committed to the SDT concept or see it as innovative. There is considerably more interest in building on and strengthening existing organisations (CBOs).

Where NGOs have linkages with existing CBOs, these have continued. On the whole, evaluation has suggested that the BUPP has had a positive impact on NGO-community relationships and communities have greater confidence in NGOs, although this positive impact has to be seen in the light of BUPP's ability to provide resources and to assist in leveraging inputs from government. •

Municipal action toward NGO partnerships

The opportunities and constraints of the non-governmental sector differ with context and with organisation, but the following issues form a basis for municipal consideration and action:

☐ Convergence of objectives

In some cases, it is possible for non-governmental organisations to maintain and fulfil their own specific goals at the same time as meeting the project objectives established by the municipality. In Ahmedabad, in order to meet programme requirements established by their municipal and private sector partners, the NGO Saath compromised the short-term process, viewing the long-term objective of community development and the integrated approach to service delivery to be more important than battling other priorities early in the project.

☐ Understanding NGO potential

Municipal partnerships with NGOs appear to work most effectively when municipalities have developed an understanding of the roles that NGOs can play. This requires an acknowledgement that the NGO sector provides a potential resource for municipal activities in both policy and implementation. Municipalities that involve NGOs in strategy formulation and project preparation are inherently developing a more participatory project more likely to address community needs in the design stage.

☐ Building on Existing Links

Existing community-NGO links provide a substantial basis for effective partnerships. Successful partnerships are built on existing trust and confidence and communities may not necessarily trust an NGO imposed through the project. Municipalities can also build on existing initiatives and relationships with NGOs, or on the work NGOs have already initiated. NGOs familiar with municipal practices are more likely to anticipate bureaucratic requirements and form effective partnerships, but the partnership takes time to evolve.

☐ Ensuring clarity of roles and responsibilities

Municipalities and NGOs unfamiliar with government partnerships frequently form open and ill-defined partnerships. A clear lesson from the case studies is the need for clarity of roles and responsibilities. Projects troubled by disagreements are frequently caused by a lack of clarity over responsibilities of partners at the various stages of the project cycle. In Ahmedabad, even though formal contracts and agreements were drawn up, in practice the description was too general and did not define particular responsibilities at each stage of the process. In Bangalore, however, the lack of investigation at the project design stage meant that assumptions were made as to the role NGOs could play. During the project this did not prove possible and the project management (PSU) had to assume a greater role than expected (see Box 5.12).

☐ Establishing a management interface

NGOs frequently complain that municipal staff do not understand the processes of community development and their role in mobilisation. A key dimension of the problem is the tendency for municipalities to allocate responsibility for NGO co-ordination to middle or lower level administration. It is essential that relationships are built at management level as well as field level.

Box 5.13

Developing NGO Relationships
Cochin Urban Poverty Reduction Project Pilot Phase

In early 1995, at the commencement of the pilot phase of the Cochin Urban Poverty Reduction Project (CUPRP), there was no established tradition of NGOs working in partnership with the Corporation of Cochin (CoC). In practice, NGOs in the south Indian city tended to be small and provide a narrow range of support to small geographical areas and numbers of households. While there are now over 120 non-governmental organisations working in Cochin, there is neither a co-ordinating mechanism nor an NGO prominent in working with the poor or with environmental improvements. The government and non-governmental sectors have, typically, functioned in isolation and lack respect for each other's activities. NGOs generally fear the burdensome bureaucracy of the CoC, the failure of the CoC to fulfil promises, and the risk of government interference in their work. The municipality has seen the NGO sector as disorganised and unaccountable for their actions.

In late 1995, as an integral part of the Cochin Urban Poverty Reduction Project pilot phase, a team from the CoC approached the residents of Kissan Colony (approx. 200 households) with a proposal to undertake a programme of poverty reduction activities in their colony. A multi-disciplinary team from the CoC, consisting of the Project Co-ordinator and Senior Executive Engineer, the Project Officer (CD), the Lady Medical Officer and a designated Community Organiser, convened to work with communities to carry out both physical infrastructure and social activities. At that time, the reputation of the Municipality was that of a dysfunctional organisation which frequently made empty promises. This seriously hindered attempts by the team to establish a Community-municipal partnership project. The community in Kissan Colony displayed a complete lack of trust in the municipality at the outset; they did not welcome the pilot proposal and thought it would be short-lived, waste their time and ultimately fail.

In the light of this impasse, the CoC team approached the NGO that was well established in the area. A well-attended Community-Corporation meeting was then convened by the NGO (Sisters of Mercy) in their rooms within the colony. The content of the meeting was essentially a one-sided presentation (the CoC said they would introduce the project on that occasion and the community could respond on the following occasion). The Corporation explained the basic structure and the components of the donor-funded project and the participatory mechanism to be adopted for the planning process. Minutes of the meeting were produced to formalise the process.

Despite the efforts of the CoC team, the participatory nature of the project was still not well received. A meeting with NGO leaders was held and the NGO agreed to intervene by first showing their support for the Corporation efforts, and then by explaining to the community the nature of the CoC objectives and intentions. This was carried out over a series of formal and informal meetings. With time, trust and familiarity, the NGO created a bridge between the community and the municipality that enabled further discussion.

As a result of this and other relationships that developed between the CoC and local NGOs, the CoC co-ordinating team gained, quite unintentionally, considerable experience of working with the non-governmental sector. Through this experience CoC officials began to recognise the possible role of NGOs in the implementation of the main phase of the CUPRP.

Key lessons from the partnerships established in this pilot phase included:

- NGOs can provide an important entry point to establish community-municipal relations;
- NGOs can be important actors in building and maintaining community confidence in the project;
- NGOs can provide important psychological support for the community to take on a participatory role (particularly in the execution of the construction works themselves);
- NGOs can build capacity and underpin community contracting with management and accounting support skills;
- It is essential to work with NGOs already established in an area (community mobilisation was far less effective where unknown NGOs were brought into neighbourhoods and had to win the confidence of the communities).

(Cochin Case Study)

☐   Developing effective management systems

Municipal-community partnerships require management. Management approaches can be overlooked, or imposed, without discussion, by the municipality. Municipalities that acknowledge the importance of community ownership, decision-making and self-reliance frequently establish independent mechanisms (such as steering committees) to involve NGOs in project management.

☐   Developing trust and confidence

In most contexts there is a degree of mistrust between NGOs and government, and it is necessary to build greater understanding of the barriers between the government and non-government sectors. It is necessary to differentiate between fact and fiction. Similarly, NGOs need to build confidence in government, to be convinced that government intentions are genuine. Many project partnerships falter when the government does not keep their end of the bargain. Committed NGOs fear losing credibility when municipal partners do not, or are not able, to keep promises.

It is essential that municipalities become familiar with the capacity of the NGO sector, develop an understanding of the potential role that NGOs can play in forming effective partnerships for delivering services, and develop skills to foster effective working relationships. Municipalities can therefore tap into an under-utilised resource for implementing poverty reduction initiatives, including the delivery of services and infrastructure to poor areas.

Notes

1. Paul first identified these instruments as: user groups, community workers or committees and fieldworkers. See Paul (1987) p5

2. The deputation of such workers to Community Development Departments leaves Health Departments understaffed. As a result some COs are expected to carry out multiple community development and health roles, and often do so indefinitely.

3. The key issues of community development processes are developed in detail elsewhere, including Eade (1997).

Box 5.14   ## The Role of the NGO
Ahmedabad Slum Networking Project Pilot Phase

In 1995, the Ahmedabad Municipal Corporation (AMC) entered into an innovative partnership aiming to bring together the community, the NGO sector and local industry in a collaboration to improve the quality of lives of the poor people of Ahmedabad. The partnership was developed in the context of significant and powerful support from the municipality and other key secondary stakeholders. Four influential figures dominated the process at project inception: the Municipal Commissioner, the Deputy Municipal Commissioner, an industrialist, and a consulting engineer. Each played a key role in facilitating the development of a formal and carefully planned partnership.

The Slum Networking Project (SNP) pilot included three primary components: in-slum infrastructure, citywide infrastructure and community development. A primary aspect of the project was the financial basis of the partnership (Box 4.13). The municipality, the community and the private sector partner each contributed 33% of the costs to the in-slum infrastructure works. The secondary and primary levels of infrastructure were financed entirely by the Corporation. For Community Development activities, a 33% contribution was provided by the NGO and 70% from the AMC.

The Ahmedabad Municipal Corporation assumed the role of co-ordinator and facilitator of the project and partnership. They established the project rules, identified the slum areas to be included in the project and implemented the citywide infrastructure works. Initially, however, the key force in the development of the partnership was Arvind Mills, the private sector partner. The Managing Director of Arvind Mills had, for many years, supported programmes assisting the poor in Ahmedabad. Within the pilot project, Arvind Mills was given responsibility for the implementation of the in-slum works. At the same time, the comparative advantage offered by the private sector partner was to be utilised in the skills development and employment generation component of the project.

A locally based NGO, Saath, with experience in CBO formation, micro-credit and social mobilisation, was brought in to underpin the partnership with the community. Compared with other local government in India, the AMC has a history of developing sustainable relationships with NGOs, although involvement in direct decision-making processes has been limited. In the pilot project, however, the Saath role proved to be central to the whole partnership, not just in the community development activities for which they had responsibility. They provided the linking mechanism from the community to the municipality and from the community to Arvind Mills. More specifically, this role included:

- explaining projects and finances;
- facilitating and training communities in forming CBOs and community development skills;
- negotiation and dispute resolution;
- providing and explaining technical options;
- motivating community financing and payment;
- mediating between community members and between the AMC and the community; and
- facilitating savings and credit programmes.

SEWA Bank, a well established urban co-operative bank for self-employed women in Ahmedabad, mobilised the community finances, acted as the financial intermediary and carried out the financial management of the project.

The key partner in the alliance, however, was the group of slumdwellers in Sanjay Nagar whose commitment enabled municipal action. Despite this, the role and responsibility of the community were explicitly prescribed through a top-down decision-making process imposed by the AMC. The outlined responsibilities are, in practice, rules and conditions which the community must accept. They include:

- the formation of a Neighbourhood Group and special interest groups;
- a financial contribution;
- the creation of a corpus fund for future maintenance;
- agreement to co-operate with and monitor the construction work and performance of the contractor to ensure quality of infrastructure construction and service provision;
- the operation and maintenance of the services to ensure ongoing access and performance;
- participation in the health and socio-economic programmes; and
- 'creating the right environment' to achieve a successful partnership and sustainability of the initiative.

   (continued in Box 5.15)

Lessons in Municipal–NGO Partnerships

Box **5.15**

Ahmedabad Slum Networking Project Pilot Phase

A vast number of individual and collective lessons were learned from this one innovative and ambitious pilot. These lessons led to a number of fundamental changes in the approach to the replication process. Perhaps the most successful element of the SNP was the approach that the AMC took towards establishing an effective interface with the community. From the outset the AMC acknowledged the need for a skilled mediator and a force for social mobilisation. The AMC filled the gap in its own expertise by inviting an NGO to join the partnership. However, the delegation of community mobilisation tasks was only accompanied by a limited role in handling key problems and issues.

In many ways, the experience of the SNP pilot strengthened the municipality's resolve to work with NGOs and consolidated the role of the NGO in municipal activities concerning the poor. The AMC relied heavily on the expertise of the NGOs involved in the collaboration, recognising the skills and extensive experience in the NGO teams not only in community development and social mobilisation but in finance, shelter, education and awareness building. As a result, the AMC depended on the NGO to interface with the community.

Saath acted as a social intermediary representing the community's interest with other partners, building municipal capacity and supporting community initiatives. Frequently Saath supported the community when they were on unfamiliar territory. Saath came to the partnership with established relationships to the slum dwellers, and to the AMC (having successfully worked with the AMC on the Community Health programme). Saath brought to the project ideological and practical experience of integrated slum development programmes, and a flexibility and open-mindedness to work with communities, the municipality and the private sector. Saath was able to develop relationships with political representatives, stressing the non-political role they played in promoting community development.

The partnership was, however, also plagued with difficulties and tensions which arose out of different working cultures and, to some extent at least, a lack of understanding of the constraints of each partner. One of the primary roles played by Saath was in the facilitation of the residents association necessary to meet the formalities of the project. Like any municipality acting as a service provider, the AMC was also focused on outputs, on services functioning within a given period. Community organisations therefore had to be formed, mobilised, registered and functioning within a year. Despite Saath protests, this was carried out. The formal CBO (8 men and 3 women) was ultimately only formed towards the completion of the physical infrastructure work and has been more concerned with the community development activities. This longer term objective has countered the hasty process of establishing the organisation. Saath has facilitated capacity building within the CBO such that it now acts as a development-oriented organisation for Sanjay Nagar.

The AMC also internalised much of the decision-making at policy level before the project commenced, and to some extent during implementation. NGO involvement only commenced after the structures and systems were already in place, and were marginalised over certain key issues.

Saath also found that the municipal actions or lack of actions impacted upon their work and their credibility with the communities. In the second pilot slum of Pravinanagar-Guptanagar, despite the community contribution of Rs. 2 lakhs (approx. $5000), little visible activity toward planning for infrastructure improvements led to an increasingly hostile community. Saath's credibility, built up over many years, was seriously damaged.

Despite these difficulties, the greatest challenge for the municipality proved not to be the partnership with the community or the NGO, but with the private sector actor. The failure of the municipal-private sector partnership is characterised by the juxtaposition of a bureaucratic municipality with tight controls on expenditure and auditing beside an unconstrained private sector organisation with a flexible and spontaneous approach toward financing and financial management. Despite the benefits of working with a private sector partner (the financial resources, the efficient work structure and the management capacity), the AMC found the working method of Arvind Mills overly assertive and demanding. Arvind, on the other hand, found the AMC to be slow at making and operationalising decisions, and slug-gish in mobilising resources. This alliance ultimately proved unsustainable and, whereas the NGO-Corporation partner-ship has developed in the main phase of the project, the municipal-private sector alliance has been buried. •

(Ahmedabad Case Study)

Andrew Cotton

The Internal Capacity
of the Municipality

6

Overview

Typically, municipalities are orthodox, hierarchical and compartmentalised organisations, frequently dysfunctional and under-skilled and slow to adopt the changes necessary to fulfil their statutory functions. Municipalities are also the implementation arm of national, state or provincial policies, and, in most cases, municipal reforms are needed to create a supportive framework for community participation. The key constraints of the municipal organisation and the primary areas of change needed to implement policy are discussed in this chapter.

In order for municipalities to facilitate participatory processes in the delivery of services and infrastructure, they must change fundamental aspects of the way they do things. Community participation is not fostered if municipal officials are unskilled or if the development of participatory skills is affected by staffing systems that do not facilitate effective work practices. Participation does not evolve in municipal contexts where well entrenched systems and procedures hinder the community from becoming involved in planning, implementing or managing the services intended for their use. Participation cannot develop in an organisational structure that marginalises poverty reduction initiatives and divorces participatory activities from mainstream municipal functions. Participation also cannot develop without sound financial and administrative principles, and it certainly cannot take hold in a milieu where attitudes are inundated with doubt and scepticism.

A primary aspect of capacity building for community participation is clearing a path within the municipality to 'let participation in'.[1] Without internal efforts, the municipal status quo may remain anti-poor, detached and inaccessible and will block the development of participatory initiatives. The important role of senior management (discussed separately in Chapter 7) is critical to bring about the change necessary to create an effective and responsive municipal organisation.

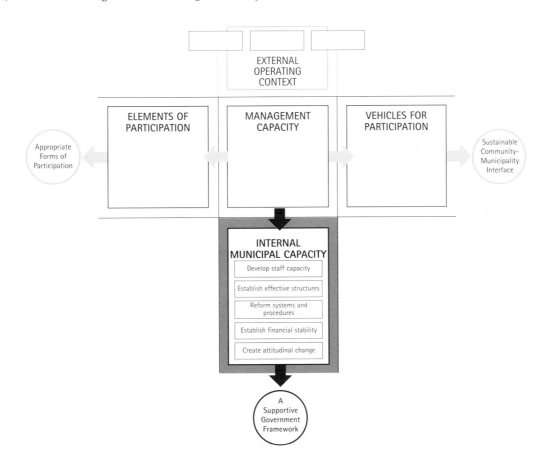

6

Box **6.1**

Issues and Impacts of Staff Capacity
Comparative Table

	Key aspects of staffing	Primary impacts of staffing
Surat Municipal Corporation (ongoing service activities)	• Staff reforms through organisational, procedural and management change. • Capacity building amongst senior managers to match responsibilities, but no particular focus on improved skills for remainder of staff.	• Improved commitment of staff to perform jobs and improved capacity of municipality to meet municipal functions. • Increased responsibilities for zonal level brought staff closer to the people and improved accountability.
Ahmedabad Municipal Corporation (SNP)	• Staffing strategy focused on management staff and professionalisation. Skilled staff were recruited. No significant training initiatives.	• New staff more open to participatory approaches, private sector participation and procedural reform. • Staffing reform and subsequent changes built public confidence in municipality.
Bangalore Municipal Corporation (BUPP)	• Lack of staff skills to support participatory methodologies. • Policy to keep salaries to government payscale and contract status offered.	• Isolated participatory project implementation. • Extreme difficulties to recruit and keep staff.
Corporation of Cochin (CUPRP)	• Senior management staff constantly transferred. • Staff trained in participation transferred. • Insufficient skills across departments at all levels of management and implementation.	• Staff transfers removed the skill base of the project team. • Lack of continuity has caused problems in progress of main phase. • Staff without participatory skills blocked the efforts of those with skills.
Kerala State Government (KPPC)	• Significant capacity building programme undertaken through structured and formal processes. • Voluntary technical corps created to provide support to government officials.	• Training provided was insufficient and inadequate, hindering municipal implementation process. • Weak municipal skills and undeveloped attitudes towards participatory forms of planning diminished the impacts of policy.
Municipal Corporation of Visakhapatnam (VSIP, CHISII)	• Multi-disciplinary training for all departments in participatory strategies and processes. • Training based on practical staff experiences. • Managerial level training addressed institutional aspects of participation.	• Well trained and broad base of professionals with understanding of participation and commitment to approach. • Evolution of participatory approaches in second stage.
Colombo Municipal Corporation (UHSP)	• Training focus on providing municipal-community interface officials with skills for community mobilisation. • Lack of opportunities for replication and use of skills. • Lack of training, awareness and orientation programmes for other officials on participatory development.	• Initial interface with communities effective and successful in developing groups and micro-planning processes. • Later, insufficient trained staff to meet mobilisation objectives. • Training officers in micro-planning tools valued by communities.
Faisalabad Development Authority (FAUP)	• Planned capacity building with focus on participatory strategy. • Focus on PMU staff, followed to some extent by training municipal engineers and line agency officials. • Emphasis on promoting and supporting community-led activities. • Focus on providing technical skills to social organisers, and participatory skills to engineers.	• Skills well developed within PMU. • Significant improvement in levels of awareness of participatory objectives and processes outside project management unit, although limited commitment due to lack of ownership of approach.

Municipal Staff Capacity

Perhaps the most important message for municipal managers is that participatory activity requires special skills which come with planned learning opportunities, experience and training. In most cases, the individual and collective capacity needed for promoting community participation in the delivery of services and infrastructure is unlikely to pre-exist to any substantial degree within a municipality. In general municipalities have relied on:

- staff who have not been exposed to the principles and practices of participatory approaches; or
- technical staff who have been 'thrown in' to interact directly with communities in the belief that no particular skills are needed, so no training or skills development have been provided; or
- community development staff who are allocated the 'job' of participation and may be trained and gain experience in isolation from the rest of the municipality.

In order to build staff capacity in the skills needed to develop participatory processes, it is necessary to determine what the existing staff capacity is, and what capacity is needed to meet participatory objectives. Developing capacity in relation to ultimate objectives ensures that efforts are targeted, planned and meaningful. In addition to skills development, a strategic approach to staff capacity building should confront the institutional practices that also affect staff willingness and ability to play a sustainable role in community participation.

This section seeks to outline some of the key aspects of a staffing strategy aimed at community participation and to provide illustrations of municipal experience in this area (see Comparative Table, Box 6.1). Evidence clearly shows that staff capacity building does not, on its own, produce a supportive municipal context. Ideally, it is carefully linked to the other elements of municipal reform discussed throughout this chapter.

Skills Development

In order to improve municipal capacity for effective and ongoing participation, skills are required which enable officials to work with communities, carry out municipal functions, implement policies, and manage urban environments. It is essential that staff skills are assessed and a training/capacity building strategy is formulated. This will involve consideration of whose skills should be built, how they should be built, and by whom. It may also mean filling gaps with skilled professionals from outside the existing body of municipal staff.

Through the lessons of the case studies, key aspects of a training strategy have been identified. These are illustrated in the adjacent boxes and outlined below.

☐ Horizontal Skills Development

While experience suggests it is essential to have a custodian of participation within the implementing agency, such as that seen in the role of the Health Inspectors in Colombo (see Box 5.2), it is also clearly evident that participatory processes are not integrated into municipal functions effectively when poverty, participation and communication skills are seen as a 'technical' or 'sector' skill confined to one department. Community participation must be seen as a 'process' skill taken up, to some extent at least, by all departments. A training strategy aimed at improving the skill base of the municipality should therefore have a 'horizontal' emphasis, i.e. skills should be developed in all disciplines associated with poverty and the delivery of services to the poor, and should not be confined to community development departments. Improving the knowledge base of the whole municipality will emphasise the importance of participation and begin to improve the status of the task. Training and awareness building should therefore include engineers, planners, health and community development workers, as well as administrative decision-makers (see Box 6.4).

Box **6.2**

Training in Participatory Approaches and Methodologies
DFID Slum Improvement Projects India

The skills development initiatives developed in the DFID Slum Improvement Projects in five Indian cities, including Visakhapatnam, provide a range of experiences and lessons for the training of municipal staff in participatory approaches and methodologies. In 1994, a formalised approach to skills development was established following an agreement between the donor (then ODA) and municipal partners that the Slum Improvement Projects (SIPs) needed to be more participatory in their approach. In the initial stages this took the form of one-off training events organised by the ODA Field Management Office, but with time and increased confidence, this approach evolved into a series of linked interventions involving different municipal actors.

In the first stage, the Community Development staff were trained in participatory methodologies (PRA) through a series of 3-day training workshops conducted by local PRA trainers. The aim was to give participants practical tools to use with communities to plan and monitor programmes. While the training was successful in generating enthusiasm for the tools and approaches, in practice few participants were able to utilise these newly acquired skills as senior managers were unfamiliar with the method and unconvinced of the benefits. The rigid procedural framework within which staff worked meant that few were willing or able to innovate without management support. In order to overcome this problem, a two-day workshop was held in Calcutta for Project Directors, CD managers and other senior influential staff from the projects. This training introduced management-level participants to PRA methodologies but also focused on the objectives of participation and institutional change. In order to raise the profile and attract participants, the internationally renowned PRA advocate, Robert Chambers, was brought in to conduct the training. This proved successful and gave credibility to the promotion of PRA. The training was followed by a number of senior officials participating in an overseas study tour to Indonesia and Sri Lanka. This aimed to expose managers to examples of community participation in other urban contexts and to provide extensive opportunities for peer group debate over the benefits and possibilities of participatory processes.

In a second stage, a more structured approach was designed to capitalise on the interest generated by the senior managers' training. This built on the interest generated in a smaller number of projects. This stage was considerably more intensive and action-focused than earlier training initiatives and included:

- initial training of trainers for core training teams from each project (made up of CD, health and engineering staff);
- project level training of health, engineering and CD staff by core training teams;
- integration of PRA into selected project activities with regular support from local consultants;
- back-up from the DFID as necessary e.g. to encourage management support; and
- a follow-up workshop for core trainers to share experiences.

One of the main constraints to the integration of participatory approaches into planning and implementation of infrastructure was that the infrastructure programmes were managed by engineering staff. CD staff had little if any influence because of their relatively low status and rigid organisational structures. Engineering staff were therefore identified as a priority group for training in participatory approaches. This was achieved by integrating a participatory component into a UK-based training course for project engineers. Experience showed that this training was most effective when facilitated by fellow engineers.

The key lessons from the SIP experience of skills development in participation include:

- the importance of convincing senior managers and influential individuals of the benefits of participatory approaches;
- the need for strategic planning of training;
- the importance of starting with a participatory discussion and analysis of the constraints as perceived by municipal officials;
- the need for technical and moral support from trusted outsiders, especially local consultants;
- that training of engineers in participatory approaches is perhaps more essential than training CD staff because of their key role in planning and delivery of infrastructure;
- that training will be most successful when accompanied by changes in organisational practices and procedures such as team work and community action planning: and
- that changes in institutional attitudes and behaviour are critical to genuine partnership approaches. •

(Visakhapatnam Case Study)

☐ Vertical Skills Development

Many municipalities have launched into participatory projects by dispatching unskilled, poorly paid and low status officials to the field to work with communities. Unsurprisingly, the development of participatory processes has been limited by the capacity of this interface. However, this is not to say that fieldworkers alone need knowledge and understanding of community participation. Many skilled fieldworkers have lacked the support of managers who are skilled in and committed to community participation and as a result they are unable to make any sustainable progress in building community partnerships. Skills development in participatory approaches must therefore be established with a 'vertical' emphasis, starting with the most senior officials (such as the Municipal Commissioners, immediate deputies and departmental heads) and building out skills at lower levels of the municipal hierarchy.

☐ Target training to suit staff roles and responsibilities

The types of skills and knowledge required will depend on municipal roles and responsibilities. An important step in the training strategy will be a Training Needs Assessment that defines the skills and knowledge available and the training needed for each municipal role. It is essential that skills development is targeted.

- Senior managers need to establish a working knowledge of the principles of participation, the opportunities and mechanisms for achieving this participation, the constraints that may affect efforts, and most importantly the role of management in alleviating constraints and promoting participation to create a receptive environment.
- Technical officers require a deep understanding of participatory processes, the mechanisms, tools and techniques for implementation. They also need to develop the technical skills and knowledge that promote community participation (such as low cost, appropriate technologies and labour-based approaches to construction).
- Community Development workers, often without formal education, need participatory skills training and experience, but they may also need to develop confidence and management skills. If they are expected to discuss project-related matters with communities, they also need knowledge of basic service options.

This may mean that multi-sector training in the principles of participation is supplemented by single-sector training. Multi-sector training will facilitate a team approach while specific sector training will provide the opportunity for officials to develop their ideas and knowledge within their own professional teams. An outline of the skills required for participatory processes is provided in Box 6.6.

☐ Address perceived ideas and constraints

Experience suggests that municipal officials perceive different constraints to community participation and are concerned with different issues. It is vital to approach the training of officials with an understanding of the constraints they perceive in their own institutional and social framework. To this end, it is necessary to establish the views of municipal officers at the outset of the process and to tailor training packages to address specific concerns (for instance, building standards or the risk associated with community contracting initiatives). It may also be necessary to disaggregate the benefits of participation and to highlight specific benefits to each audience. In Faisalabad, the training package developed for WASA officials was tailored to suit their training needs and explained the benefits of participation in terms of their individual and institutional functions (see Box 6.3).

☐ Select trainers and training forums to suit the audience

The experience gained in the formal training programme introduced by the DFID in the India Slum Improvement Projects (see Box 6.2) emphasises how important it is to carefully select *who* the trainers are and *how* learning will take place. For instance, senior managers will not respond well to classroom situations but often respond immediately to the exposure and knowledge gained from field visits and discussions with municipal peers in other urban municipalities. They also

Box **6.3**

Formulating and Tailoring Training Programmes for Municipal Officials
Faisalabad Area Upgrading Project

The Faisalabad Area Upgrading Project placed a high degree of emphasis on training and skills development in the early stages of the project. Training events were primarily intended to develop the capacity of the Project Management Unit (PMU) Social Organisers working in the field, but attempts were also made to involve the PMU management staff, including the Additional Project Director and the Administration and Finance Officer. There were 8 full-time trainees.

The approach to training centred on building skills in PRA methods and techniques. Over a period of intensive training of about 5 months, in-house lectures and exercises were organised together with visits to other projects and exposure to training events organised by other projects and programmes. The latter included the Orangi Pilot Project, the Baluchistan Rural Support Programme and the work of Aurat, a Pakistani NGO that provides support and training for women. An external social development consultant led the in-house training initially through classroom-based activities but without fieldwork exercises because of the concern that the trainees would give the community false expectations. This approach proved unsatisfactory and an experienced Pakistani social development consultant was appointed after 3 months and trainees were then encouraged to work in the field. Although the length of this training input has been considered excessive, it provided the Social Organisers with a very strong participatory outlook that has served the project well.

Training of project managers was less successful, and a number of key lessons were learnt as the project progressed. In the first instance, project managers were invited to attend the same training sessions as the Social Organisers. However many did not see the need or relevance of the training to their position and role in the project. As a result, the management received only limited skills development in practice, and a strong field team proposing participatory methodologies found themselves in an unreceptive hierarchical government context. This undermined their efforts in the field and ultimately in the sustainability of the project approach.

Similar problems have arisen in relation to the line agencies directly linked to the project. Without simultaneous training and experience, these officials also find themselves at odds with the well-trained and committed Social Organisers. While some officials have absorbed some understanding of participatory procedures in the course of their interactions with FAUP staff, they are some way from having a detailed awareness and commitment to the project approach. These officials and the project itself would have benefited substantially from training events targeted at their own needs and roles.

Training continued throughout the project, but with less intensity than that attempted during the early stage. Ongoing training initiatives included:

- overseas training for a limited number of project personnel, covering general social development, gender, project administration;
- specialist short courses organised by non-government organisations and private-sector training organisations (mostly week-long courses in gender, aspects of social development, credit and finance and management techniques); and
- regular half-day and full day in-house seminars led by consultants, project personnel and external local specialists.

Three key lessons were learnt from the training approach adopted on the Faisalabad Area Upgrading Project.

- The failure to draw in project management meant that the skills of fieldworkers were not supported at higher levels of management and led to high levels of tension in the PMU. Training in participation *must* include those managers responsible for the delivery process.
- The failure to engage with those working outside the PMU such as WASA officials led to blockages in the delivery process. There is a need to inform line department officials of the participatory approach and its potential benefits and to supplement and adapt the technical skills of these officials so that they can contribute to participatory approaches.
- The lack of attention to the mechanisms for making participatory initiatives happen has meant that participatory principles have not always been converted into the participation of communities. There is a need to focus on mechanisms which officials can utilise to develop active participation. •

(Faisalabad Case Study)

respond to well known experts. Junior engineers and health professionals accustomed to formal learning may respond to classroom-based activity, may gain from field visits, but may not have the confidence to openly discuss issues with other municipal staff. Extension workers may learn most effectively through participatory workshops and closely monitored fieldwork. The decisions of *who*, *where* and *how* should form an integral part of the training strategy.

☐ Develop an ongoing process of training

Municipalities frequently send one staff member to one training workshop in participatory approaches or cost recovery, and treat this as an isolated event. Instead, training strategies need to incude ongoing support and continuing skills development. The impacts of training should then be monitored and steps taken to adjust approaches to ensure more effective results and that skills are aligned with the evolving nature of community participation. At the outset, for instance, fieldwork officials may need to focus on techniques for working with communities, but at a later stage they may need to focus on evaluation tools or appropriate technologies.

Staffing Policies and Practices

It is important for municipalities embarking on skills development to acknowledge that capacity is not limited to improvements in skills alone. Staff with excellent community skills will benefit from staff policies and practices that support their efforts in the field. For instance, the numbers of staff allocated to community work, the nature and extent of their allocation to a project, their perceived status and the terms and conditions of their jobs, all affect their capacity to implement participatory processes and to work with poor communities. It is essential therefore that municipalities exert as much control as possible and ensure that staff policies are favourable to participatory endeavours. In contexts where good management practices have been institutionalised (such as job definition, transparent recruitment and promotion procedures), a more positive and satisfying work environment exists and commitment to participation has increased.

☐ Staff appointment systems

Decision-making over the appointment or allocation of staff to participatory service delivery projects needs to consider:

- the skill base of the officials appointed;
- the numbers of staff required;
- the salary level and seniority of the officials;
- the terms and conditions of their employment.

Each of these factors is likely to affect the efficacy and sustainability of the municipal interface with the community (see Chapter 5).

Evidence of problems encountered in a number of contexts illustrates the impact of inappropriate staff appointment procedures on the ability and willingness of staff to perform allocated roles. In Pakistan, for instance, **political appointments** at Deputy Director level can undermine participatory activities carried out by Community Organisers. Promotion systems in some Development Authorities favour status and connection over sectoral skills and knowledge. Such appointments are clearly demotivating for staff working closely with communities who would benefit from appropriately skilled management to direct and foster their work. In Colombo, a lack of fieldwork staff has meant that interaction with communities has been constrained by availability and time. More recently, communities complain that they do not see the allocated municipal representative regularly. Unfortunately, the CMC has had little power to increase **staff numbers**.

The experience of the Bangalore Urban Poverty Project is rather different. Skill gaps identified in the Project Support Unit (PSU) and in the Corporation included participatory tools (social mapping, action planning and animation), group skills

Box **6.4**	**Pyramidal Training Programme**
	Kerala People's Planning Campaign

In early 1996, the State Government of Kerala launched the Kerala People's Planning Campaign (see also Boxes 3.2 and 5.11) which aimed to involve the people of Kerala in the development of the 5-year plan and annual budgetary plans for all aspects of development in their local areas. Capacity building was seen as a crucial ingredient of the process and a strategy was developed by the State Planning Board Campaign Cell to produce rapid, widespread results across the entire state. A number of features were prescribed for this capacity building programme. For instance:

• the programme was to be designed to reach the broadest number of people possible to a level needed to produce viable development plans;
• the capacity building process was to be linked to the publicity and promotion of the reform of the planning process; and
• the programme was to be developed with a limited budget employing as few paid staff as possible.

One of the key problems identified at the outset was that local level officials lacked the technical skills and understanding of the processes of decentralisation to meet the objectives of the campaign. The training therefore focused on the development of skills of both elected local representatives and a supporting structure of local officials. In order to reach the broadest number of people, resource persons were trained through a pyramidal (or cascading) approach previously adopted in the Kerala Total Literacy Campaign. This involved the training of Key Resource Persons (KRPs) at state level. These KRPs trained District Resource Persons who then trained the Local Resource Persons at municipal level, responsible for the facilitation of the Ward Conventions and the primary mechanism for the planning process. The numbers of people initially envisaged were underestimated. In the second stage, 660 state level, 11,800 district level, and 100,000 local level resource persons participated in the training programme.

A key aspect of the strategy adopted was to precede each and every stage of the planning process with a training event focused on the information and skills needed for the successful completion of that stage. This included the goals and philosophy behind decentralisation and the people's planning process, the legislative provisions and campaign phasing, participatory and planning methodologies and techniques, the documentation process, sectoral development, integrated development and the role of scheduled castes and tribes and women. Local government and management institutes led training initiatives of various forms (training camps, lectures, participatory workshops and project clinics) dependent on the trainees and objectives. The strategy for the formal training was implemented with great flexibility and a willingness to adapt to gaps and weaknesses. The process also relied heavily upon indirect and informal learning processes.

Despite the broad and rapid response that was achieved, the key lessons arising from this approach were the dilution of training and information transfer by the time it reached the local level and that training alone did not produce the capacity required to produce viable plans. In response to those lessons, capacity building was broadened to include:

• the formation of task forces responsible for leading at municipal level and supported by trained resource persons;
• the identification of future training approaches methods such as project clinics, models, demonstration wards, and inter-ward study tours;
• the development of the Voluntary Technical Corps (discussed in Box 5.11) to underpin the planning process with technical skills;
• the appointment of full-time Municipal Campaign Co-ordinators to initiate feedback and exchange, to improve integration, and to introduce mechanisms for addressing cross-cutting issues; and
• the development of plan guidebooks and sectoral handbooks to provide guidelines and document the lessons learnt in the Campaign.

While the institutionalisation of the training process is still in its early stages, a significant achievement has been seen in the attitudinal change brought about through the training and campaigning process. Despite the initial scepticism, the lack of quality in training and information transfer, and the financial and resource constraints, the training process still brought about significant reform. It created a foundation for ongoing improvement of planning skills and greater empowerment of the people of Kerala as a resource for development planning and decision-making in Kerala. •

(adapted from Isaac, 1999)

(conflict resolution, group dynamics) as well as leadership development, training skills and micro-finance. When the PSU explored the possibility of employing professionals from the NGO sector to fill these skill gaps, project procedures (specifically that **staff salaries** conform with government pay scales) resulted in an inability to recruit the skilled professionals required.

Local government in India is increasingly recognising the need for appropriate appointments and for skills to match responsibilities. However, it is difficult within rigid institutional staff structures to reorganise posts and to build greater depth in skilled staff. As a result, many Indian municipalities wishing to bring in particular skills or to boost community development departments have avoided the constraints of appointment systems by taking on staff on fixed term **contracts.** These steps, seen in Indore to boost the team of community organisers, in Cochin to bring in accounting skills, and in Ahmedabad to appoint qualified middle managers, have had mixed success.

A number of factors appear to influence the efficacy of contract appointments:

- the degree to which contract staff members are accepted by fellow staff members;
- roles and responsibilities and the degree to which these are matched by support from administrative and political leaders;
- the nature and extent of skills in municipal systems and procedures, and the extent to which they are assisted by their colleagues;
- the consideration given to their prospects at the end of the fixed contracts; and
- the degree to which newcomers can remain unaffected by negative institutional culture and fulfil the task allocated to them.

Staff transfers

Staff transfers also have a significant impact on the sustainability of participatory processes in a municipality. Municipalities attempting to establish participatory processes generally do not have a supply of skilled individuals to draw upon, and the transfer of key individuals can create extensive setbacks if they cannot be replaced. In a few cases, these transfers may be brought into effect because their participatory skills are needed elsewhere. More commonly, however, transfers are politically motivated. Skilled staff, versed in community-led processes and advocacy, for instance, frequently cross paths with senior officials and municipal councillors not fully in agreement with participatory strategies and processes, and promptly find themselves transferred. The loss of these skills can seriously hamper project progress and a constant turnover of staff creates discontinuity, demotivation and disruption. The 'vertical' skills development approach discussed above helps to create ownership of the process at leadership level and to reduce conflicts leading to transfers.

Incentive structures

Staff capacity is also affected by formal and informal incentive structures. These structures need to be reformed in accordance with good practice but must also take account of changing roles within the municipality. For instance, engineers are typically judged on their ability to undertake projects to meet time, cost and quality parameters. If engineering staff are instructed to incorporate community participation into their work, the evaluation of their performance (and thus promotion and salary) must be refocused to include participation and sustainability indicators.

Box **6.5**

Staffing Reforms
Surat Municipal Corporation

Prior to the outbreak of the plague and the appointment of a new Municipal Commissioner in 1995, the Surat Municipal Corporation was beset with unmotivated and unskilled staff, many of whom were unable or unwilling to carry out their responsibilities. The reforms introduced into the Corporation included changes to staffing policy to improve staff performance of allocated tasks and staff take-up of new procedures. This was achieved largely by on-the-job training that improved the knowledge and skills of those staff exposed, through field visits, to inadequate services and deteriorating infrastructure. This was neither a smooth, flexible process, nor one welcomed by the staff, but the speed at which the reforms were undertaken by SMC management did not allow for staff objection or retribution.

A number of areas were targeted to bring about change in staff capacity. First, efforts were made to **improve the status of staff working in poor areas** of the city. For instance:

- Anganwadi (kindergarten) teachers and workers traditionally provide an important entry point for poverty reduction initiatives in slum areas. They have substantial knowledge about children and household circumstances in their neighbourhood, and as such have proven to be of great assistance to municipal officials. However, their low salary of Rs. 400 and Rs. 200 per month respectively (approx. $10 and $5) under a state government grant did not acknowledge their role. In order to provide them with greater status and respect, and greater incentive to work towards a cleaner environment, the Corporation now pays them a supplementary salary.

- The massive upgrading and cleaning programme also prioritised the neighbourhoods occupied by the sanitation staff themselves on the basic premise that staff motivation and standards would improve if their own living conditions were improved. As a result, sewerage systems, water supply, roads, street lighting, sanitation and conservancy services were upgraded in municipal sweepers' colonies.

Second, a **multiple-worker system** was introduced in slum areas to co-ordinate the welfare and health activities undertaken by the Corporation. The multiple-worker system makes one fieldworker responsible for a population of about five thousand persons, and includes municipal services such as health, community development, mother and child care, malaria control and immunisation. This integrated system aimed to counter the overlaps and gaps in targeting the poor that were commonplace under a system divided between different officials and departments. The single point responsibility was associated with a systematic and regularised approach to field visits that improved the frequency and the certainty of municipal visits. Slum residents now know the date, time and purpose for each visit by the Multiple Worker, and can plan accordingly.

The **Sanitation Department** of the SMC was a target of the capacity building process. This was brought about by a broad range of changes and incentives.

- Staff numbers in the sanitation department were increased by 10-15% in all zones.

- Roles and responsibilities were clarified to ensure staff could not deny their responsibility for activities. The distinction between works and responsibilities was removed. All staff in a Zone, including Zonal Officers and sweepers, were held responsible for the conditions and problems of an area.

- Grievances demotivating the sweepers (unpaid leave, medical bills, etc) were also resolved.

The fieldwork procedures introduced gave senior management ample opportunity to monitor the performance of staff in the field. In order to recognise the efforts of individuals in the field, particularly those who were poorly paid, but whose work substantially improved the health standards of the city, the Commissioner introduced a system of awards and personal letters to acknowledge and thank those who had performed well.

Despite the formal and resolute manner in which the Municipal Commissioner approached the staff reforms in the SMC, the process significantly improved the status of those staff working with the poor. Many of these community workers comment on the concern the Commissioner showed for their welfare. They admired his leadership and the visible impacts of the reform process. •

Skills Required to Promote Community Participation

Summary Table

Box **6.6**

Skills	Actors	Skills required to promote participation
Community skills	**Municipal Managers** (and senior officials of line departments and agencies)	Need to develop a basic understanding of the principles of participation and the processes to be undertaken by their staff: • the elements of participation • the vehicles for participation
	'Interface' staff (interacting directly with the community)	Require detailed knowledge of the elements of participation, including: • problem identification • needs assessments • understanding of community perceptions of their poverty, the nature of poor communities and constraints to participation • understanding objectives of participation • awareness of options for community roles • tools and techniques of participatory planning (PRA) management and implementation (social mapping, interviewing, focus group discussions, microplanning) • techniques for enhancing the role of the community in decision-making • participatory monitoring Require detailed knowledge of the vehicles of participation: • assessment of community capacity • development of community organisations • training and development of community leadership • support for women and vulnerable groups, understanding of gender needs and relations • group dynamics and consensus building • negotiation and dispute resolution • household finance and micro-finance • working with NGOs
Technical skills	**All implementing staff** (CD staff, planner, engineers) require a general level of knowledge. **Technical staff** should have detailed knowledge in each of their subject areas. Participatory skills complement existing technical skills, they do not replace them.	• participatory planning • options for upgrading services • levels of service options • low cost technology options • labour-based approaches • community contracting options • mechanisms for ensuring technologies meet the needs of women • land tenure and regularisation • assessment of technical, economic, environmental and social feasibility • alternative forms of procurement • assessments of affordability and willingness to pay criteria and cost recovery options • options for operation and maintenance
Administrative and management skills	**Managers, project and administrative staff** In addition to understanding the principles of community participation, managers need to understand organisational reforms.	• strategic planning • organisational skills • project management • financing systems and sources • working with external actors • impacts of organisational structures, systems • human resource development, staff management • attitudinal reform • monitoring and evaluation

6

Box **6.7**   ## Municipal Structure
Comparative Table

	Organisational Structure	Primary Impacts of Structure
Ahmedabad Municipal Corporation (SNP)	• Project managed through special project cell (SNP cell) managed by the Deputy Municipal Commissioner • Separate from Engineering Department and Community Development cell.	• Project prioritised • Effective management • Development of staff capacity delayed as there was little transfer of skills. • Unclear departmental ownership of completed project interventions.
Bangalore Municipal Corporation (BUPP)	• Project managed through semiautonomous project management unit called a Project Support Unit and under the control of a Steering Committee • Entirely separate from municipal functions.	• Little dissemination of skills and capacity to mainstream municipal departments and staff • No staff specifically allocated to co-ordinate • No regular contact • Isolated and remote • Sustainability of project interventions unlikely through municipality.
Corporation of Cochin (CUPRP)	• Pilot phase managed through PMU • Organisational arrangement reorganised in main phase through municipal line departments • Project management placed in the Urban Poverty Alleviation Department.	• Project is perceived as community development project and is not considered as a part of mainstream municipal activities • Lack of support from engineering department • Low status of UPAD has resulted in significant marginalisation.
Surat Municipal Corporation (ongoing service activities)	• Activities carried out by line departments • Emphasis placed on the role of the Zonal Departments • Undeveloped community development department and participation limited to monitoring activities.	• Accountability developed through structural and procedural reforms provided a strong impetus for improved service delivery. Also provides a receptive context for broader participatory initiatives, but not yet tested.
Municipal Corporation of Visakhapatnam (VSIP, CHIS II)	• Established Urban Community Development (UCD) wing became project management office • Technical staff seconded to UCD • Project and non-project activities separated.	• CD and participatory activities marginalised by taking on the larger multi-sectoral work • UCD lost identity and mainstream role • CD Staff marginalised • Effective co-ordination of PR initiatives, and integration of participation • Established the role of the UCD department in any poverty-related service works.
Colombo Municipal Corporation (UHSP)	• Managed by Community Development Department in a high status and well established Public Health Department.	• Location gave the department status and added influence • Community perceptions improved by the central positioning of the Community Development Department.
Faisalabad Development Authority PMU (FAUP)	• Managed through a Project Management Unit functioning independently from the municipality, development authority and line agencies. Management staff not committed to participatory approaches.	• Participatory activities and skills marginalised in separate unit • Activities not integrated into mainstream municipal activities • Efforts to create ownership in the WASA required to link initiatives.
Aswan City Council (NUP)	• Managed through a PMU semi-detached from mainstream government departments • Senior personnel seconded from Housing Directorate assisted in establishing links • Gradual transference to municipality as project progressed.	• PMU structure facilitated the establishment of participatory processes and transfers passed skills on • Significant impact of personnel disseminating skills in parent departments.

Effective Municipal Structures

The departmental structure of a municipality and the manner in which community participation is integrated into that structure is one of many internal decisions which will affect the capacity of the municipality to first establish, develop, and then to integrate and sustain participatory processes. Municipal experience suggests that there is a great deal of leeway for differing organisational arrangements. These range from isolating participatory projects in project management units to mainstreaming projects through line departments (see Box 6.7). Yet despite the diversity of organisational structures that have been tested, some promoted by donors, it would appear that organisational structures which effectively develop, integrate and sustain participatory processes are difficult to achieve. Some of the key models for service delivery in municipalities, and the blockages to the integration and sustainability of participatory processes that result from organisational structures, are discussed below.

Organisational options for service delivery to the poor

☐ The central role of the Engineering Department

Traditionally, municipal structures tend to be hierarchical and have evolved to suit policies and implementation processes where the municipality is the provider and the poor are beneficiaries. The arrangement found in most municipalities that lack exposure to community participation is one in which Engineering Departments have sole responsibility for infrastructure provision and Public Health Departments provide solid waste services. As departmental status is often associated with high spending power, engineering departments are in a position to dominate decision-making, and supply-driven solutions are often implemented in isolation, with little co-ordination with the other departments working with poor people.

In such a municipal context, the Community Development Department (if it exists) generally has a low status and is marginalised within the organisation. Community Development Departments have low budgets and staff are often poorly qualified. Department heads are less senior and less powerful than Engineering or Health Departments, they are less established, they are perceived as marginal and no more than a project necessity. They often employ more women than other departments. The lack of status means that co-ordination with the Community Development Department is rarely prioritised and frequently undermined. If responsibility for community participation has been handed to the Community Development Department, and not considered as a responsibility of all, the participatory process has, in practice, a low priority. In such a situation, limited project-based results may be possible, but it is unlikely that participatory processes will be integrated into mainstream municipal functions.

☐ Project Management Units

Many decision-makers have responded to the domination of engineering-led solutions and sought to increase the focus on participatory processes by opting for independent project management units (PMU). A PMU can offer the opportunity to develop a unified, multi-sectoral team outside routine municipal functions and can enable the introduction of new techniques, such as community participation.

While this organisational structure has been seriously criticised because it removes ownership from the mainstream municipal departments and ultimately risks sustainability, in terms of participation a PMU does allow for the testing and development of participatory approaches and provides a small cell of positive attitudes. This is valuable in contexts where participation is threatening to existing structures and participatory processes would not have had the opportunity to evolve if they had been placed centrally in the municipality. There are cases where PMUs facilitated the initial development and gradual integration of participation within a municipality in this way.

Box **6.8**

The Limitations of Project Management Units
Bangalore Urban Poverty Project

As the main objective of the Bangalore Urban Poverty Project (BUPP) was the creation of an innovative mechanism for multi-agency co-operation in urban poverty reduction, the project was intended to provide an institutional structure with sufficient autonomy for experimenting with new approaches in urban poverty reduction. The main mechanism for partnership between the key partners (the Bangalore Municipal Corporation and the Karnataka Slum Clearance Board) and the project was a specially constituted Steering Committee headed by the Secretary for Urban Development with representation from senior officials in BCC, KSCB and other concerned agencies.

A Project Support Unit (PSU) was set up as the executive arm of the Steering Committee - a semi autonomous unit with its own staff, budget and management systems. The independent nature of this unit meant it could operate in a more flexible manner than might be the case if the project were located within the Corporation or the Slum Clearance Board. Through the Steering Committee, it would nevertheless be responsible to the main urban development agencies. The key role of this unit was seen as supporting other more permanent agencies involved in poverty alleviation to help them fulfil their roles more adequately.

As the Corporation was perceived to have insufficient resources for developing new approaches to poverty reduction, at the outset it was envisaged that the Municipal Corporation would work closely with the PSU on all matters relating to slum upgrading and habitat improvement. The decision to ensure that the PSU would remain independent was seen as particularly important in the context of the Bangalore Municipal Corporation, where community development falls under the broad remit of the Additional Commissioner rather than a specially constituted Urban Community Development (UCD) cell. The Corporation has been slow to form an urban poverty cell and in the absence of any substantial capacity to undertake multidisciplinary, participatory urban poverty activity, it was felt that it would be more effective to establish a well trained independent unit, through which the city could channel resources for urban poverty reduction.

Neither the Corporation nor the PSU have been guided by any coherent strategy which has indicated the main roles and responsibilities of each of the main project partners. Indeed, senior corporation staff highlighted this as a major gap in the whole BUPP approach. A key problem appears to have been the lack of any clearly defined operational plan or framework for the project identifying and allocating responsibility for the main outputs and activities. This is especially critical in a project emphasising the concepts of partnership and convergence.

Within the Corporation there has been a lack of any clear understanding on the part of senior line staff as to how to build and maintain an effective partnership with the project. There have been no staff specifically assigned to act as liaison between the project and the Corporation and no line staff allocated duties relating to the partnership. This has meant that there has been no regular contact between the PSU and key line departments in the Corporation and no structure established within which this could happen. In the absence of such a structure, partnership activities have been completely ad hoc. This has resulted in the project being seen as isolated and remote. Corporation staff have lacked skills in the areas that the project has been attempting to promote, and the structural arrangements have not enabled capacity building.

This BUPP model of urban poverty reduction was designed to bring together government and NGO actors within a single institutional framework as a semi-autonomous body. This case demonstrates both the strengths and weaknesses of creating a separate organisation for urban poverty reduction outside the structure of municipal government. Whilst such a structure clearly enables a greater measure of independence and innovation, with greater opportunities for NGO involvement in decision-making and implementation, it also highlights the weaknesses of such a model, which tends to be seen by the wider urban governance agencies as external and incidental to their work. At the same time it shows that, whilst the greater opportunity for experimentation has generated benefits in relation to new and more participatory ways of working with the poor, these are neither wholly innovatory nor sufficiently substantial to offset the disadvantages of its separation from the mainstream municipal government operations. •

Conversely, other experiences of project management units have revealed that capacity frequently remains isolated. The lessons learnt in Bangalore (see Box 6.8) and Faisalabad indicate that skills development is not easily transferred from the PMU to the municipality, opportunities for synergy and informal dissemination within the municipality are missed and the process lacks ownership and commitment within the broader municipal forum. This loss is critical to municipal capacity building and can considerably outweigh the small gains of an isolated unit.

Management through Line Departments

Unlike the PMU model, many multi-sectoral poverty reduction projects are organised and managed through the line departments of the municipality, with the aim of mainstreaming poverty-related activities. Under the guidance of skilled management, line departments may engage in the project objectives and sustain interventions in the post-project stage. This arrangement is generally considered preferable by donors who are looking for mechanisms that promote the sustainability of the project outputs.

Yet this model encounters problems relating to the status and capacity of the host department managing the delivery process. For instance, in Visakhapatnam the process of hosting a large slum improvement project undermined the previous responsibilities of the Community Development Department and threatened its ongoing existence (see Box 6.9). In the Cochin Main Phase,[2] management responsibility was placed with the Urban Poverty Alleviation (UPA) Department in order to promote the importance of community participation and social inputs within project delivery, and to avoid the domination of engineering-led solutions in the process of improving environmental conditions. In practice, however, the selected department has a low status and is marginalised within the Corporation of Cochin (CoC). The contribution of the CoC Engineering Department was not effectively facilitated and the services component of the project stalled. The problem was further exacerbated when the UPA department was moved from the Corporation headquarters and the physical distance between the Engineering and UPA Departments made it more difficult to obtain the interest and commitment needed for effective engineering inputs.

Conversely, in Colombo, the placement of the Community Development Department within the Public Health Department in the Colombo Municipal Corporation illustrates how high status departments and effective managers can underpin participatory initiatives (see Box 5.2).

Project Cells

Another organisational model for both multi-sectoral and infrastructure projects is the project cell. Not as isolated as the PMU, a project cell functions within the municipal organisation, has a core staff and draws on the resources of other technical departments as required. In Ahmedabad, such a separate cell has been created and is one of the many responsibilities of the Deputy Municipal Commissioner. It sits outside both Community Development and Engineering Departments but within the control of a senior mainstream municipal manager. Engineers and town planners are deputed to the project and the community development activities are carried out by an NGO. On the one hand this arrangement has ensured that the Slum Networking Project was prioritised by the municipality. On the other, the organisational arrangement has meant that there has been little transfer of community, poverty and participation skills to any line department normally responsible for these municipal functions.

Zonal Offices

Another model of organisational reform is the devolution of power to the sub-municipal (or zonal) level. The intention of this shift, illustrated by the Surat Municipal Corporation (see Boxes 6.5 and 7.2) is to place the responsibility for effective service delivery and public health management closer to the communities and problems, and to make the municipality more accountable for their performance. Through this reorganisation in Surat, the responsibility for the city, ward

Box **6.9**

Municipal Structure

Municipal Corporation of Visakhapatnam

The Municipality in Visakhapatnam has had an Urban Community Development (UCD) Department since 1979. UCD activities were extended in 1982 with support from UNICEF through the UBS Programme. The emphasis of the UCD programme during this period was in developing community participation in planning and implementation of slum upgrading, health, education, literacy and community and women's development activities. The emphasis on community participation was reflected in the staffing of a UCD wing dominated by community development staff. Technical expertise was provided from relevant departments (primarily engineering and health) on request.

After the inception of VSIP in 1988, the UCD wing became the Slum Improvement Project Office. This move changed the nature and the structure of the UCD. Rather than a community development department working with other departments on specific programmes, the VSIP Project Office seconded in engineering, planning and health staff, and functioned independently.

This integrated structure proved convenient for project implementation and provided a number of immediate and long term opportunities and advantages:

- allowing urban poverty programmes to be co-ordinated through one department;
- enabling community participation to be recognised as a legitimate component of urban poverty programmes;
- developing a cadre of staff with professional competence and extensive experience of working with communities and government;
- establishing the UCD staff as key members of the team who the engineering department automatically consults and involves in the planning and implementation of infrastructure in low income areas; and
- creating a body of experience and institutional learning which can be utilised in the planning of new programmes.

Despite these benefits, the structure also created a number of institutional problems. Although the Project Memorandum viewed the existence of the UCD department as a major advantage for project implementation, in practice the project design appears to have contributed to its marginalisation over time. The project is clearly designed as a shelter project 'integrating' community development and health activities, rather than a community development programme. Recruitment of engineering and health staff into the UCD resulted in CD staff effectively being sidelined to implementing community development activities, and the process of organising the poor into neighbourhood groups for collective action became marginalised. By the time CD activities were incorporated into an implementation manual they had been reduced to the administration of a set of specified activities.

In addition, many of the UCD staff members, including those formerly employed under the UCD wing, now have unclear status in the MCV. Although the department had a long established identity in MCV and the staff were funded fully by the municipality before the beginning of the project, the ODA intervention, which included the payment of UCD staff salaries for 8 years and redefined the department as a Project Office, and the organisational approach to the project, had the effect of de-institutionalising the department within the municipality. The problem was initially aggravated by the fact that neither the State nor National Government led a regularisation of Urban Community Development Departments. In the current context, even though the 74th Constitutional Amendment allocates this function to municipalities, and higher levels of government commit more and more resources to urban poverty alleviation to be managed through UCDs (now Urban Poverty Alleviation (UPA) departments), the marginalisation problem continues. There has been strong pressure from elected representatives to disband the department.

Seconding engineering, planning and health staff to UCD also meant that there was a separation of 'project' and 'non-project' health and engineering activities during the project lifetime. This has resulted in little cross-fertilisation of ideas between project and non-project staff. It also means that there has been no development of permanent mechanisms for co-ordination between UCD and other departments, either for poverty or non-poverty focused work. One of the major issues is that UPA programmes have yet to be mainstreamed as a regular municipal function. They are considered in the same light as health and education sectoral programmes and have a different institutional status. Social perspectives are not generally integrated into the health and education programmes as organisational expertise lies in the UCD department. As a result, 'participation' is only perceived as relevant to activities undertaken through the poverty reduction project or programmes.

(Visakhapatnam Case Study)

and neighbourhood levels of infrastructure and service delivery was not then subdivided between departments. The structural reform that took place in Surat aimed at tackling and managing service delivery problems in the areas where they occurred. Zonal offices were given responsibility and held accountable for the performance of water, sanitation, solid waste (and other) services. Parallel procedural changes ensured the transparency of activities at the zonal level. Communities can visit their zonal office to make complaints and access information and assistance. While this has undoubtedly resulted in a cleaner city and much improved services to poor areas, community participation was only envisaged in terms of the monitoring and evaluation, and was not an integral objective of the reorganisation.

Identifying appropriate management structures

In summary, the various models highlight a number of important issues that should be considered in the selection of appropriate municipal structures. These include:

- identifying the impacts of organisational structure on community decision-making and the evolution of participatory processes;
- creating space for establishing participation and building confidence at the outset;
- improving the access of communities to the municipal institution;
- considering the transfer of skills versus the loss of skills developed in temporary organisations;
- addressing the implications of hierarchy and status of departments and managers and the capacity of a department to function effectively; and
- delegating to lower levels versus improving the profile of participatory initiatives.

As the delivery of services and infrastructure to the poor is frequently a marginalised and low status task within the municipality, and incorporating the participation of the poor can accentuate this marginalisation, the organisational arrangements within the municipality for promoting community participation will have a significant effect on the benefits of the participatory project and the sustainability of the participatory process. Yet efforts to protect the process frequently result in a lack of integration and sustainability, while efforts to mainstream the process can result in domination, marginalisation of departments and compromise of participatory objectives. Effective structures are difficult to achieve without significant attitudinal change throughout the whole municipality. Structural change should be co-ordinated with other elements of municipal reform (such as skills development and procedural change) and a strategy formulated which responds to the participation envisaged and the vehicle of delivery adopted.

Box **6.10**

Systems and Procedural Reform
Surat Municipal Corporation

The development of management capacity in the Surat Municipal Corporation (see also Box 7.2) was closely linked to the introduction of new systems and procedures relating to municipal functions. These changes were fundamental and reflected the spirit of change in the municipality. The procedural reforms addressed monitoring, maintenance, management and information, planning and procurement and construction procedures.

Monitoring and Maintenance Procedures

A fundamental change that led to the improved sanitary conditions of Surat was the formalised and prescribed approach to field visits by municipal officials. Changes to fieldwork procedures had two main aims: first, to improve monitoring and, consequently, the efficiency of service delivery; and second to build a clearer understanding of the nature and impacts of service deficiencies (specifically, solid waste, water and sanitation) experienced by poor people.

Field visit procedures were developed which:

- **increased management presence** – all levels of management were directed to spend 5 hours in the field every day, including the Municipal Commissioner and Deputy/Zonal commissioners;
- **introduced joint visits** – senior management was expected to accompany Ward Sanitary Inspectors and Sub-Inspectors to develop a greater understanding of the scope of their work and the problems they encountered;
- **focused on the poor areas** – at least 50% of the time allocated to fieldwork was to be spent in slum areas to enhance knowledge of the poor and their problems;
- **increased random visits** – unannounced visits were carried out to improve the performance of middle and lower level staff; and
- **promoted immediate action** – radio communication was established to facilitate rapid responses to environmental problems (the previous requirement for written authorisation was removed).

Each zone was managed and monitored through a **pyramidal structure** that resulted in prompt identification of problems in the field, immediate notification to zonal offices and actions by officials responsible for rectification. This process brought about greater interaction between levels of management and implementation staff within the Corporation, and between the Corporation and the communities themselves. It significantly enhanced the accountability and effectiveness of decisions made and has, to some extent, improved the skills of those previously shielded from the problems of the field. In the SMC, this change in culture became known as a change from 'AC to DC' (from Air-Conditioned Offices, to Direct Chores).

The SMC also introduced a **system of micro-managing** problem areas of the city in an effort to rectify the imbalance in the allocation of resources within the city. This resulted in the identification of nuisance spots; systematised removal of waste on streets; collection of waste in containers and dustbins; cleaning areas surrounding waste bins and containers; twice daily cleaning and removal in high traffic areas (such as markets and densely populated areas); daily group meetings and visits. With this procedural change, the coverage of solid waste collection increased from 35% to 95% with an additional investment of 10%. The quantity of solid waste removed increased by 60%.

In order to redress public grievances and to rectify environmental problems in the city as quickly as possible, a **system of reply cards** was established for both sanitation and engineering complaints. Procedures for sanitation complaints were introduced which stipulated immediate response and set down deadlines for actions. For instance:

- the AMC response time to public health complaints about dead animals, water leakage and solid waste collection was limited to 24 hours;
- the response time for engineering complaints such as lighting, building debris and drainage was also amended to 24 hours; and
- complaints such as removal of dirt and waste, exposure to insecticides, and blocked drains, repair of standpipes, public roads and new drainage connections required action within 24–48 hours.

The complaints system promoted transparency and accountability by requiring Zonal Offices to respond in writing to the citizen making the complaint. In more than 90% of cases, complaints were being addressed and problems resolved within the stipulated time period.

(continued in Box 6.11)

Municipal Systems and Procedures

Local government has generally been characterised by the burdensome and bureaucratic nature of procedures and systems. In many cases communities complain that such systems make municipalities inaccessible and restrict the degree to which they can, in practice, become effective partners. Cumbersome systems affect community morale and trust can be lost if procedures are overly bureaucratic and slow to produce results. Municipal efforts to involve communities in service delivery projects can benefit substantially from strategic and practical revisions to well-entrenched municipal procedures that constrain community participation. Experience suggests that there are viable solutions to most procedural constraints to participation and in many cases these solutions may already be possible under existing legislation and procedures. Frequently, however, procedures are formulated at higher levels of government and municipalities must apply for waivers and approvals to bring about even temporary procedural change (see examples of methods of producing change in Box 6.12). This process of changing established procedures can prove extremely difficult without the support of high level political and administrative management.

Some of the procedures affecting municipal capacity for community participation are discussed below.

Financial Management Procedures

In many municipalities undergoing reform, procedural change has focused on improving the processes used to manage municipal functions. Foremost amongst these are reforms to financial management such as computerisation, accounting procedures, budgeting and budgeting control procedures as well as MIS for billing and collection of property tax. Reform brings about improved information, greater transparency and accountability to the public, and greater flexibility. These are all necessary for establishing effective and sustainable partnerships with external organisations. In Ahmedabad and Surat, for instance (see Boxes 6.10, 6.11 and 6.13), municipal reforms focused on getting the ground rules right. They focused first on ensuring that the strategic capacity of the municipality was in order and then carried out procedural reforms in association with organisational, financial and staffing reforms. In Ahmedabad this was accompanied by the Slum Networking Project, which introduced community cost-sharing successfully because the Corporation had visibly rectified its financial status.

Many municipalities initially base procedural change on a need to mobilise additional resources with community funds, but rarely recognise that this move changes the role of the community from beneficiary to co-financier, and that places a responsibility on the municipality to perform. Problems frequently appear to occur due to the annual budgeting process, restricting expenditure to budgets prepared well in advance, and restricting the flow of funds to suit financial years. Despite the success of Ahmedabad in mobilising community funds, the municipality failed to make their financial contribution in a timely manner because the project was budgeted for the following financial year and the AMC was unable to release funds earlier. This affected community trust and threatened to involve communities in additional cost. Ultimately, the private sector partner, not constrained by the inflexibility of budgeting procedures, was able to cover the municipal contribution temporarily.

Project Planning Procedures

In the context of an effective and sustainable municipality, procedural change in relation to services and infrastructure is not onerous but a part of an integrated effort to greater efficiency. In most municipalities, however, procedural change only occurs at the project level. It requires significant commitment on the part of the initiator and visible and immediate benefits if it is to become sustainable. Changes to project planning and design procedures (such as those in Kerala and Colombo, discussed in Chapter 4 and illustrated in Boxes 4.8 to 4.10) can be absorbed if the will and the management

6

Box **6.11**

Systems and Procedural Reform
Surat Municipal Corporation

Contract Procurement Procedures

A contractual system of **unit rates** was introduced by the SMC in 1995-6 to facilitate immediate appointment of contractors for construction works. Through this mechanism of locally approved unit costs, the Municipality is now able to award works to any competent agency without inviting tenders. Works undertaken under the unit rate system include small works such as the construction of pavements and street paving in poor areas, laying of sewers, water supply and storm water drains, construction of compound walls, maintenance of buildings, planting of trees, construction of communal pay toilets and erection of street lighting poles.

The implementation of the unit rate system has had significant impacts, specifically:

- facilitating emergency work to be undertaken without delay;
- easing the workload of Zonal Officers normally responsible for estimating and decision-making (Zonal managers can now sanction works up to a limit of Rs. 2.00 lakhs (approx $5,000));
- standardising the costs of similar works (to the same standards and specifications) in different zones; and
- reducing administrative procedures and time for tendering routine works, including operation and maintenance works.

In order to expedite the completion of works essential to improving the environmental conditions of the city, the SMC management introduced procedures for the **management of small works** that placed time constraints on the construction programme. A time limit of six months was placed on works facilitated through the unit rate system. The enforcement of this procedure has encouraged junior engineers responsible for supervision to minimise delays in completion of works. Should they fail to bring the work in on time the procedure requires them to submit a six-page explanation to the Commissioner. (As the submission is to be written in English, most engineers prefer to focus on ensuring the works are completed).

The SMC also implemented a number of steps to improve the contract procurement system (such as estimating, tendering and contracting). Apart from the introduction of the unit rate system and the time limits for completion of small works projects, a Research and Analysis Cell was formed. All estimates costing more than Rs. 2.00 lakhs (approx. $5000) are reviewed by the Research and Analysis Cell in order to minimise discrepancies in the preparation of estimates and tender documents. Heavy penalties were introduced for delays. Procedures enabling the use of professional consultants were also established to hasten the speed at which the municipality could undertake contracts.

Planning Procedures

In order to re-establish regulation and control over development in Surat, the SMC introduced rigorous enforcement of the regulations controlling construction and development. This enforcement was widely implemented and had a particular impact on those developers and contractors that, for many years, had functioned in an unregulated climate. The Development Control Team responsible for enforcing regulations identified illegal constructions, served notices, marked buildings (with the required setbacks and other statutory obligations) and instructed immediate demolition. While in some cases residents and owners themselves demolished the illegal sections of the buildings, in others (particularly buildings owned by powerful, well connected businessmen) the demolition would be imposed. To avoid potential difficulties, the Municipal Commissioner would ensure he was present when the demolition started.

Other forms of encroachment, particularly by the poor (petty traders, slum dwellers etc.), were given the same level of attention. The Municipal Commissioner visited the areas and discussed the problems of public health or congestion with the communities. In most cases, he identified the primary causes of the specific environmental problem and informed the encroachers of actions to be taken by the SMC. While there was little opportunity for the community to participate, the impact of this equitable approach indirectly improved relations between the poor and the SMC. Rarely had the poor citizens of Surat been witnesses to the removal or demolition of buildings owned by the non-poor. ●

(Surat Case Study)

commitment are there to do so. Other procedural changes needed to bring about effective participation may include land management and planning and building regulations. In some cases these may lie outside municipal responsibility and efforts will be needed to waive or relax regulations to legitimise informal settlements and service and infrastructure initiatives and promote community shelter initiatives.

Procurement Procedures

Procurement procedures of municipalities form a key part of the professional responsibility of engineers and are well established in administrative systems. Typically, service contracts in municipalities are let through a linear process of surveys, designs, document preparation, estimates, invitation to bid, tenders and award of contracts. If community participation is to be effectively incorporated, this linear process must not only be changed to facilitate the iterative design implied by demand-responsive approaches, but must also be moderated so that municipalities can involve communities in implementation stages of projects.

For instance, conventional procurement procedures limit options for communities to act as contractors for construction works because poor communities are not able to:

- raise and risk the money required for the tender deposit;
- risk under-pricing in a formal tender;
- raise the capital for the security deposit; and
- secure the funding necessary to cover start-up costs.

A variety of pro-poor procedures have been developed to breakdown the barriers to community involvement in construction. These include:

- **Unit Rates:** In order to ensure fairness, a system of unit rates can be used as the basis for communities to price contracts and for municipalities to make payments. The system is simple and transparent. In Kerala, under the People's Planning Campaign, the municipality carried out estimates based on unit rates devised for the local area and 'beneficiary committees' undertook to complete the works at no more than 5% over the estimated cost. A procedure is being established for local market rates to be updated on a yearly basis. (See Box 6.11 on the introduction of unit rates in Surat.)

- **Waiving tender deposits and security deposits:** In order for poor communities to tender and win contracts it is necessary for municipalities to relax onerous contractual requirements by informal waiver or government order. Municipalities forcing communities to risk capital for deposits threaten the participation process and/or force communities to take out loans from moneylenders at high interest rates. It is unlikely that community contracting initiatives will develop in this situation.

- **Advances to cover start-up costs:** Experience suggests it is possible to facilitate mechanisms that assist communities to mobilise resources for start-up costs (to purchase the materials and equipment necessary to begin construction). Examples of municipal actions that assisted communities to obtain funds include the Kerala State Government order which facilitates direct advances to beneficiary groups. This compares with the earlier situation in Kerala, during the Cochin Urban Poverty Reduction Project Pilot Phase, where formal change was not forthcoming and a municipal official secured the advance on behalf of the community (see Box 4.12). While unsustainable, such informal practices provide helpful lessons to sceptical bureaucrats and frequently build the confidence to enable more formal mechanisms to be established in subsequent initiatives.

6

Box **6.12**	**Procedural Change** Comparative Table		

	Procedure	Change	Method of introducing change
Surat Municipal Corporation (ongoing service activities)	• Performance Monitoring • Operation and Maintenance • Contract Procurement	• Random checks • Increased presence in field • Reply Card Complaint System • Unit Rates System • Procedures introduced for small works contracts	• Change to procedures driven by and brought into effect by Municipal Commissioner • The immediate and noticeable benefits produced eased the difficulties of introducing change
Ahmedabad Municipal Corporation (SNP)	• Financial management • Staffing procedures • Operation and Maintenance	• Property taxation • Octroi tax • Revised standards and qualifications. • Qualified middle management staff introduced on contracts. • Reply Card Complaint System	• Change introduced by Municipal Commissioner • Enforcement of existing legislation • Changes introduced by Municipal Commissioner
Corporation of Cochin (CUPRP)	• Contract Procurement	• Earnest deposit • Security deposit • Mobilisation payment	• Procedures bypassed or waived informally • Personally facilitated by Municipal Engineer
Kerala State Government (Kerala People's Planning Campaign)	• Planning processes • Construction costing • Contract Procurement	• 5-year budget and plan through compilation of ward level plans • Unit rates • Preferential award to beneficiary group at estimated cost	• Government Order • Government Order
Bangalore Municipal Corporation (BUPP)	• Planning processes	• Planning procedures replaced with micro-planning in identified slum areas • Joint Bank Accounts	• Waiver
Colombo Municipal Corporation (UHSP)	• Planning • Dispute Resolution	• Town planning procedures replaced with Community Action Planning • Multi-levelled system introduced to resolve community disputes.	• Government Order
Faisalabad Development Authority (FAUP)	• Contract Procurement • Project planning • Project Expenditure • Building Standards	• Joint Bank Accounts • Community planning initiatives • Implementation Committees responsible for project finances disburse funds. • Developing appropriate cost-effective standards of construction	• Waiver • Written agreement

Operation and Maintenance Procedures

Procedures for operation and maintenance have been subject to varying degrees of neglect due to a lack of resources and commitment in local government. The development of procedures, through which communities can become involved in reporting on malfunctioning services and the maintenance of infrastructure, has been very successful in Ahmedabad and Surat. In both cities a system of reply cards for sanitation problems legitimises community involvement and institutionalises community participation in monitoring the operation and maintenance role performed by the municipality (see Box 6.10).

Key lessons in relation to procedural change

A number of lessons concerning procedural change are provided by municipal experience and are outlined below. These point toward the importance of integrating change in systems and procedures with other areas of internal municipal reform to create a more receptive environment for community participation.

- Support for procedural reform can be achieved quickly once evidence is provided as to the benefits of change.
- Blockages caused by existing systems and procedures can be identified and procedural change brought into force with the political and administrative will.
- Procedures and monitoring systems that promote accountability and transparency reduce corrupt practices and decision-making for personal gain, and promote community trust.
- Procedural change is necessary to improve community access to information.
- Procedures must change if the municipality is to change its roles and relationships with external actors.
- Procedural change is closely linked to attitudinal change at municipal level, and is underpinned by the efforts of higher levels of government.

The need for senior management support to lead the process of reform is essential (see Chapter 7). In tandem with other elements of municipal reform, capacity building with municipal managers should include exposure to projects where procedures have been revised to incorporate communities in service delivery processes. Training needs assessments, skills development and procedural change will be closely linked to capacity building activities.

Box **6.13**

Financial Reform
Ahmedabad Municipal Corporation

In the last five years the Ahmedabad Municipal Corporation (AMC) has improved its financial status significantly. In the early 1990s the Corporation was operating annual deficits and capital financing was declining as a percentage of annual expenditure. In 1992-3, total revenue receipts were Rs. 198 crore (US$50m), with a deficit of Rs. 21 crore (US$5.25m) against expenditure. In 1995, the AMC operated a financial surplus and for the last 3 years the financial status of the Corporation has steadily improved. By 1997-8 the AMC showed total revenue receipts of Rs. 550 crore (US$140m) and a surplus of Rs 90 crore (US$22.5m) against expenditure. (1 *crore* equals 100 *lakhs*, approx. US$250,000). Ahmedabad is financially now one of the healthiest municipal corporations in India. The combined effects of focused management, attitudinal change and procedural reform resulted in substantial changes in the total revenue and capacity of the Corporation to carry out municipal functions.

The primary factor behind this financial turnaround was the appointment of a skilled financial manager and senior IAS officer as Municipal Commissioner in 1994 (discussed in Box 7.3). During his 3-year tenure in Ahmedabad, the Commissioner developed a strategy toward rapid financial reform and self-sufficiency of the municipality which targeted the octroi tax, property tax and the development of public-private financial partnerships. This was underpinned by the utilisation of existing legislation and aggressive enforcement of standards and procedures.

Substantial reform to the operation of the existing **octroi tax** included improvements in the assessment systems and rationalisation of the tax collection procedures. Octroi (a 'regressive' tax which is paid on all goods being sold within the Corporation boundaries) now represents 70% of the annual AMC revenue and, on a daily basis, offers a strong, stable and buoyant source of revenue. The reform was managed by the Municipal Commissioner himself, who is reputed to have been unforgiving, requiring hourly reports and initiating midnight visits to collection points to alleviate delaying tactics and corrupt practices by tax collectors. These tactics generated a massive inflow of funds and permanently eradicated the precedent of non- (or late) payment.

At the same time, change in the property litigation procedures removed many constraints limiting the collection of **property tax** in the AMC area. In 1993 over 50% of property was untaxable due to litigation. New systems were introduced to remove the overwhelming backlog, the overtly litigious behaviour and lengthy court battles. Litigants are now required to pay 70% of the court costs in advance. The AMC is also implementing a new area-based framework for the property-tax assessment which is expected to improve further transparency and efficiency of collection systems.

Improved accounting and financial **management systems** introduced in the AMC, including the computerisation of property tax and octroi tax, and the separation of the loan account to trace cash flows, led to more transparent and accountable financial management of municipal operations.

The financial turnaround in Ahmedabad led the AMC to launch **municipal bonds**. In January 1998, 1,000,000 bonds were released with a rating of AA. This initiative was fully subscribed and raised Rs. 100 *crore* (approx. US$25m) to be utilised specifically for improvements to the water supply to Ahmedabad and the implementation of a sewerage scheme in the east of the city.

While the municipality has certainly improved its access to resources, it is also strategic in the manner in which it is approaching a large range of projects requiring expenditure. The cost recovery aspect of the community participation in the Slum Networking Project (Box 4.13) is no different in principle from the private-public partnership approach that the AMC adopted for the maintenance of a number of major parks and roads. In this respect, the AMC has begun to redefine its **role as a facilitator** and co-ordinator rather than the traditional municipal role of provider. The stability of municipal finances clearly enabled the AMC to embark upon these partnerships and to develop a cost recovery approach with communities. The competent and transparent management of municipal finances together with the professionalisation programme and the implementation of poverty-focused initiatives has improved the way the AMC is perceived by NGOs and communities.

Despite the enormity of the task and the constraints which still hinder the Corporation from meeting objectives and effectively involving communities, the AMC provides an illustration of a local government willing and able to build the foundations for the roles and responsibilities required by decentralisation. The case also highlights the importance of other aspects of municipal reform, particularly the impacts of capable staff and effective procedures which must accompany financial reform if a supportive context for evolving forms of participation is to be created. •

(Ahmedabad Case Study)

Financial Stability

Municipal finance is one of the key elements of urban management and an important factor determining the capacity of the municipality to initiate and maintain partnerships with communities in service delivery. The primary purpose of including a discussion on municipal finance in this chapter is to emphasis the importance of financial capacity and stability as a basis for effective participatory processes.[3] A financially healthy municipality provides opportunity. Service delivery and maintenance represents the most capital intensive component of poverty reduction initiatives and both adequacy and buoyancy of municipal finances affect the capacity of local government to enter into partnerships.[4]

First, the municipality has the financial resources for **expenditure on infrastructure works.** Whether or not service delivery involves cost recovery in whole or part, the municipality may incur costs at the micro, meso and macro levels in order to ensure the services delivered are reliable and meet consumer needs.

Second, the financial stability of the municipality and the improved capacity of the municipality to fulfil municipal functions can **create greater trust** in the institution and its leaders, and greater confidence in municipal initiatives. Apart from improving relationships, this creates the potential for, and promotes, investment and financial partnerships. For decades, local government has failed to fulfil municipal functions. As a result, most poor communities and the NGO sector have little confidence in municipal ability and little trust in municipal promises. Evidence suggests that this mistrust is abated as municipal finances develop and expenditure becomes visible. Communities, NGOs and businesses appear more willing to enter into municipal partnerships and to contribute financially toward service delivery objectives. This visibility generates further trust and mobilises more resources. (It is, of course, more likely that insolvent municipalities have a greater need to introduce community participation processes to gain from the financial resources that communities may have to offer. Yet it is in this context that communities are least likely to be drawn to the idea of paying for services.)

Third, financial stability promotes **accountability and transparency** of financial management. This appears to lead to other elements of reform, promoting greater flexibility and accessibility of communities to participate in entrenched municipal functions.

Financial reforms undertaken in various municipalities illustrate that both strategic and practical changes are required, which include:

- **strategic financial planning:** realistic budget formulation/strategic revenue generation;
- **sound financial management:** effective control/accurate information about expenditure, revenue and loans;
- **rationalisation and enforcement of tax provisions:** removal of constraints, effective collection systems, monitoring and enforcement procedures; and
- **partnerships in municipal functions:** attracting outside investment (private sector, international investment) to relieve the municipality of some areas of expenditure.

The case study of municipal finances in Ahmedabad illustrates each of these points. It provides an example of a large Municipal Corporation in India that seized its obligation under the national decentralisation policy to become self-sufficient and to serve the people of the city. It established a capacity to raise finances for recurrent costs and large capital expenditure, and to alleviate recurrent costs through partnership arrangements with the private sector (see Box 6.13).

6

Box **6.14**

Municipal Attitudes
Viewpoints and Attitudinal Change

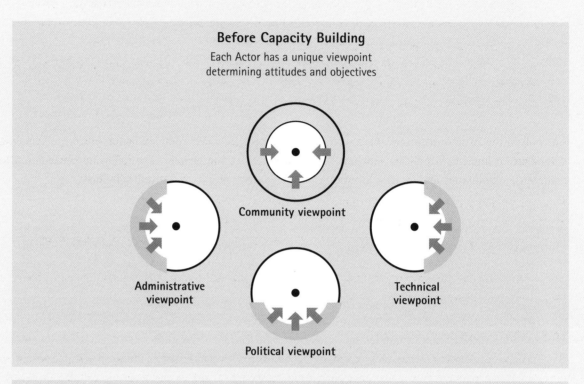

Before Capacity Building

Each Actor has a unique viewpoint
determining attitudes and objectives

Community viewpoint

Administrative
viewpoint

Technical
viewpoint

Political viewpoint

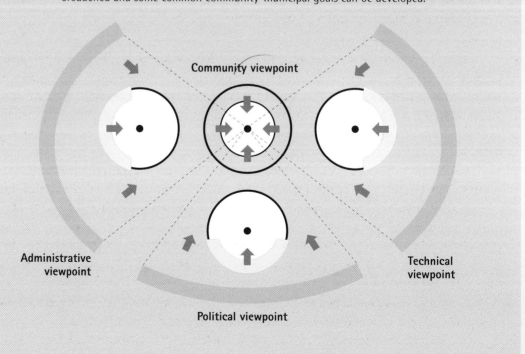

After Capacity Building

Actors maintain their existing viewpoints but through exposure and capacity building perspectives are
broadened and some common community-municipal goals can be developed.

Community viewpoint

Administrative
viewpoint

Technical
viewpoint

Political viewpoint

Attitudinal Change

Perhaps the most critical issue of those discussed throughout this guide and that which both precedes and follows any discussion on the formation of effective community-municipal partnerships is the issue of attitudinal change.

- How can attitudes be changed to enhance capacity?
- Does enhanced capacity in the form of better skills, better understanding and a supportive operating context bring about a sustainable change in attitudes toward community participation?
- Why is there such resistance to community participation?

Not only is the issue of attitudes the most critical, it is also the most complex factor which municipalities must address if they are to implement policies aimed at the participation of the people. The following discussion attempts to disaggregate the cumulative and indistinct notion of 'unsupportive municipal attitudes' by first:

- acknowledging that municipal attitudes are not always similar;
- identifying the attitudes and underlying rationale of different actors; and by
- acknowledging the poverty dimension which influences the way officials perceive participation.

Notwithstanding the enormity of the task, experiences of municipalities to date highlight some of the steps which can be taken to initiate attitudinal change.

The rationale of municipal actors

Different actors within the municipality may oppose or fail to support community participation for entirely different reasons. It can be argued that attitudes within municipalities stem from either a political, administrative or a technical base. The viewpoint of each of these municipal officials, while in part overlapping, stands in stark contrast to the viewpoint of the community. Attitudes of each actor involved are formed from different objectives, values and capacities. This idea, represented diagrammatically in Box 6.14, draws on Goulet's concept of rationalities of development.[5] This aims to create a greater understanding of how attitudes towards participation develop. For instance, in a municipal context it is possible to envisage a situation where:

- The administrative official is concerned with maintaining the status quo, with minimising change (and in some cases preserving established mechanisms for rent-seeking). Seen from the viewpoint of the administrative official, there is no benefit of community participation apart from the potential of cost sharing. Conversely, the disruption to the status quo, to the functioning of normal procedures, structures and hierarchies, the creation of additional work, and potentially the loss of rent-seeking opportunities, creates practical reasons why community participation should be avoided.

- The administrative viewpoint is closely aligned to the political representative, whose aim is to retain power and assume greater control. (The work of the administrative official is a political act in so much as it involves discretion in the allocation of resources.) The political viewpoint errs towards preserving the status quo of social and political institutions that facilitate power. Community participation threatens the perception that politicians are benefactors. It challenges the nature of social and political institutions by redefining roles and responsibilities.

- The technical official has developed his attitudes from another viewpoint that essentially looks towards instrumental objectives and concrete ends. This is prescribed through formal education and reinforced through professional affiliation. The municipal engineer, for instance, has a responsibility for the completion of infrastructure projects. That is the purpose of his/her work. The success of that service delivery is measured in terms of the degree to which the time, quality and cost have been achieved in relation to a predetermined brief. The participation of a poor community does not directly fit into a rational framework from the technician's viewpoint. Indeed, the notion of

Box **6.15**

Municipal Attitudes and Administrative Culture
Ahmedabad Municipal Corporation

The case of Ahmedabad illustrates the broad range of attitudes towards the poor, participatory processes and municipal reform which can be found within a municipality. The reform process in the Ahmedabad Municipal Corporation (AMC) was led by the administrative wing of the Corporation, and was achieved through the skilled and committed management of a reformist Municipal Commissioner, his supporting management team and his successor (see Boxes 7.3 and 7.4). In particular, the administration was characterised by attitudinal change toward management processes. The viewpoint of the senior managers was that the AMC could, like any other organisation, function efficiently and autonomously. A strategic approach was developed to attain this end. The desire for the status quo was replaced at the senior management level by the desire for reform which would bring with it greater achievements, greater respect and higher status.

These attitudes and the viewpoint generating them were not shared by all. Lower levels of administrative staff did not initially welcome change, clinging to the status quo and the need to retain existing structures and methods. The reform process, however, was relentless and led from the top. A message was disseminated that the inefficiencies of the existing staff were no longer acceptable. Skilled managers were also employed to introduce a new force and a new attitude of professionalism within the Corporation.

The institutionalisation of participatory approaches within the AMC has been slower to evolve than that of a new management culture. To some extent this is due to the approach developed with external partners that shifted responsibilities and redefined the role of the municipality to that of facilitator. Despite the efforts of the AMC to build a partnership with communities, and the support of two successive pro-poor Deputy Municipal Commissioners in implementing the Slum Networking Project (SNP), municipal attitudes have focused on output and ease of implementation. This has limited the decision-making role (and thus the empowerment) of the poor in their development.

From a technical perspective, the SNP was the work of a local consultant with fixed ideas on the strategic framework and details of appropriate service delivery. While the approach was developed with insight into cost-effective technologies and the need to integrate service provision into the overall infrastructure network of the city, the approach envisaged technical output-oriented ends and was not, initially, developed with an explicit focus on meaningful community participation. This is clearly exemplified first by the lack of choice given to poor communities in the types and levels of service offered under the umbrella of the project; and second by the attitudes and behaviour of technical officials. Engineering and planning staff had little understanding of poverty and the needs of the poor at the outset of the project, and they had no opportunity for broadening their viewpoint through skills or orientation courses. They did not recognise that their viewpoint or understanding of the project was very different in means and ends from that of the community they served. They had no familiarity with working with the poor and no basis on which to build the relationship. One junior AMC engineer supervising the construction of a sewer at Sanjay Nagar, financed in part by the community, commented that he had no need for skills in participation and did not see the need for community involvement, that his work was purely technical in nature.

While technical officials still have not undergone any significant formal skills development, the ongoing process of working with the poor has, over time, begun to change attitudes. NGO officials suggest that those AMC officials who have continuously worked with the poor during the pilot of the SNP have, through exposure and experience, developed a far greater insight and sensitivity to their needs. This change is visible and significant. At the same time there is still a reluctance to involve the poor communities in technical decision-making, mainly because it is felt that communities do not have the knowledge of technical matters to meaningfully contribute to these decisions.

On the political side, the short tenure of the Mayor of the AMC has continually resulted in a concern for short-term and visible achievements. Community participation, by its nature, takes time to establish, and one year is insufficient to see significant achievement in participatory processes. As a result, the political wing has been slow to pursue participatory and other long-term objectives and has been resistant to institutional change which would not bring immediate, visible results. This difference became particularly evident during the process of implementing financial reforms. Despite the legislative provision for the enforcement of tax, the decision to compel citizens to meet tax obligations was not popular amongst the political wing of the AMC. The rigorous measures introduced demanded political conviction and the willingness of the council to look beyond the short-term political cycle to the long-term financial health of the city of Ahmedabad. Ultimately, the political patronage lost due to rigorous enforcement of tax obligations was recaptured when the expanded financial capacity of the municipality led to improved services, large infrastructure projects and opportunity for more contracts for more contractors. The political will was thus generated through the single-mindedness of the administrators. •

participatory decision-making disrupts the technical rationale s/he would apply to planning service provision. Participation in implementation confuses norms of procurement. At an individual level, participation redefines the engineer's professional role, threatens the mystique and perceived superiority surrounding his/her technical knowledge and the decision-making process over capital works, and encroaches on established performance and monitoring criteria.

In contrast to these attitudes, **poor communities** are primarily seeking to improve the quality of their lives. Their viewpoint is of a marginalised group, able to see, but unable to achieve the benefits of economic growth or to access improvements to standards of social and physical services. Communities lack choice and focus on survival. Their attitudes are a result of this position; they seek services and infrastructure and empowerment and improved access to, and control over, information and resources as a means to this end.

While this may be an oversimplified view of communities' needs and objectives, the key point is that the attitudes are very different from the municipal actors 'responsible' for bringing about change to their physical environment. One of the fundamental problems hindering the implementation of participatory policy and building alliances is the very different rationality that motivates the different actors involved. The diversity of these viewpoints and the diversity of the rationale determining the behaviour must be recognised in order to bring about change.

The poverty layer

The lessons of those municipalities which have initiated community participation reveal the need to bring about change to discriminatory attitudes towards poor communities. In the area of service delivery to the poor, this 'poverty layer' must be understood and addressed. The negative attitudes towards participatory processes found in a number of the municipalities examined were associated with a set of prejudices and misunderstandings. These include:

- a basic antipathy to the poor as a social group;
- a belief that the poor are incapable of meaningfully contributing to environmental upgrading because they lack the education and skills; and
- a belief that the poor are poor because they are lazy.

These attitudes not only create an incapacity to work with the poor, but affect other officials' capacity to work effectively. In India and Pakistan, as already discussed and illustrated, the task of going out into poor areas is not valued and community development staff are often marginalised for working with the poor. The disaggregation and identification of causes for prejudicial and ill-informed attitudes provide a starting point for bringing about attitudinal change.

Addressing unfavourable attitudes

Seen in this context, to rely on a low-status Community Development Department or on one individual Community Co-ordinator to develop sustainable community participation is incongruous. Attitudes are diverse, complex, layered and deeply engrained. They are not easily changed and certainly not changed from below. Addressing attitudes will vary according to the actors involved, their backgrounds and their viewpoints and rationale.

Municipal managers can initiate attitudinal change by:

☐ Recognising different attitudes and viewpoints

Municipal leaders must recognise the different viewpoints and fundamental attitudes existing in the municipality, acknowledge their validity and accept that they may not be conceptually reconcilable. It is the task of the municipality as facilitator to bring together the viewpoints and needs of actors into a practical evolving partnership.

Box **6.16**

Involving Engineers in Participatory Processes
Actions, Problems and Solutions

Typical actions and attitudes of engineers involved in orthodox service delivery

- prescriptive top-down methods of planning for services and infrastructure;
- resistance to involving communities in decision-making processes;
- tendency to opt for 'informing' and 'consulting' rather than pursuing forms of participation which focus on decision-making processes;
- tendency to resist moves which replace conventional contracting arrangements (and provide opportunities for officials to receive informal incentives);
- preference for posting in departments carrying out major public works (as against low profile service delivery to poor areas, or operation and maintenance);
- output-oriented objectives lead to indicators showing quantity completed rather then appropriateness, use, efficiency, sustainability;
- technical preferences prioritised in planning and design and resistance to exploring options with communities.

Problems experienced by engineers in municipalities introducing participatory processes

- lack of experience in working in multi-disciplinary teams and working with women;
- absorbing demand-led processes and requirements into strategic planning for meso and macro levels of infrastructure provision;
- overcoming view that technical knowledge and objectives are all-important and superior to other social objectives;
- the multiple and conflicting demands on their time and performance.

Key elements to building capacity of engineers for participatory processes

Long Term

- Ensure **syllabus of engineering courses** includes and prioritises community participation in the delivery of services and infrastructure to the poor. This formalisation of the approach in university/college education (when attitudes are still being developed) is essential to introduce a new attitude to engineers who join municipalities. Education should include the concept of community ownership, participatory methodologies, multi-disciplinary working, and the role of the engineer in promoting sustainable forms of development.
- Develop greater commitment to participation amongst the broader engineering profession through developing support for participatory approaches in professional associations and including participation in registration examinations.
- Provide opportunities for engineering staff to **broaden their understanding** of the whole context of poverty and the means to poverty reduction.

Short term

- Identify and disseminate the **benefits** in terms of the engineer's own goals at the present time (quality of construction, programme, costs, maintenance).
- Develop mechanisms for **training** engineers both within the hierarchy of engineers and within a multi-sectoral group.
- Ensure individual champions and **senior engineers play a key role** in skills development initiatives; promote exposure to similar contexts where engineers can see the role played by their peers.
- **Identify common interests** (such as the cost-effective operation and maintenance of tertiary services) as effective starting points for participation.

This is the dynamic found in Surat. The Municipal Commissioner brought with him the desire to reform and to develop the capacity of the municipality to manage the urban environment effectively. The reforms introduced (rapidly and without popular approval) proved existing systems were not functioning, proved power structures could be overcome, and that change would bring about a cleaner city. The evidence brought about attitudinal change because the viewpoint of the politicians, the administrators and the technicians changed. Politicians saw the benefits of an improved economy, administrators saw the benefits in terms of increased power, and technicians saw improved quality, reliability and efficiency in service delivery.

Broadening all actors' understanding of the overall context

The narrow rationale of various actors means that their understanding of the practical needs and aspirations of the poor is limited. Developing this understanding is essential if social and economic objectives are to be met. This does not deny the critical importance of technical or financial factors, or the importance of particular bureaucratic procedures, but it means that these issues should be seen in the context of other social priorities and objectives. Municipal managers should identify those areas where basic information can inform staff and ensure it is included in skills development programmes.

Identifying Common Interests

A first step in addressing potential conflicts is to identify common interests and to develop officials' capacity to see their role as a part of a larger system. The broader picture of social, environmental as well as economic, technical and political factors opens municipal actors to the concept of community participation.

The rationality theory discussed above fails to recognise that the work of municipal officials, like all human action, can be driven by diverse interests. The suggestion that politicians and senior administrators are driven by power motives and financial gain is to a large extent true, but there are, of course, many who are also committed to serving the community and are able and willing to take on community participation if they are exposed to its benefits. Tapping into this diversity and negotiating a path towards common interests and objectives is a difficult task.

It is generally the role played by local champions, but ultimately is the responsibility of municipal leaders. It is necessary for municipal managers to develop a clearer idea of what the driving factors and attitudes are. The committed manager will ask, for instance, whether administrative staff are only concerned with preserving the status quo and adhering to routines; whether political representatives are only concerned with power and control and the preservation of social and institutional structures; and whether technical professionals are only concerned with physical outputs and levels of investment in services.

Highlighting gains in terms of benefits to administrative, political or technical roles

A key aspect of bringing about attitudinal change is ensuring that individuals and staff are able to see the benefits in the process: benefits to them personally, benefits to them in their municipal role, benefits to the department and benefits to the municipality as a whole. It has already been stressed that skills development should focus on exposing the potential benefits of participatory processes through demonstration projects and pilot initiatives.

Identifying keys and mechanisms to motivation

Developing an understanding of the keys to unlocking demotivated staff and mobilising or assisting in the reorientation of attitudes is an important part of the process of changing attitudes. While some may respond to incentives and rewards, more commonly, municipal experience highlights the tendency for municipal officials to place a priority on improving their role in municipal functions. This may be ultimately followed by the reward of improved status, higher salaries and promotion, but this is unlikely to be immediate.

6

Box **6.17**   **Addressing Municipal Attitudes**
Possible Actions for Attitudinal Change

Capacity remains unchanged

Response A
Deny importance of rationale and try to change viewpoint

Response B
Ignore and do not include actors in participatory processes

Manager imposes participatory approaches on all staff without understanding of the source of the attitudes and viewpoints
Unconstructive Responses

Addressing Attitudinal Problems

Constructive Responses
Manager develops understanding of different viewpoints and their impacts on attitudes and outcomes

Work with these attitudes

Aim to broaden attitudes

Response C
Recognise and validate different viewpoints and attitudes

- Identify common interests
- Highlight benefits for each actor (Politicians, Administrators, Technicians)
- Identify keys to motivation (incentives, mechanisms, standards)

Response D
Broaden understanding of context of municipal functions

- Expose a range of municipal officials to participatory activities and opportunities
- Identify skills development (individual champions, mentors)

Capacity is enhanced

In Surat, middle level managers were motivated to meet the demands of greater efficiency precisely because it was led by respected senior managers and resulted in a greater sense of achievement in their jobs (see Box 7.2). They received no financial reward for significant change in performance, but were publicly shown the gratitude of management. The Commissioner of Surat recognised this key to motivation at all levels. In the process of cleaning up the city, the motivation of the sweepers was given the highest priority (see Box 6.5).

One of the key lessons in bringing about change in the attitudes of technical professionals is illustrated by the DFID-funded Slum Improvement Projects in India (see Box 6.2) where it has been repeatedly shown that engineers listen to their seniors, and that leaders, mentors and heads of professions are the only effective vehicle for imparting information and developing skills.

☐ Broadening experience of working with the poor

A lack of exposure and experience exacerbates unfavourable attitudes towards the poor and towards participatory processes. Typically, municipalities have limited the interface role to a small team of fieldworkers. This approach does not encourage broader municipal understanding of the poor, or participation, and hinders the work of those involved. Exposure and familiarity facilitate attitudinal change and provide greater support to those working directly with communities. Increasing the numbers of municipal officials involved and spreading responsibility for community participation to a multi-disciplinary team helps to develop a deeper base to the processes and begins to remove previous perceptions and stigmas associated with working with the poor.

Promoting positive attitudes towards community participation can produce the greatest change in municipal capacity and in perceptions. The actions and issues described above are only a start to the process of attitudinal change that will primarily come about through first-hand experience and knowledge, through those invloved seeing the immediate benefits to themselves and to the communities, and through the evidence of sustained improvements.

Notes

1. Blackburn (1998) p3
2. The municipal responsibility for 'slum improvement projects' has shifted in DFID-funded projects in India over a ten-year period. This change reflects the lessons learnt of different organisational arrangements. The earliest projects were managed through Project Management Units, and while these were hosted in UCD departments in municipalities (and engineering departments in Development Authorities), they were managed by influential engineers. Due at least in part to the scale and budgets of the projects, they suffered from a lack of focus on community development and participation and an emphasis on engineering-led approaches and outputs. Later poverty reduction projects, such as that illustrated by Cochin, address broader aspects of poverty, and management arrangements have been reconsidered. These too have ultimately proved problematic.
3. Best practice of municipal financial reform is documented elsewhere. See Davey (1993).
4. Financial health is generally understood in relation to adequacy and buoyancy of finances. Adequacy means there are enough funds to fulfil municipal functions and buoyancy means the funds are accessible and available for expenditure.
5. Goulet (1986) pp310-317. See also Abbott (1996) pp155-162, for a description of the role of the professional in the participation process.

The Management Capacity
of the Municipality

Overview

The most critical factor in establishing sustainable participatory processes in a municipality is gaining the active support of senior management. Without committed and knowledgeable management, efforts at lower levels, no matter how skilled and innovative, will be limited in scope and replicability. Municipalities are hierarchical organisations; change comes about slowly and is generally brought about by respected leaders. It is therefore essential that decision-making officials understand and are fully involved in initiating and developing participatory approaches within the municipality.

Experience supports the contention that, in most municipalities, the integration of participatory processes into service and infrastructure delivery functions is dependent on the support of 'champions' occupying senior management positions in the municipality. Case studies show, without exception, that the commitment of senior decision-makers has been crucial to provide a driving force for community participation and to bring about the necessary internal reforms within the municipal machinery. They alone have the authority and power to induce change and to begin the process of capacity building towards the elements, vehicles and municipal reforms necessary for community participation to become sustainable and effective.

This chapter considers the problems and actions of senior managers. It emphasises the factors which constrain effective management but are largely outside the control of the municipality. This brings the discussion back to Chapter 3 and the influence of the external operating context. It also outlines some of the elements of effective management drawn from the case study illustrations.

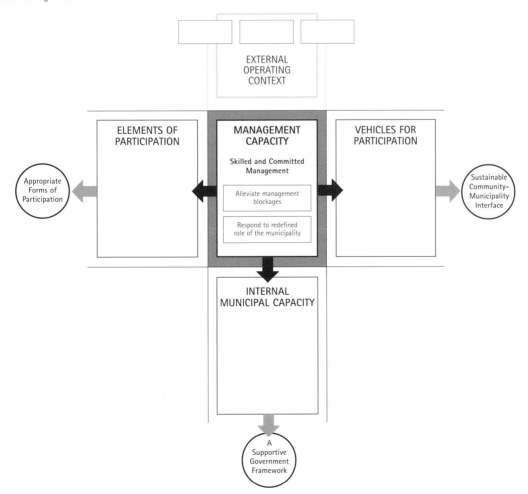

7

Box **7.1**   Municipal Management
Comparative Table

	Key management characteristics	Primary impacts of management
Surat Municipal Corporation (ongoing service activities)	• Municipal Commissioner was the champion of a significant reform process. • Commissioner developed widespread commitment to municipal reform. • Delegation of responsibilities to secondary tier of management. • Promotion of accountability and transparency of municipal action and performance. • Objectives pursued relentlessly, unperturbed by political opposition.	• Sustainable change in capacity of municipality to perform municipal functions. • Significant change in the environmental conditions of the city. • Transparent and accountable organisation and staff. • Formal systems established for public participation in monitoring and evaluation of municipal performance.
Ahmedabad Municipal Corporation (SNP)	• Municipal Commissioner was the champion of a significant reform process. • Second tier of managers were able implementers of the reform process. • Skilled financial management. • Professionalisation of municipality as an organisation. • Relentless pursuit of objectives.	• Financial state of municipality turned around (effective taxation systems and confidence in financial management). • Issue of municipal bonds. • Development of partnerships with private and non-governmental actors. • Improved credibility of municipality.
Kerala State Government (Kerala People's Planning Campaign)	• Political champion (Chief Minister) led the reforms to budgeting and planning processes. • Leadership at state level supported local level initiatives. • Training and capacity building of municipal managers acknowledged and intended but not sufficient to achieve objectives. • Managers unable to bring about immediate change at lower levels.	• Strategic and structural framework established to support initiatives. • Political influence facilitated immediate change to procedures. • Foundations for multi-dimensional reform and community partnerships. • Foundations for change in administrative culture. • Lack of implementation capacity affected outcomes.
Bangalore Municipal Corporation (BUPP)	• No clear management focal point within government. • Lack of commitment to, and management isolated from, project objectives and implementation.	• Lack of ownership of the project from the outset, declining further. • Lack of institutional learning of participatory processes and poverty reduction responses.
Corporation of Cochin (CUPRP)	• Senior management capacity set back by constant transfers. • Lack of understanding of participatory objectives and lack of commitment to project methodology. • Donor initiative and lack of management commitment to concept.	• Lack of ongoing commitment to participatory strategies. • Loss of management capacity developed through project. • Project delays, community insecurity. • Lack of management support for field staff promoting participation.
Municipal Corporation of Visakhapatnam (VSIP, CHIS II)	• Frequent changes in Commissioner and Project Director.	• Decreasing understanding of participatory objectives throughout project. • Poor continuity / major disruption to project implementation; in later stages little support for participatory approaches. • Poor performance clearly linked to lack of managerial commitment.
Faisalabad Development Authority (FAUP)	• Frequent changes in Director General. • Managers unskilled and uncommitted to participatory processes. • Lack of a champion at senior level, processes externally driven.	• Difficulties in convincing officials / politicians of viability of approach; • Lack of commitment led to conflict within PMU.
Aswan City Council (Nasriya Upgrading Project)	• Supportive champions in two successive and long-term Governors.	• Influence of Governors led to national replication of participatory processes

Understanding the constraints to effective municipal management for participation

Like most forms of government in developing countries, the hierarchical nature of municipal institutions is in conflict with the participatory ethos. In most municipalities the CEO has extensive power (e.g. Municipal Secretary, Commissioner or City Clerk). Municipalities make decisions from the top, and are themselves non-participatory with lower levels of staff in most of their activities. Indeed, many are even battling with the concept of involving politicians in decision-making, as they have enjoyed complete control for many decades. A few key decision-makers at the top (but normally only the CEO) direct the workings of a large amorphous organisation. Thus the fundamental nature of the institution is the antithesis of that embodied in the concept of community participation. It is also a key reason why small-scale successful participatory initiatives are not readily integrated into municipal organisations. Communication between those implementing participatory activities on the ground and those making the decisions at the top is, more often than not, very limited. Fieldworkers have no access to senior management and there is little dissemination of the achievements of their work with poor communities.

Perhaps ironically, but nevertheless predictably, the introduction of community participation into municipal functions has been most successful when it is championed at the highest level of municipal management. This is a reflection of the authority and control at this level. Participation cannot develop where municipal managers do not have the knowledge and commitment to create a supportive context in which staff are enabled and encouraged to work with communities. Evidence clearly indicates the debilitating effects of inadequate management on participatory efforts. It is seen in the lack of commitment in Bangalore and Faisalabad, and the constant transfers in Cochin and Visakhapatnam (see Box 7.1). The starting point for municipal capacity building for participation is in establishing skilled and committed management able to analyse the blockages to community participation and to build a municipal context which is supportive of a partnership approach.

A number of factors constrain the development of management able to promote community participation, and many, if not all, lie outside municipal control. The factors identified in the case studies are discussed below.

☐ The lack of status of the municipal institution

The lack of status and the perceived low importance of municipal administration are primary constraints to the establishment of effective management. Despite the exceptions seen in Ahmedabad, Surat and other innovative municipalities, skilled managers are not attracted to or asked to take on the municipal CEO role. It is without status and a less attractive post than positions in higher levels of government. In India, for instance, decentralisation policies have not been accompanied by a change in this practice and perception. In Pakistan, the Faisalabad Area Upgrading Project has lacked local high level support from the outset. As a result, institutional learning has been difficult to achieve and progress and sustainability have been undermined (see Box 3.5).

☐ Bureaucratic inertia

While 'reformists' can be found in many contexts, there is still an overwhelming majority of municipal managers who would prefer not to initiate change, who would prefer to wait for policies to be tried and tested by others than be associated with innovative development initiatives. There can be no doubt that participatory approaches in the delivery of services and infrastructure challenge many aspects of municipal management. In any sector community participation may be resisted in preference to conventional approaches on the grounds of control, output and time, personal careers and remuneration or just simply preserving the status quo. In the case of infrastructure, where the capital-intensive nature of the municipal service has resulted in an established pattern of informal incentives for administrative and political representatives, this resistance is accentuated.

7.2   ## Management Reform
Surat

In 1995, some 8 months after the outbreak of the plague in Surat, the state administration of Gujarat appointed an IAS officer to the post of Municipal Commissioner in Surat Municipal Corporation. A skilled and committed reformist, the appointed Commissioner embarked upon a process of reform which utterly transformed the municipal operations and the urban environment, particularly the environmental conditions in poorer, mismanaged areas of Surat.

The management reforms which led to significant improvement in municipal capacity were twofold. The first step was in the delegation of powers, and the second was in the strengthening of the management core of the municipality into an accountable and responsible team.

Delegation

The key reform of management introduced was the extension of the powers of the Deputy Municipal Commissioners responsible for managing the departments and zones of the municipality. The decision-making powers granted to the Zonal Commissioners empowered them to undertake the management of zones independently, and this unprecedented delegation was accompanied by the authority to sanction works up to Rs. 2 lakhs (approx. $5000) without the prior permission of the Municipal Commissioner. As a result of reorganisation and reform, the Zonal Commissioners now have dual responsibilities. They are responsible for planning, monitoring, implementing and managing zonal activities and also for the efficient functioning of the sectoral departments in their charge.

The exposure of the Zonal Commissioners to citywide decision-making created a greater body of knowledge at zonal level about macro-level policy, implementation constraints and opportunities. This has meant that zonal level responses to the community about service delivery problems are now more direct and reliable. Empowering the zonal offices has meant that decision-making is, simultaneously, closer to the service problems and closer to the people. It has had a marked impact on accountability. Operation and maintenance standards improved significantly, and problems of repair and operation and maintenance, which arise on a daily basis, are dealt with immediately.

Monitoring

The key co-ordinating and unifying mechanism introduced was the daily management meeting. This system of daily report-back meetings with the management team enabled the Commissioner to monitor the performance of each zone and the progress being made across the city. All senior officers with delegated powers (Deputy Commissioners, Zonal Commissioners and Zonal Officers) were expected to attend the management meeting every day (including holidays) with the Municipal Commissioner.

The meetings provided a forum for joint decision-making, direct instruction and feedback. The agenda included:

- problems to be resolved;
- monitoring and evaluation of decision-making and fieldwork;
- performance against targets;
- planning and management of activities;
- formulation of new policy and feedback on policy implementation; and
- key learning experiences.

The meetings proved to be a successful mechanism through which senior managers were unified into a force for action, developed ownership and understanding of the decisions made, and had a commitment to implementation.

Each Zonal Commissioner was also assigned the task of creating a framework for monitoring sector activities. The monitoring indicators, methods and actions required were identified and developed jointly during the daily monitoring meetings with the Commissioner. This collective, regular and formal discussion ensured that all Zonal Commissioners and Heads of Departments:

- understood the objectives and purpose of monitoring, developed the method and field requirements for collection of reliable data and accessible presentation and analysis; and
- developed confidence in the appropriateness of decisions made; and
- were rewarded for their contributions on monitoring and supported in achieving objectives. •

(Surat Case Study)

Technical and prescriptive orientation of the second tier

Technical Managers (such as Municipal Engineers and Chief Town Planners) also play a key role in institutionalising participatory processes at an operational level. Municipal Engineers, for instance, frequently have responsibility for contract procurement and explicitly or implicitly determine the degree to which their staff implement participatory policy. In such hierarchical organisations and cultural contexts these figureheads generally have significant influence over operational staff, such as junior engineers. The example set by the Municipal Engineer is likely to affect the performance of the whole department. Some senior engineers are at the tail-end of a long professional career characterised by top-down, prescriptive procedures. This experience and their technical education are the basis of their prescriptive approach to project development and execution. In the early stage of the People's Planning initiative in Kerala, many officials in these posts had little experience of, or commitment to, participation, and they had little incentive to adopt new approaches or to change attitudes. As a result, many of the smaller municipalities were unable to maximise the opportunities for participation established by state policy.

Training, appointment and transfers by higher levels of government

The appointment of the Municipal CEO is normally made by the state or provincial level of government. The criteria used for selection aim to meet a range of political and administrative requirements, none of which includes capacity to promote community participation. In some large municipalities there is evidence that this approach is changing, and that managerial appointments are being made with an eye to the reform and overhaul of local level bureaucracies. This is rarely the case in smaller municipalities, where status does not attract managers with the necessary skills, where the need for change has not been prioritised, and where the tendency for change is dampened by the perception that their role is one of reacting to government directives.

Evidence also suggests that the degree to which the state or provincial strategy promotes consistent municipal policy and implementation, and trains and positions municipal managers to carry out that policy, fundamentally affects the sustainability of changes brought about by individuals. Regular transfers, whether they are political or administrative, are a constant reality of municipal operations. Developments towards an enabling environment or a pro-poor municipal policy are frequently dismissed by a change in management, yet consistent and effective management capacity is particularly important in contexts where appointments are of a limited duration.

The lack of skills to create an enabling environment

The nature and scope of the municipal manager's role has changed considerably with decentralisation policies, with the need for revenue generation and the responsibility for all aspects of development. No longer can managers automatically rely on funds from the state, or expect higher levels of government to accept responsibility for ailing municipal performance.

If they are to meet the demands of decentralisation, municipal managers must identify new ways of planning and managing the city. However, without skills development, existing municipal managers do not necessarily have the skills to change the pattern of their work, to establish partnerships or create an environment conducive to inputs by external organisations. Most municipal managers (with the exception of some trained at higher levels of government) have limited experience of the concept of the 'enabling environment', of financial reform or introducing challenging new methods for performing municipal functions.

Box **7.3**

Key Management Issues
Ahmedabad

The transformation of the Ahmedabad Municipal Corporation (AMC) from 1994 onwards was initiated and championed by a senior Indian Administrative Service (IAS) officer. At the time he was appointed to the AMC, the Corporation was heavily bureaucratic, overstaffed and underskilled and in severe financial difficulties. This Municipal Commissioner particularly focused on reforming the financial status of the AMC (discussed in Box 6.13), on the integration of municipal functions with the private sector (including the development of a partnership approach to slum improvement (see Boxes 5.14 and 5.15)) and on the professionalisation of the AMC staff.

The 'systematic professionalisation' of the human resources of the AMC was established as a municipal function under the portfolio of a Deputy Municipal Commissioner (Administrative) with the aim of creating a sustainable system and implementing professional principles of urban governance and management. Indicative of this drive towards professionalism, the Municipal Commissioner developed a skilled second tier of three Deputy Commissioners, also experienced IAS officers on deputation from the state administration. This focus on recruiting effective managers was reflected at the next level of management in the creation of a professional managerial cadre designated as Assistant Managers. This cadre was created by appointing managers with MBA and Chartered Accountancy skills on fixed term contracts. The AMC intention is to groom this team of qualified staff to take up senior management positions in the future. In order to meet the needs of the reforms in the AMC, significant revision was also made to the qualifications required for posts at lower levels.

The strategy of introducing a management team into the AMC removed the long established dominance of the Engineering and Finance Departments and Departmental Heads. Given the large number of recruits, the Municipal Commissioner created another force within the AMC which could not be overlooked or undermined with ease. The young professionals are willing and able to implement reform processes as they are not burdened with a commitment to bureaucratic procedures. Opponents of the newcomers argue that the young professionals do not have enough administrative knowledge to undertake the tasks assigned to them and need the constant support of more established colleagues. This issue and the obvious disruption to normal promotion opportunities (based on time served) led to unrest and ill-feeling in the first years.

The Municipal Commissioner was supported in this management and financial reform process by a senior and longstanding official of the AMC. Familiar with the weaknesses and inefficiencies of the Corporation, and well known to municipal staff and key individuals outside the Corporation, the Deputy MC provided an important link and vehicle through which reforms were introduced. This Deputy Commissioner was also a force behind the implementation of the community partnership approach adopted for the Slum Networking Project (SNP).

A number of other key individuals, both political and administrative, assisted the Municipal Commissioner in the process of reform and in developing community partnerships. There was some appreciation and understanding of participatory objectives and benefits, and for this reason the SNP was pursued and given the space to develop. However, understanding of participation significantly declines amongst officials at lower levels. It can be argued that the AMC has paid insufficient attention to developing internal capacity at implementation levels which ensure the municipality itself is an effective partner.

Despite the significant improvements, and the development of a team of managers able and willing to lead a comparatively transparent and accountable municipality, there is still a question mark over the manner in which staff are deployed and the management of crisis situations. It is reported that successful assistant managers perform more than one role for a majority of the time, significantly reducing their effectiveness and developing unsustainable management patterns. They are drawn to high profile departments, and are required to leave allocated posts to deal with crisis situations. This is particularly noticeable in the management of the Slum Networking Project which has, more recently, received criticism due to the haphazard approach to management.

Notwithstanding the difficulties in implementation and the questions placed over the mechanisms employed for sustaining change, the strategic reorganisation of management within the AMC has resulted in the creation of an enabling environment and significant improvement in municipal capacity to fulfil statutory functions. Public perception of municipal performance has increased dramatically. •

Elements of effective management for community participation

Despite the enormity of these constraints, some municipalities are led by skilled managers committed to reform, the creation of enabling environments and open to the participation of civil society. They provide a set of lessons for consideration at municipal and state/provincial levels of government.

Developing a cadre of municipal managers appropriate to the redefined municipal role

In order to ensure that decentralisation policies are actively implemented at lower levels of government, it is necessary to create a link between the responsibility handed to local government and the skills of the managers appointed to lead the process. Either managers must be appointed who are already skilled and sensitive to the objectives of decentralisation, participation and enabling environments, or skills and knowledge must be developed.

The role of influential managers is critical when there is little or no policy promoting participatory processes. In this context committed managers provide the driving force to pursue participatory objectives, they facilitate action, and provide the ongoing motivation and robustness to enable processes to take hold. Replicating pilot projects and approaches is very difficult, if not impossible, without senior officials' commitment, and their ability and willingness to mobilise funding and staff to extend participatory processes. In the city of Ahmedabad, for instance, the commitment and vision of an innovative municipal commissioner enabled a community-municipality-private sector partnership to develop (see Box 7.3). This support increased confidence in the municipal efforts, rallied the support of junior staff and ensured the procedural change necessary to facilitate new working methods and the inclusion of external actors in municipal functions.

In all policy contexts, a broad base of skilled managers is essential to ensure that efforts are not impaired by a change in leadership. All innovative initiatives, including participatory projects, lose significant momentum and direction when project champions who have nurtured change from the outset are replaced. A larger base of skilled management trained to implement policy and create enabling environments would help to ensure that transfers do not have overwhelming effects on projects. In India, for instance, the highly respected Indian Administrative Service could be broadened to include a cadre for municipal management. This would reflect the intent of decentralisation policy and would raise the status of the municipality.

Effective management for community participation is then characterised by municipal CEOs mobilising the municipality toward participatory processes, and specifically:

- promoting and disseminating the intent of policy, or formulating municipal policy;
- supporting fieldworkers and understanding the political nature of their work;
- focusing middle management on the importance of participation and ensuring that implementing staff have the seniority, skills and training to achieve participatory goals;
- introducing new processes, procedures and systems into municipal work culture;
- providing an example to staff and deputies and attempting to change the attitudes of municipal employees.

If managers do not 'own' and promote the new approaches, they are unlikely to initiate change to the culture of their organisation. This is the case with the introduction of all new processes. It is particularly essential in the case of community participation, which is not always seen as a more 'advanced' process (such as information technology), but as one which 'lowers' the performance of technical tasks.

Box **7.4**

The Changing Role of Politicians
Ahmedabad Municipal Corporation

The role of local politicians in the Slum Networking Project (SNP) in Ahmedabad has changed dramatically. When the slum networking concept was introduced in 1995, the political wing of the Ahmedabad Municipal Corporation (AMC) was not well established. Political leadership of the AMC was in its infancy. Unlike state level representatives, elected officials at the local level have no training or orientation in key issues of governance and most had not been exposed to participatory processes involving poor communities (or to other forms of non-governmental partnerships). At the same time, senior administrators throughout India were unaccustomed to working with politicians. In this context, the SNP concept, which promoted community participation, was introduced to the political wing of the AMC. Unsurprisingly, the council neither understood nor accepted the concept of the partnership, and particularly opposed the cost-sharing approach central to the SNP process. The politicians saw this as a direct challenge to their capacity to provide for their constituents and, by extension, to their capacity to hold on to the votes of the poor in Ahmedabad. Despite these objections, the shift towards participation of communities, NGOs and the private sector in municipal functions was strong, and was also being reinforced by external agents (such as multilateral aid agencies). As a result, the administrative wing of the AMC was able to pursue the project approach it proposed.

In Sanjay Nagar, the first and most publicised of the pilot areas, most of the slumdwellers were not politically aligned with the local representative. The Councillor's credibility with the residents of Sanjay Nagar was low and he was not particularly threatened by the project processes and goals. Nevertheless, early in the process a few slumdwellers sought his support and consequently he made efforts to discourage the community on the promise that he would secure free services for them. Concerned that this move could undermine the pilot if it gained momentum and spread through the slum area, the Sharda Trust representative responsible for the partnership convinced the Councillor of the potential merits of the project and the possible benefits for him if the project was successfully completed. The Councillor was also consoled that the other actors (AMC administrators, the private sector partner or the NGO partner) did not have a political motive and that the results of the project would only be attributed to him. This argument enabled the project to continue with a local representative who neither hindered nor contributed to the project. He was not included on the Steering Committee set up for the project and did not play a role in the decision-making process.

The pilot project originally envisaged upgrading in four slum areas, and in another area, Sankalchand in Chali in Berhampura, the impact of Councillor intervention produced a different outcome. (Basic infrastructure in this area was originally constructed for 200 households, and the increase in population to the current level of 400 households has left the area grossly underserviced. There is only minimal water available at different times of the day and the lack of adequate drainage during the monsoon is a serious threat to the health of the residents.) The NGO Saath had been working in this slum since 1989, and had won the trust and confidence of the local slumdwellers. As a result, they convinced the residents to join the SNP. However, when the local representative heard the residents intended to participate and to contribute to the cost of the works, he held a meeting to convince them it was not necessary. This opened the door to doubt. The elected representative then offered to pave roads inside the slum from the Councillor's budget and to expedite the construction of toilets. In this case, the residents opted out of the pilot SNP project.

In another slum in the pilot project, Pravinagar-Guptanagar, the local representative was more supportive and steadfast from the outset. He encouraged the residents to join the project and to pay their contribution in order to upgrade the infrastructure and services in their area. He actively imparted the message to slum residents that free services were not a viable option in the current municipal climate and that it was in their interest to contribute to the costs. This built willingness amongst the residents and a successful partnership with the AMC.

Since the inception of the project in 1995, there has been a shift in the stance of the ruling party of the AMC. Once politicians saw firsthand that slum residents were willing to pay and that the initiative would not threaten their power or voting base, they have supported the project. Many have become advocates of the cost-sharing approach. Ownership has also changed. The political wing now claims credit for the Slum Networking Project and is using it as a key aspect of their election campaign. The elected representatives who blocked the early pilots are now promoters of the project and, in a turnaround, are asking the NGO Saath to encourage more communities to join the SNP partnership. •

(Ahmedabad Case Study)

Delegation

The lessons learnt to date highlight the importance of broadening the second tier of management and delegating responsibilities within the municipality. The decentralisation of staff powers and responsibilities to the Zonal Level Commissioners in Surat (Box 7.2) significantly improved the accountability of the municipality to the citizens of the zone. Management reform in Ahmedabad (Box 7.3) focused on boosting skill levels to create a core management team, supported by qualified middle management. In other cities in India, notably Calcutta and Cochin, senior engineers with the vision and skills to adopt participatory approaches have had significant influence. Training in the aspects of participation, the benefits and problems, as well as options for achieving participation, enables this second tier of management to facilitate capacity building within their teams, and thence to pursue partnerships with the non-government and private sectors.

Developing the role of politicians in community participation

Local politicians are key figures in the development of municipal capacity to work with communities. Elected members can provide an important link to communities, underpin participatory efforts or drive participatory processes. Evidence from countries such as India and Sri Lanka, where democratic representation is now assured for local government, clearly shows that political as well as administrative arms of the municipality are primary actors in the development of sustainable participatory processes. Political commitment, Councillor involvement and Councillor skills have a significant impact on the capacity of the municipality to implement participatory projects, but politicians do not necessarily welcome the participation of their poor constituents. Many political leaders perceive community participation as undermining their political power and voting base.

In order to establish this political commitment, however, significant levels of awareness and capacity building are generally necessary. An important step is mitigating perceptions that community participation is a threat to politicians' power. Many politicians, such as those in Ahmedabad described in Box 7.3, have recognised the benefits of participation (for themselves and their constituents) and devised ways to become attached to the success of community partnership projects. In so doing, whatever their motive, they have raised awareness of the potential role of the community and built wider confidence in the process. The converse situation, illustrated more recently in Colombo, results in projects which are accorded low priority and risk being marginalised from mainstream council activities.

Skills Development

An essential, if obvious, requirement to build the capacity of management within municipalities is the development of skills. This skills development, described in detail in Chapter 6 and itemised in Box 6.6, must include both administrative and political arms of management. Managers need to develop a basic understanding of the options for organisational reform needed for a supportive municipal context, the principles of participation and the processes that need to be undertaken by their staff. Capacity building for politicians is also needed to focus on developing an understanding of the benefit of participatory approaches before they can develop skills in promoting community participation. Municipal training programmes should include modules for councillors to assist them in meeting their electoral responsibilities. In addition to improving knowledge on poverty and participation, training for politicians will include policy and decision-making, communication, negotiation and leadership, management and facilitation. In India, state level training institutions, such as ILGUS in West Bengal and KILA[1] in Kerala, have developed courses for municipal councillors and are overrun by the demand for such skills development.

Notes
1. Institute for Local Government and Urban Studies (ILGUS) and the Kerala Institute of Local Administration (KILA).

Framework for Action

The strategic framework developed throughout this guidebook provides municipalities with a comprehensive picture of the elements of capacity building that can influence municipal attempts to extend or establish community participation. The framework for action, described in the strategic framework diagram (Box 2.1) and reproduced below, highlights four primary components of capacity building and the aims of each component.

The following pages provide an overview of the various elements of municipal capacity building for participation. The framework is intended to provide a broad checklist of the issues that should be considered and prioritised in the development of a capacity building strategy for municipalities in all parts of the world. These elements are, of course, indicative and not all will be relevant to every context.

The illustrations from the various case studies show that opportunities and constraints vary considerably, and that local solutions responding to the context are frequently the most effective and expeditious. By extension, this points to the need to tailor capacity building strategies to suit the external, institutional, social and resource constraints of the municipality. Trainers and capacity builders are encouraged to build on the strengths and opportunities identified in particular contexts, and to develop the ability to identify specific solutions to various municipal and community constraints.

The specific nature of training options in different countries and, furthermore, in different cities makes a discussion on training providers outside the scope of this sourcebook. Municipal officials embarking on (and donors funding) capacity building programmes will need to identify appropriate training institutions that can play a central role in the skills development central to building municipal capacity for community participation.

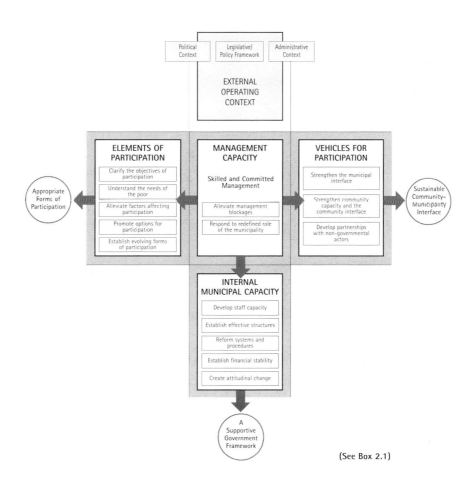

(See Box 2.1)

8

Box **8.1**

A   The Elements of Participation
Appropriate Forms of Participation

1	**Clarify objectives of participation**	Build understanding of the objectives of participation and their implications • instrumental objectives • empowerment objectives • project objectives • acknowledge objectives may differ
2	**Build understanding of the poor and their needs**	Build understanding of the dimensions of poverty in the municipal area • characteristics and causes of poverty • key problems and needs • vulnerability • disaggregating the group categorised as poor • participatory needs assessments
3	**Alleviate factors affecting participation**	Build understanding of the nature of communities • dynamics and power relations in the community, heterogeneity of urban communities • assets of community (skills, education etc) • factors constraining participation (illiteracy, gender inequalities, cultural beliefs and practices) • factors affecting participation (marginalisation, domination, political views)
4	**Promote options for participation throughout the project cycle**	Build understanding of the factors which specifically affect participation in service delivery • types of service • levels of service (neighbourhood, ward, city) • stage of service delivery (project, operation and maintenance) • quality of service delivery (standards, technological options for services) • labour based approaches Develop understanding of potential role of communities throughout the project cycle • project identification/needs assessments • micro-planning and project design • project implementation (contracting and management) • project financing • participatory monitoring and evaluation
5	**Establish evolving forms of participation**	Build understanding of the potential forms and indicators of participation • exploitative participation • from information participation to co-operation and mobilisation Build understanding of the basic parameters of effective and sustainable participation • appropriate participation • mutually beneficial participation • evolving participation

B   The Vehicles of Participation
A Sustainable Community-Municipal Interface

Box **8.1**

6	Strengthen the capacity of the municipality to interface with poor communities	**Identify constraints and opportunities of existing municipal vehicles for participation** • actors (status, skills, numbers) • roles and responsibilities • relationships (to management, to other departments) **Develop effective fieldwork interface** • location of interface staff • essential members of multi-disciplinary team • vulnerabilities • links to higher levels of management • external support **Develop an effective management interface** • senior management • line management • politicians and local champions **Develop understanding of the capacity of the community to become a partner** • constraints and opportunities of existing instruments • skills, knowledge and access to information • vulnerable and marginalised groups
7	Strengthen community capacity and the community interface	**Develop organisational capacity** • formation of community groups, building on existing CBOs • evolution of groups • domination/representativeness • mechanisms for inclusion of women and vulnerable groups • dispute resolution **Develop community skills** • assess existing skills and training needs • leadership skills • tailor training opportunities to suit communities and vulnerable groups • access to information
8	Develop partnerships with non-governmental actors	**Develop understanding of the potential role of NGOs** • strengths and weaknesses of existing NGO relationships • NGO skills and experience in policy and implementation • NGO links to communities • identify key gaps in expertise which NGO sector can fill **Define roles and responsibilities for NGOs** • mediation with community • capacity building of community and municipality • community development support/ gender awareness • post-project sustainability **Develop effective interface with NGOs** • skills • status • formal and informal mechanisms • mutual trust and confidence

8

C Internal Municipal Capacity
A Supportive Government Framework

Box **8.1**

9	**Develop staff capacity**	**Develop and implement skills development strategy** <ul><li>Horizontal skills development</li><li>Vertical skills development</li><li>Target training to suit staff roles</li><li>Address perceived constraints</li><li>Select trainers and forums to suit audience</li><li>Develop an ongoing training process</li></ul> **Reform staffing policies and practices** <ul><li>Staff appointment systems</li><li>Staff transfers</li><li>Incentive structures</li></ul>
10	**Establish effective municipal structures**	**Identify organisational constraints for participatory service delivery** <ul><li>Central role of the engineering department</li><li>Project management units</li><li>Management through line departments</li><li>Project cells</li></ul> **Identify appropriate organisational options for participatory service delivery**
11	**Reform systems and procedures**	**Identify constraints of existing procedures** <ul><li>financial management procedures</li><li>project planning procedures</li><li>procurement procedures</li><li>operation and maintenance procedures</li><li>monitoring and evaluation procedures</li><li>appropriateness of regulatory framework to the poor</li></ul> **Instigate reforms to procedures constraining participation**
12	**Establish financial stability**	**Develop accountability and transparency of municipal finances to promote community confidence** <ul><li>strategic financial planning</li><li>better financial management</li><li>partnerships and outside investment</li></ul>
13	**Create attitudinal change**	**Develop understanding of the rationale of municipal actors** <ul><li>administrative</li><li>technical</li><li>political</li></ul> **Acknowledge the impact of discrimination against the poor** **Address unfavourable attitudes** <ul><li>recognise different attitudes and viewpoints</li><li>broaden understanding of the overall context</li><li>identify common interests</li><li>highlight benefits for each actor</li><li>identify keys to motivation and change</li><li>broaden knowledge of poverty</li></ul>

D   Management Capacity
Skilled and Committed Management

Box **8.1**

14	Alleviate management blockages	Understanding the constraints to effective municipal management for participation • lack of status of the municipal institution • bureaucratic inertia • technical and prescriptive orientation of second tier of management • training, appointment and transfers by higher levels of government • the lack of skills to create an enabling environment
15	Respond to redefined role of the municipality	Elements of effective management for community participation • developing a cadre of municipal managers appropriate to the redefined municipal role • delegating responsibility • developing the role of politicians in community participation • skills development

Background to **Case Studies**
Appendix A

The framework set out has been derived from an analysis of municipal experiences in participatory processes. The Building Municipal Capacity for Community Participation research was initially carried out through a series of studies undertaken in municipalities in India, Pakistan, Sri Lanka and Egypt. These 10 case studies provide a range of lessons, learnt in diverse social, political, institutional and administrative contexts. The meaning of 'participation' in these situations, and the processes adopted to delivering services varied considerably.

The boxed illustrations throughout the text draw heavily on case studies carried out by local and UK consultants as follows:

Ahmedabad:	Mihir Bhatt and Janelle Plummer with Rajendra Joshi
Bangalore:	Richard Slater
Cochin:	Janelle Plummer and Mr K Gopalakrishnan
Colombo:	Richard Slater
Faisalabad:	Community Action Planning and Kevin Tayler
Kerala:	Mr K Gopalakrishnan and Janelle Plummer
Nasriya:	Ahmed Eiweida and Kevin Tayler
Shrouk:	Kevin Tayler and Ahmed Eiweida
Surat:	Sharadbala Joshi and Janelle Plummer
Visakhapatnam:	Sue Phillips

A brief background statement of each case study and its relevance to the research is provided below.

Ahmedabad

The case study carried out in Ahmedabad (Gujarat, Northwest India) provided the research with specific lessons concerning the development of vehicles for participation and the changes possible within a municipality to create a supportive context for participation. First and foremost, it provides a potent illustration of the power and impact of an effective, skilled and committed municipal manager. The appointment of a Municipal Commissioner willing to disrupt conventional practice and to disturb the status quo resulted in a financial turnaround unprecedented in Indian history. This financial reform was accompanied by a process of internal municipal reform that focused on the professionalisation of the institution and included significant staff and procedural reforms. These internal reforms underpinned the **Ahmedabad Slum Networking Project (SNP)** which aimed to involve communities in a development process to improve the environmental conditions of poor neighbourhoods. Early pilots were characterised by the broad partnership approach (including the Corporation, NGOs, the private sector as well as communities), an emphasis on cost recovery, and the notable combination of both participatory and prescriptive approaches throughout the project. The relationship between the NGO sector and the Corporation is illustrative of potential partnerships. Despite the rhetoric of participation, the SNP did not, in its early stages, display a shift in decision-making or in attitude, but later reports suggest that there has been an evolution in both participatory decision-making and attitudinal change amongst municipal officials.

Bangalore

The **Bangalore Urban Poverty Project** (Karnataka, India), supported by the Netherlands Government, provides an interesting juxtaposition to the 'home grown' initiatives in that it rigorously pursued donor objectives for participation. This objective was facilitated through the placement of project management in a separate unit away from the potential constraints of conventional municipal procedures. The project emphasised the role of NGOs in community development and mobilisation, acknowledging the limited skills in community participation in the Bangalore City Corporation. The

BUPP developed two institutional instruments for implementation: a steering committee at decision-making level, and the Slum Development Teams at the community level. The project advocated a formalised approach to decision-making. The key lessons of the Bangalore case study for building municipal capacity for community participation were found in issues such as project ownership, roles and responsibilities of partner agencies, the functioning of steering committees, and the role of politicians.

Cochin

The **Cochin Urban Poverty Reduction Project** (Kerala, India), supported by the British Department for International Development, was developed as a multi-sectoral poverty reduction project. In its pilot phase the project particularly provides useful illustrations of small scale participatory processes in the context of a problematic operating context. These included, particularly, innovative community contracting initiatives, the informal development of relationships with local NGOs, and the procedural constraints and solutions to facilitating new methods of service delivery. The main phase of the project was formulated by external consultants through an intensive design process and was commenced in a context of political and institutional change. The project has since suffered from a lack of ownership, administrative and attitudinal constraints and by the lack of a project champion within the senior management of the Corporation. The marginalisation of poverty-related issues, the lack of a driving force at municipal level, and the early transfer of trained staff have had significant effects on the capacity of the municipality to develop effective community participation.

Colombo

The case study undertaken in Colombo, Sri Lanka, considers the efforts of a number of governmental institutions, particularly the Colombo Municipal Corporation, in the development of participatory instruments and methodologies for the implementation of the Urban Basic Services and the **Urban Housing Sub-Programme of the Million Houses Programme**. Colombo is well known for the development of an extensive and seemingly sustainable network of Community Development Committees and the successful adoption of Community Action Planning methodologies as the primary mechanism towards the planning and development of poor urban groups. Apart from the lessons of participatory planning and group formation, the Colombo case study provides strong evidence of the influential role of politics and the importance of political support for promoting sustainable participatory processes. It also provides a comparative example of the impacts of locating participatory initiatives within municipal line departments. Located in the Health Department of the CMC, the participatory initiatives enjoyed the status of that department and the support of a strong departmental head in the CMC.

Faisalabad

As the only case study in Pakistan, the **Faisalabad Area Upgrading Project** (FAUP), funded by the DFID, provides an illustration of the difficulties of managing and promoting community participation within an unsupportive legislative, political and administrative context. The separation of the project management from the line departments of the municipality and line agencies has meant that a participatory project was developed outside government. On the one hand, this has enabled the piloting of innovative participatory approaches in the constrained social and cultural context of Pakistan; but on the other hand it has resulted in isolated efforts which do not appear replicable within existing institutions. The FAUP also provides the guidebook with illustrative material on extensive training and skills development programmes and on the important role of the project interface in mobilising communities.

Kerala People's Planning Campaign

The **Kerala People's Planning Campaign** (KPPC) is a statewide initiative aimed at involving the people of the state of Kerala, India, in the planning and development processes of all sectors. The KPPC aimed and established a process for people-led planning for the development of the ninth 5-year plan for the state. It is a notable exception to the other case studies in a number of respects. First, it was underpinned by a supportive legislative and policy context and was led by politicians. Second, it illustrates the potential (and the problems) of massive replicability of participatory planning processes (poor and non-poor). Third, while it acknowledged the need for extensive capacity building to achieve objectives, the early stages of the campaign were hindered by sceptical municipal officials, and the lack of skills and organisational capacity needed to produce viable and integrated results. The impacts of the process have been equally notable. With a political directive, significant and rapid procedural change was implemented to enable municipalities to act.

Nasriya

The **Nasriya Upgrading Project** (NUP) is a GTZ-supported project in Aswan in Egypt. The project provides an illustration of participatory planning in the particular social and institutional context of Egypt. Managed through a PMU, the project design sought to bypass the difficulty of initiating new processes into existing structures, and succeeded in introducing the concept of participation in this narrower field. However, this decision, while constraining the integration of participation into line departments, has had a demonstrative effect, raising officials' awareness and influencing national level policy-makers. The transfer of skills to municipal level officials has been established, to some extent, by the close linkages established between local agencies and by project mechanisms such as the secondment of staff. Two important lessons can be learnt from the project. One is that benefits will be gained from continuity at the highest level of project management. The second is that weaker forms of participation at the outset can be an effective starting point for the development and institutionalisation of more comprehensive approaches to participation.

Shrouk

The **Shrouk Programme**, a national level initiative in Egypt, is technically a rural initiative which was included in the case studies because of the central place it occupies in the country's plans for towns as well as villages, and the extent to which it highlights issues of replicability. The participatory element of the programme was led by an academic champion able to influence policy-makers to formulate a community approach to development. The Shrouk process is heavily dependent on civil society inputs but has not built the capacity of officials at the municipal level. In this respect, the project demonstrates a lack of municipal engagement with participatory processes.

Surat

The Surat case study (Gujarat, India) was included in the research not so much because of successful participatory initiatives as the significant and unprecedented achievements in municipal reform. It provides an illustration of the municipal reform necessary to bring about sustainable change in the capacity of the municipality to fulfil its functions (particularly the access of the poor to adequate infrastructure and services). The capacity of the Surat Municipal Corporation was built through a strategy which started with the appointment of a strong leader committed to the process of reform and to building commitment from the public at large, the media and with staff of the SMC. This was supported by the creation of a core management team and by specific procedural reforms which built accountability to communities and sustainability. The procedural and staff reforms created a balance of autonomy and monitoring of zonal activities and enabled a decentralised response to environmental problems. The accumulative result brought about the transformation of a dysfunctional organisation into one that provided effective and accountable urban management. The approach toward participation was concerned with monitoring municipal performance and accountability, rather than strong forms of participatory decision-making.

Visakhapatnam

The **Visakhapatnam Slum Improvement Project** (VSIP) and its successor, the Chinagadili Habitat Improvement Scheme, are DFID-funded projects developed in a supportive external operating context in Visakhapatnam in the state of Andhra Pradesh in India. The projects provide exemplification of the complexities of community group formation and the issues of representativeness, gender relations and domination. The Chinagadili experience highlights the lessons of institutionalising a Project Steering Committee, which involves communities in strategic decision-making. The VSIP case study also highlights the value of a Community Development department committed to promoting and training officials in community participation. It exposes some of the structural issues of locating participatory projects in separated units and outside line departments, and also some of the primary issues concerning staff systems and policies. The extended programme of poverty reduction in Visakhapatnam highlights institutional development processes and the nature of evolving participatory processes.

References

Abbott, J (1996) **Sharing the City** Earthscan, London.

Akbar, O (1990) 'The Nasriya Upgrading Project' **Shelter and Urbanisation** Conference Paper, GOPP, Cairo.

Amis, P (1994) 'Urban Management Training, Action Learning and Rapid Analysis' in IIED **RRA Notes: Special Issue on Participatory Tools and Methods in Urban Areas** IIED, London.

Arnstein, S R (1969) 'A ladder of citizen participation' **Journal of American Institute of Planners** vol XXXV p19.

Banerjee B et al (1997) **Participatory Planning and Monitoring in Chinigadili Habitat Improvement Project CHIS II** Unpublished, DFID, Delhi.

Batley R (1983) 'Participation in urban projects: meanings and possibilities' in Moser, C (1983) **Evaluating Community Participation in Urban Development Projects** DPU Working paper no.14.

Bernard, A et al (Ed) (1998) **Civil Society and International Development** OECD.

Blackburn J (Ed) (1998) **Who Changes?** IT, London.

Cernea, M (1988) **Non-Governmental Organisations and Local Development** World Bank Discussion paper no. 40, World Bank, Washington DC.

Chambers, R (1989) **Farmer First: Farmer Introduction** IT, London.

Chambers, R (1994) 'The Origins and Practice of Participatory Rural Appraisal' in **World Development** vol 22 no.7 pp953–969.

Chambers, R (1994) 'Participatory Rural Appraisal: Analysis of Experience' in **World Development** vol 22 no.9 pp1253–1268.

Connell, D (1997) 'Participatory Development: An Approach Sensitive to Class and Gender' **Development in Practice** vol 7 no.3 pp248–259.

Creative Associates International Inc. (1996) **Options for USAID Assistance to Shrouk** Unpublished report prepared for USAID/Egyptian Ministry of Local Administration.

Davey, K (1993) **Managing Growing Cities: Options for Urban Government** DAG, University of Birmingham.

Devas, N and Rakodi, C (1993) **Managing Fast Growing Cities** Longman, Harlow.

DFID (1995) **Notes on Stakeholder Participation** DFID, London.

Eade (1997) **Capacity Building** Oxfam, Oxford.

Eiweida, A (1997) **Aswan Urban Development Projects- Nasriya Upgrading Project, Documentary Report on the Infrastructure Activities** GTZ, Aswan.

Goulet, D (1986) 'Three Rationalities in Development Decision-Making' **World Development** vol 14 no.2 pp301–317.

GTZ (1991) **Objectives Oriented Project Planning: Documentation of ZOPP 5** The Nasriya Upgrading Project GTZ, Aswan.

GTZ (1992) **Nasriya Upgrading Project – Aswan (Egypt)** Nasriya Upgrading Project GTZ, Aswan.

GTZ (1994) **Objectives Oriented Project Planning, Documentation of ZOPP** The Nasriya Upgrading Project, GTZ, Aswan.

Gulati, I and Isaac, T M (1998) **People's Campaign for Decentralised Planning: An Experiment in Participatory Development** State Planning Board, Trivandrum.

IDS (1996) **Introductory PRA Methodology pack** IDS, Brighton.

IDS (1996) **PRA Policy Pack** IDS, Brighton.

IDS (1996) **PRA Tools and Techniques Pack** IDS, Brighton.

IIED (1994) **RRA Notes: Special Issue on Participatory Tools and Methods in Urban Areas** IIED, London.

Isaac, TM (1999) **Decentralisation, Democracy and Development: People's Campaign for Decentralised Planning** State Planning Board, Trivandrum.

Jones, S (1995) **Main Findings Cochin Urban Poverty Profile Study** Unpublished, Overseas Development Administration, Delhi.

Lewin, C (1986) **Nasriya Upgrading Project: Project Study and Proposal** Annex no. 8, Aswan and Cairo.

Madbouly, M (Undated) **Capacity Building of Local Government in Managing and Delivering Urban Services in Egypt** Unpublished paper.

Mayfield, JB (1996) **Local Government in Egypt: Structure, Process and the Challenges of Reform** The American University in Cairo Press, Cairo.

McAuslan P (1993) in Devas, N and Rakodi, C **Managing Fast Growing Cities** Longman, Harlow pp236–264.

Montgomery, R (1997) **Micro Planning Notes, Cochin Urban Poverty Reduction Project** (unpublished) UPO DFID, Delhi.

Moser (1983) **Evaluating Community Participation in Urban Development Projects** DPU Working paper no.14.

Moser (1989) 'Community Participation in Urban Projects in the Third World' **Progress in Planning** vol 32 part 2.

Narayan, D (1993) **Participatory Evaluation: Tools for Managing Change in Water and Sanitation** World Bank Technical Paper no.207, World Bank, Washington.

Narayan, D (1995) **The Contribution of People's Participation** ESD Occasional Paper Series no.1, World Bank, Washington.

Natraj, VK (1997) **Bangalore Urban Poverty Project Review Mission Supplementary Report** Dutch Ministry of Foreign Affairs, Unpublished.

Oakley and Marsden (1984) **Approaches to Participation in Rural Development** ILO, Geneva.

Overseas Development Administration (1987) **Project Evaluation Committee: Visakhapatnam Slum Improvement Project**

Palmer, M, Leila, A and el Sayed Yassin (1988) **The Egyptian Bureaucracy** Syracuse University Press, New York.

Paul, S (1987) **Community Participation in Development Projects** World Bank Discussion Paper no.6.

Peltenburg M, et al (1996) **Building Capacity for Better Cities** IHS, Rotterdam.

Pretty, J and Chambers, R (1994) **Towards a Learning Paradigm: New Professionalism and Institutions for Agriculture** in Scoones and Thompson (eds).

Schübeler, **Participation and Partnership in Urban Infrastructure Management** UMP Policy Paper no. 19 World Bank, Washington.

Scoones, I and Thompson, J (eds) (1994) **Beyond Farmer First: Rural People's Knowledge, Agricultural Research and Extension Practice** IT, London.

Smith, BC (1998) 'Participation Without Power: Subterfuge or Development?' **Community Development Journal** vol 33, no.3 July, pp197–204.

Srinivasan (1992) **Options for Educators: A Monograph for Decision-makers on Alternative Participatory Strategies** PACT, NY.

State Planning Board, Kerala (1997) **Selected Articles for People's Campaign for Ninth Plan** State Planning Board, Trivandrum.

Sundaram, PSA (1994), **Study on Replicability of ODA funded Slum Improvement Projects in India** Overseas Development Administration, Unpublished.

Tayler, K and Cotton, A (1993) **Urban Upgrading Options and Procedures for Pakistan** WEDC, Loughborough.

Tripathi, D (1998) **Alliance for Change: A Slum Upgrading Experiment in Ahmedabad** Tata McGraw-Hill, New Delhi.

University of Birmingham, Development Administration Group (1997) **Summary Draft Report: Impact Assessment Study of Visakhapatnam Slum Improvement Project** Department for International Development, Unpublished.

University of Birmingham, Development Administration Group (1997) **Impact Assessment Study: Visakhapatnam Institutional Study** Department for International Development, Unpublished.

UPO (1997) **A Gender Equality Strategy**, Unpublished, DFID, New Delhi.

Index